THE FINE ART OF LITERARY FIST-FIGHTING

THE FINE ART OF LITERARY FIST-FIGHTING

How a Bunch of Rabble-Rousers,
Outsiders, and Ne'er-do-wells
Concocted Creative Nonfiction

Lee Gutkind

Yale
UNIVERSITY PRESS

NEW HAVEN AND LONDON

Yale University Press books may be purchased in quantity
for educational, business, or promotional use. For information, please e-mail
sales.press@yale.edu (U.S. office) or sales@yaleup.co.uk (U.K. office).

Set in Yale and Alternate Gothic No2 type by Integrated Publishing Solutions.
Printed in the United States of America.

ISBN 978-0-300-25115-9 (hardcover : alk. paper)
Library of Congress Control Number: 2023938994
A catalogue record for this book is available from the British Library.

This paper meets the requirements of ANSI/NISO Z39.48-1992
(Permanence of Paper).

10 9 8 7 6 5 4 3 2 1

For Montgomery Culver, with my deepest appreciation for his friendship
and support during my earliest days of dreaming of living the writing life

CONTENTS

CONTENTS

PART 2

PART 3

CONTENTS

PART 4

THE FINE ART OF LITERARY FIST-FIGHTING

INTRODUCTION

I am often asked: "What is creative nonfiction?" Or, in some cases, "What the *hell* is creative nonfiction?" The answer—or answers—can be complicated because creative nonfiction may mean different things to different people, a characteristic that makes this form so elusive and alluring.

On its very baseline creative nonfiction is a literary genre. Some people call it the fourth genre, along with poetry, fiction, and drama. And it's an umbrella term for the many different ways one can write what is called creative nonfiction. Memoir, for example, personal essay, biography, narrative history, and long-form narrative reportage may all fit under the creative nonfiction umbrella. Recently, as it has evolved, there have been offshoots to the genre such as specu- lative nonfiction, auto(biographical) fiction, lyric essay, and the visual essay, to name only a few.

Writers who write creative nonfiction are very different in voice, orientation, and purpose. But what they have in common is that they are, in one way or another, writing true stories that provide information about a variety of subjects, enriched by relevant thoughtful ideas, personal insight, and intimacies about life and the world we live in. And this scope and variety are exactly what make creative nonfiction significant and, these days, so incredibly popular.

"Freedom" and "flexibility" are words I like to use when defining creative

---

nonfiction, for the genre invites writers to push boundaries and open doors, offering them the opportunity to use all of the techniques of the fiction writer (or the poet) — dialogue, setting, description, inner point of view (seeing the world through the eyes of the person they are writing about) — in order to capture a reader's attention and enlighten and intrigue them through nonfiction.

There are very few rules for writers of creative nonfiction. You can predict the future, speculate about the past, or imagine what could have happened or what someone might have been thinking, as long as you don't violate the reader's trust, and in the process your own credibility. There are, however, limits to the freedom and flexibility that make creative nonfiction so attractive and compelling — legal, ethical, and moral issues that are challenging and, in many ways, impossible to clearly define. Freedom and flexibility — and daring — are governed by responsibility, not just to the people we write about, but to those who read and publish our work.

Nonfiction itself has had a bad rap in the literary world. For a long time, it was commonly believed that writing nonfiction was generally inferior to the writing of poetry and fiction. "Nonfiction is a pleasant way to walk," Larry McMurtry once wrote, "but the novel puts one on horseback, and what cowboy, symbolic or real, would walk when he could ride?"[1]

I remember reading this from McMurtry, who had written a great deal of nonfiction, in addition to his many novels and stories, and feeling more than a little annoyed and, at the same time, amused. He had to be joking, I thought. Or maybe he had just fallen off his horse. I pictured the comedian Rodney Dangerfield, who became rich and famous for the line "I get no respect," which in many ways has been the story of creative nonfiction in a nutshell.

The addition of the word "creative" to nonfiction was at first controversial, but it gradually reversed the belief that nonfiction was somehow second class, a cut below poetry and fiction. It liberated all writers, journalists especially, releasing them from longstanding rules and boundaries that had been so restrictive and inhibiting. For novelists, poets, and essayists, "creative" encouraged experimentation and offered new avenues of expression. Scientists, physicians, attorneys, were intrigued by the notion of being creative and began to write true stories that humanized their professions. The interest in true stories motivated and opened doors for others who were not writers by trade to share their life experiences, finding meaning in the process and fulfillment in the connections they forged with readers.

This transition — an awakening to the potential and power of nonfiction that allowed and encouraged creativity — did not happen overnight and was not without resistance and often bitter infighting. Change was difficult for the literary, journalistic, and academic communities, steeped in tradition and long resistant to new ideas, to accommodate. Indeed, the resistance in some corners far exceeded the scale of the change itself. As I point out in this book, the change was hardly drastic and was not really, when one looks back over the history of nonfiction, much of a change at all. Writers, including familiar and famous names you will recognize, such as Daniel Defoe, Charles Dickens, George Orwell, and many others, had been writing nonfiction that was creative and imaginative for centuries. The change, the adjustment that it precipitated, had much more to do with the approach or attitude toward nonfiction rather than its content and, of course, the idea that creative and nonfiction were not mutually exclusive. That change in approach and attitude is ongoing. The scope of nonfiction today, if it can still be called nonfiction, continues to evolve.

This book documents the evolution of the genre from its controversial beginnings to the respect and legitimacy it has achieved today. It highlights some of the history of the genre — the authors and events that most inspired and affected me and other writers of the genre at the time, including the impact of the new journalism, the reemergence of the essay, the surge of memoir. This book will be eye-opening to students and beginning writers. It will open doors and opportunities for more experienced writers who want to push the limits of their work and ideas and reach new readers.

Perhaps more important, this book is about the meaning of the genre, the revolution it initiated and the incredible impact over the years that it generated not just in literature or journalism, but to the changing culture and values worldwide. It's about how women (and minorities), long ostracized by a white male good old boys' network, so much that they were sometimes not even permitted to write in their own names, in time became the dominant voices of the genre. And so very relevant today, it is about the ethics and morality that challenge writers, the behind-the-scenes revelations of how and why writers manipulate their material or, in some cases, make stuff up. This book will be of interest to all writers and to unknowing readers who may be surprised to learn that the true stories they have read and admired may not be as true as they believed. Readers will learn about the tricks of the true-story trade, like the compositing of characters, the compression of time and place, and the phrases writers often employ, like "larger reality," "the untrue truth," and "the poetic truth," to justify those embellishments. Finally, the book will tell you how and why creative nonfiction became the people's genre, how anyone with a story to tell, no matter how personal and intimate, no matter their background or education, was provided a forum and a vehicle to express themselves and justify and share their lives, their work, and their beliefs.

This book is not, however, meant to be a thorough and comprehensive examination of the history of the genre, which goes back hundreds of years and would probably require volumes; and if it were, I would not be the one to write it.

I am not, have never been, a scholar, by any means. In fact, unlike many of the students I teach or the writers I edit, I do not have a Ph.D. or MFA or any advanced degree. I was never a card-carrying journalist or a failed novelist. I was just, at the time, the middle 1960s when I started out, a hippie motorcyclist with shoulder-length hair and unruly sideburns and all of the turquoise accoutrements of the era — who was also a wannabe nonfiction writer, trying to figure out what the writing life was all about and somehow become a part of it.

Until, eventually, I stumbled into the academy, or, as many of my colleagues in the English department at the University of Pittsburgh might have then said, "barged" my way in — long before creative nonfiction became creative nonfiction. As it turned out, I was in the right place at the right time, and it is fair to say that I was somewhat of an opportunist. I realized in the early 1970s that some sort of literary transition in nonfiction and journalism was occurring, a transition that many writers, critics, and scholars, in and out of the academy, vigorously resisted. This conflict excited and invigorated me, and I instinctively, and perhaps naively and sometimes provocatively, defended it and simultaneously pushed it forward. To go back to McMurtry, I climbed on the creative nonfiction horse and rode it like hell.

Over time, mostly because of the ongoing resistance with which I was confronted, I became more than a little obsessed. In my own mind, the acceptance of creative nonfiction and the acceptance of an outsider-motorcyclist-interloper in the academy were one and the same thing. I went after that acceptance with a freewheeling or, some have said, "crazed" resolve.

In addition to starting *Creative Nonfiction*, the first literary journal to publish creative nonfiction exclusively, the publication that would become the flagship of the genre, I helped establish, despite ongoing and sometimes petty resistance from my colleagues, the first MFA program in creative nonfiction at the University of Pittsburgh, and, later, the first low-residency MFA program, at Goucher College. I started a creative nonfiction book series that led to a full-fledged book imprint. I initiated the first all-creative-nonfiction writers' conference, which brought together for the first time the most prominent voices of the genre — Susan Orlean, John McPhee, Gay Talese, Mary Karr, Joyce Carol Oates, Tobias Wolff, and George Plimpton, to name just a few — to interact with student participants who came from throughout the world to learn about creative nonfiction. These and many others, like Norman Mailer, Lillian Ross, Truman Capote, Joan Didion, brought respectability to the genre and opened doors for the generations of writers they inspired.

Over the years, with every opportunity, I have taken my creative nonfiction message on the road, across the United States and into Australia, China, Egypt, New Zealand, Ireland, England, Israel, beating the creative nonfiction drum. Later I introduced creative nonfiction into a science policy think tank. James Wolcott, in a scathing article that ridiculed the genre in *Vanity Fair* in 1997, in which he dubbed me "the godfather behind creative nonfiction," compared me, in reference to all of my drum-beating activities, to a "human octopus."[2]

My version of the evolution of the genre is rooted in the changes occurring in journalism in the 1960s and 1970s, but there are, for sure, many other ways to tell the creative nonfiction story. There are those who would begin in the sixteenth century, with Michel de Montaigne, who coined the term "essay" and is often referred to as the father of the essay.

It is certainly true that essays have always contained many elements of what came to be known as creative nonfiction, and maybe it would even be all right to say, in retrospect, that Montaigne was the first creative nonfiction writer. But the emergence of creative nonfiction, as the genre — the umbrella — is known and accepted today, did not take place until hundreds of years after Montaigne.

Essayists, however, eventually joined and invigorated the creative nonfiction movement and turned it into the rich, diverse, and legitimate genre it is today. There are probably more essayists writing creative nonfiction today than there are journalists. Even journalists these days tend to refer to their long-form work as essays. The word "article" has become somewhat of an anachronism.

A major part of the story I am telling in this book is how creative nonfiction came to be accepted in the academy — an unlikely wellspring for what started as such an unscholarly invasion of an established, conservative, and seemingly impenetrable bastion. And how over a period of years, writers in the academy, in creative writing programs, began developing a creative nonfiction pedagogy and a community for their students, and how those students and their students after that transformed a bare blip in the literary landscape into a legitimate and flourishing genre that would soon equal or outpace poetry and fiction. And how the writers in the academy brought together what were then two factions — journalists and literary writers — and how this union helped change the course, the flavor, and the direction of the growth of literary art, not just in the United States but from a global, all-encompassing perspective. And not just into the humanities, but into many other academic disciplines.

But getting to where we are today — to the ascendancy of creative nonfiction as the fourth and most active and visible genre — was a real battle, an often disagreeable and circular series of debates over long-held and outmoded ideas, over class and prejudice, over literary and journalistic turf, and, not surprisingly when writers are involved, over insecurity and self-identity and, most of all, over words. These debates went on for many years, until gradually and sometimes painfully, nonfiction that was creative was recognized as an art form equal to poetry and fiction.

More than any other factor over the past fifty years, it was what I like to call, with more than a hint of embellishment, the "literary fist-fighting" of these debates, between those who held the line and resisted change and those who defied and challenged them, that triggered an evolution of literary art, expanding its scope in ways that might have never been predicted or imagined. This is the story of how that all came about, told from the perspective of an outsider who inadvertently and reluctantly became an insider.

PART 1

CHAPTER 1

WHO MADE THIS NAME UP?

The name, or label — creative nonfiction — is new, or newish. Over the years, the genre has had many names — such as "literature of fact," "literature of reality," "belles lettres," "verfabula," "documentary narrative," "extended digressive narrative nonfiction." Or just plain old "essay." Some of these names or labels aren't very nice — or fair. Like "parajournalism," "parody journalism," "gutter journalism."

Some responses to the name and the meaning of creative nonfiction have been downright mean-spirited. James Wolcott, in his *Vanity Fair* article, lambasted creative nonfiction as "a sickly transfusion, whereby the weakling personal voice of sensitive fiction is inserted into the beery carcass of nonfiction."[1] And Michael Anderson, an editor for the *New York Times Book Review,* told a reporter from *Poets & Writers Magazine:* "Creative nonfiction, I am so sick of this bullshit. Even the term is an oxymoron. If it's creative, it's not nonfiction. If it is nonfiction, it is not creative. I don't know what it is other than people making stuff up."[2]

"Creative," as Anderson made clear, was the most contentious of the two words, especially for journalists, because to them "creative" could mean that the writer was lying, exaggerating, imagining, spinning — not truly reporting, objectively, true to fact. But even "nonfiction" has had its detractors. To some writers, the word "nonfiction" was, in a way, demeaning. For the historian Barbara W. Tuchman, a two-time winner of the Pulitzer Prize (for *The Guns of August* and *Stilwell and the American Experience in China*), the term "nonfiction" was "despicable — as if we were some sort of remainder. I do not feel like a Non-something," she insisted. "I feel quite specific."

Laboring to think of a name that might replace "nonfiction," she turned to Webster and looked up "fiction," which was defined as "opposed to 'Fact, Truth and Reality.'" Which led to her idea: "I thought for a while of adopting 'FTR,' standing for 'Fact, Truth, and Reality'"; but she then added: "Historians were actually realtors. Real Estate, when you come to think of it, is a very fine phrase and it is exactly the sphere that writers of nonfiction deal in: the real estate of man, of human conduct. But I cannot very well call us 'Realtors' because that has been pre-empted — although as a matter of fact I would like to. I wish I could get it back from the dealers in land. Then the categories could be poets, novelists, and realtors."[3]

Some writers and editors today prefer the term "literary journalism" or "literary nonfiction" or "narrative nonfiction" or just plain old "essay." But even though no one has been completely satisfied, creative nonfiction, considering all the ground it covers, over the years has worked best and has been generally accepted. Still, there will always be naysayers with caveats.

I did not make up the term "creative nonfiction." I began using it, off and on, when a colleague, a mentor at Pitt, Montgomery Culver, commented, after reading my first book, that I was "trying to be creative with nonfiction." But I did not know then that the term had been used sporadically and sparingly over the years. David Madden, a poet, essayist, and novelist, first used the term in 1959 at the University of Tennessee where he was then teaching. Half a dozen years later, at Ohio University in Athens, he taught his first class in creative nonfiction, titled "American Dreams, American Nightmares." And in 1969, Madden reviewed Frank Conroy's memoir, *Stop Time,* describing it as creative nonfiction. Around the same time, Seymour Krim, a journalist and novelist, taught a class once or twice at Columbia University called Creative Nonfiction. The term didn't quite catch on — although its roots can be traced back to a quarter century before Madden and Krim and, surprisingly, not to the United States, where creative nonfiction as a movement first emerged.[4]

The label was first introduced by the Canadian Authors Association, which had established awards in the early 1930s for Canadian authors, in fiction, poetry, and what they were then describing as "general literature" — meaning, to them, nonfiction. But submissions in general literature invariably doubled or sometimes tripled those in poetry and fiction. Which made it more difficult for those in general literature to win a prize.

What to do? Well, they were academics mostly, so of course they formed a committee and held a meeting — a number of meetings, in fact. And they realized as they examined and discussed each book that had been submitted for consideration that the general literature books could be categorized. There were books that were obviously "academic," what they described as "works of learning, bound by facts" — which would be for the scholar. And there were "works of graceful style, in which imagination played a leading part (as in essays, descriptive writing and some biographies) which would appeal to the ordinary reader." And this category they called "creative nonfiction." Not surprisingly, the "graceful style" group consistently won over more "substantial books" (such as histories), in which the authors did not "feel free to be equally selective or imaginative when dealing with facts."

With an award for the new category duly established, the inaugural winner was a political journalist, Bruce Hutchison, for his book *The Unknown Country: Canada and Her People,* which was described by the committee as "an attempt to paint a clear-cut and revealing picture of the Dominion . . . its people, its history, its virtues, its shortcomings, its joys, its sorrows."

And based on his biography, written for the awards ceremony that year, Hutchison was the perfect recipient of the first legitimate creative nonfiction award — a virtual model of how many of us creative nonfiction writers might describe ourselves years back or even today: "Mr. Hutchison claims he has no career and will continue to avoid having one. . . . His job has taken him across the length and breadth of the Dominion, to the Imperial Conference in London in 1937 (with a motor trip over most of Europe), and many trips to Washington and other parts of the U.S. He has written short stories for *Saturday Evening*

Post, Collier's, Cosmopolitan, American, Liberty. One day he hopes to return to fiction writing when he finds it no longer necessary to eat regularly."[5]

The Canadian awards for creative nonfiction continued for a number of years before fading away, mostly for lack of funding. But the debate over naming, and over the very existence of the genre, continued and grew more heated from the 1960s onward. And maybe this is not surprising, and not a bad thing. Writers are motivated by competition and provocation, powered by ego, insecurity, and their passion. Controversy, debate, challenge — the essence of acting and being contrary — leads to creativity, which is also the essence of the genre, what creative nonfiction had been and will continue to be, in the end, all about.

Moreover, if it wasn't for this "name-game" over identity, the genre might have just quietly been buried into the literary ecosystem, not as a genre like poetry or fiction or drama, but as something else — an aberration, on the fringe of the mainstream, unconventional, like maybe jazz was considered early on by music aficionados.

In some ways, in fact, creative nonfiction is exactly like jazz. It is a rich mixture of flavors, ideas, and techniques, some of which might be newly invented and others as old as writing itself. In some ways, both jazz and creative nonfiction have been discounted and undermined, considered by many purists as not quite legitimate. And it has been confronted by the same kind of critical skepticism as jazz musicians have had to confront.

Duke Ellington, renowned composer, refused to call what he wrote and performed "jazz." He once told his biographer Terry Teachout that most Americans "still take it for granted that European music — classical music, if you will — is the only really respectable kind . . . jazz [is] like the kind of man you wouldn't want your daughter to associate with."[6] Charles Mingus, another celebrated Black jazzman, felt much the same way: "To me the word 'jazz' means nigger, discrimination, second-class citizenship, the whole back-of-the-bus bit."[7]

I won't say that we writers of creative nonfiction and proponents of the label, early on or now, were in the back of the literary or journalistic bus. We weren't even on the bus. We were simply an unacknowledged part of a thing that many insisted did not exist as an entity, or, like Voldemort, that could not or should not be named.

But we needed a name, even an inadequate one, in order to define or describe

———

what we were doing and make us count. It was a question of belonging—a destination, a label, a meeting of the minds—for all of us creative nonfictionists to come together, dialogue and share our work, and earn a certain legitimacy that had been denied us from the very beginning, at least three hundred years ago. But it took a while, a very long while, for creative nonfiction . . . to become creative nonfiction . . . in name and in fact.

The story of the modern-day emergence of the creative nonfiction genre begins with another name or label—and another leader, a campaigner who did not just ride a horse but brought together an entire cavalry of writers, leading the charge with a loud and resounding symbolic "varoom."

CHAPTER 2

THE CHANGEMAKERS

I clearly remember reading for the first time Tom Wolfe's fifty-one-page introduction to an anthology, *The New Journalism*, that he had edited with E. W. Johnson. I read it right after it was published in 1973, not long after I had started teaching, and I thought immediately: "This will be the perfect teaching tool." And it was—almost.

What Wolfe had written was more than an introduction; it was like a proclamation. I could imagine Wolfe, in his characteristic white suit, standing on a stage behind a podium, in front of a crowd of admirers, waving his arms and preaching the new journalism gospel like the evangelist Billy Graham. It is not a far reach to say that Wolfe was *the* evangelist for the new journalism, and without him it is quite possible new journalism would not have ever achieved the literary status it and creative nonfiction have today.

Wolfe's introduction was actually a compilation of articles written over the previous few years for *Esquire* magazine and a really terrific article published on Valentine's Day 1972, "The Birth of 'the New Journalism': Eyewitness Report," in *New York* magazine. Much of what Wolfe was saying he had said before, as had a few others, but this introduction put it all together—his entire new journalism schtick in one definitive and detailed narrative statement.

Wolfe had two primary objectives in writing his intro. First, he meant to announce the dethroning of the novel as what many considered the pinnacle of literary success and achievement. Second, he was demonstrating that there was something happening in the literary world – over the previous decade, and maybe even much longer – that had become a movement that would propel the first new direction in literature in half a century. This is what he was calling, for lack of a better name, "the new journalism."

I personally didn't care about the first part – dethroning the novel as the pinnacle of success in literature. And I don't think anybody else did either, including some of the writers he thought would be vulnerable to this dethroning, such as Saul Bellow, John Updike, and Philip Roth, who were, according to Wolfe, "sweating it out" because of the rise of new journalism. What really resonated with me was how he took the old traditional journalism to task and put together all of the elements of this new journalism so that even non-writers, folks who had maybe never even heard of the new journalism before, could understand it.[1]

The old journalism, nonfiction, the flood of information presented to readers in newspapers and magazines at that time and in the traditional way – what Wolfe characterized as writing with "a beige tone" – could put you to sleep, he wrote. It was like painting a wall with neutral shades so whatever bits of color were in the room would stand out, a reasonable approach, perhaps, but readers were mostly bored to tears, not understanding or caring about what the writer was doing or thinking or why, and therefore losing interest and ceasing to read. "The standard nonfiction writer's voice was like the standard announcer's voice . . . a drag, a droning," he said.[2]

And it wasn't just the voice and attitude that Wolfe was rejecting, it was the literal repetitive formula, that who-what-when-where-and-maybe-why "inverted pyramid" style that so many traditional journalists adhered to when reporting news. That's when you start your story with the most important factor, usually the "who," and then place the other Ws in order of importance from that point on until all or most of the W factors were dealt with. And when you turned in your story to the copy desk, the editor could then – if there was a space problem on the page or in the paper, too much news on any given day – just lop off, delete, the less important W factors and the reader would still get the essence of the story – the most important part of the news. Very formulaic. And not that it wasn't a challenge. Not an easy task to break down a potentially complicated and many-factored idea concisely and in Ws — but it wasn't rocket science. And maybe not so creative or literary, either.

Even the feature stories were pretty much programmed and formulaic. Yes, you could lead with a clever phrase or an anecdote — something to entice the reader — but then, almost always, the reporter would just revert back to the news, the information. Maybe the reporter would end the story by tying in the anecdote from the lead in the last paragraph, depending on available space, but it didn't quite capture the potential of the story, the three-dimensionality that made the story real and memorable — what he was calling the vital elements of new journalism.

By vital elements, he meant, for one thing, the development of character. People in the story might have a distinctive appearance or manner; and they were not, always, just talking heads, providing pithy quotes. They talked to the reporter or to one another, had conversations; they dialogued. And there were status details, often symbolic of a character's behavior, their style, the way they expressed what they thought or hoped was their position in the world. The idea of objectivity, which had always been a sham, was discounted. In the new journalism, the writer had a voice; no beige tone here. Writers could observe and sometimes, in one way or the other, respond to what was happening in the story, using the forbidden "I" word in reference to themselves. All of these aspects, or as many as possible, were presented in a scene-by-scene structure that was action-oriented, and meant to keep the reader intrigued and turning pages. This — writing in scenes — was, more than anything else, the key structural aspect of new journalism.

In his introduction, Wolfe singled out a scene written by Gay Talese, then a features writer and reporter for the *New York Times,* in his *Esquire* magazine profile of the former heavyweight boxing champion Joe Louis, which starts with this scene.

> "Hi, sweetheart!" Joe Louis called to his wife, spotting her waiting for him at
> the Los Angeles airport.
>
> She smiled, walked toward him, and was about to stretch up on her toes and
> kiss him — but suddenly stopped.

"Joe," she said, "where's your tie?"

"Aw, sweetie," he said, shrugging, "I stayed out all night in New York and didn't have time —"

"All night!" she cut in. "When you're out here all you do is sleep, sleep, sleep."

"Sweetie," Joe Louis said, with a tired grin, "I'm an ole man."[3]

Encountering Talese's profile for the first time, Wolfe was amazed: "*What the hell is going on?*" he wrote. "With a little reworking the whole article could have read like a short story." Meaning that not only had Talese led with a scene, but that Talese had included other scenes that might have been rearranged so that the entire piece would flow from beginning to end just like a short story — with the informational elements fitted in more smoothly and perhaps unnoticeably as part of the narrative.[4]

Wolfe's reaction shows how uncertain journalists were at the time about writing in this way — manipulating structure, emphasizing narrative. Downgrading, in a way, the reporting? Or maybe even minimizing it, as it sometimes turned out. This was, or so it seemed in 1962, a significant departure.

Talese, in his introduction to a collection of his early work in 1970, *Fame and Obscurity,* explains that his Joe Louis piece was in some ways an experiment, or an awakening, "my first attempt at what would be called 'the new journalism'" — part of an evolution in his style. The article, Talese wrote, "opens with Louis, fatigued after three frolicsome days in New York City, arriving at the Los Angeles airport and being met by his wife . . . a scene that could have led into a short story situation; later in the article, the writing style falls back on straighter reportage, including my own uncertainty with the form at that point, but still later the approach is again scene-setting and dialogue and away from rigid reporting."[5]

Talese's profile of the Broadway director Joshua Logan, published in *Esquire* the following year (December 1963), was much less structurally erratic — a smoother and more dramatic narrative. It also demonstrated Talese's uncanny instinct to find and capture scenes — by devoting as much time as needed when researching every story (he called this "the fine art of hanging out"), to discover a brilliant flash that thoroughly illuminates the characters he profiles.[6] A more traditional journalist might have avoided or not even recognized these incidents

—

as dramatic or insightful material. Or, as he told Carol Polsgrove for her history of *Esquire* in the 1960s, *It Wasn't Pretty, Folks, But Didn't We Have Fun?* "just being there, observing, waiting for the climactic moment when the mask would drop and true character would reveal itself."[7]

While he was hanging out for his Logan piece during a rehearsal, Talese recalled in *Fame and Obscurity,* Logan and his co-star, Claudia McNeil, "got into an argument that not only was more dramatic than the play itself but revealed something of the character of Logan and Ms. McNeil in ways that I could never have done had I approached the subject from the more conventional form of reporting."[8]

Talese has been amazingly productive during his long career—he is still writing—but he will be most remembered for a scene published in 1966 taking place in a private Beverly Hills social club. Talese was on assignment for *Esquire* to write a profile of Frank Sinatra, but when he arrived in Hollywood he was denied his interview, even though it had been scheduled and promised, because Sinatra was irritable and down in the dumps; he had a cold. Suddenly forbidden to talk with Sinatra and fearing he would lose his assignment, Talese decided to follow Sinatra around, and on this night he observed quite a telling confrontation: Ol' Blue Eyes encountered a young screenwriter, Harlan Ellison, and insulted his work, the movie *The Oscar,* calling it "crap," and also Ellison's mode of dress, especially his "Game Warden boots." Talese recreated the scene, word for word, insult by insult, pretty much capturing Sinatra's imperious personality, with or without a cold. The scene itself, with many other scenes in this profile, has become one of the most memorable and talked-about "new journalism" set pieces in the history of the genre. Not long ago, in celebrating the seventieth anniversary of *Esquire*'s founding, its editors decided to reprint the best story it had ever published—"Frank Sinatra Has a Cold." It was fifteen thousand words.[9]

Not only did Talese perfect the scene and the fine art of hanging out, he and Wolfe personified something about the attitude of the movement in that they didn't disappear into the background; they didn't hesitate to draw attention to themselves and make themselves characters in their stories; you could see that in the way they dressed. Wolfe had style, panache, charisma. He was bursting, it seemed, with confidence. His writing and his persona commanded attention. This was in some ways his real mission for himself and new journalism.

Writers, whether they want to admit it or not, he told one interviewer, "are in the business of calling attention to themselves." Wolfe was masterful in that regard. And he did want attention—always—and did everything he could to make that happen, including the way he presented himself: in his white suit and vest, usually with a high-necked blue-and-white-striped shirt complemented by a creamy silk necktie—wherever he was—and whenever, summer or winter. You can see him now in all of his white-suited majesty on display in the National Portrait Gallery in Washington, D.C.[10]

Wolfe was a good-looking guy, tall and blue-eyed, with a striking mop of sandy-colored hair that made him seem even taller. Compared with other journalists at the time, he was quite an intellectual, holding a Ph.D. in American studies from Yale University. And he was fit—an outstanding collegiate athlete so naturally talented that he was invited for a tryout with the New York Giants baseball team. Perhaps, if things had gone differently for Wolfe, he might not have been breaking journalistic barriers and hitting solid literary base hits at a really high average; he would have been swinging a bat in National League stadiums and hitting home runs. And maybe even then, he might have found a reason to wear a white suit.

Wolfe's costume, as stylish and over the top as it was, was no match for Gay Talese's elaborate wardrobe. Talese's father was an old-fashioned tailor who had emigrated to Ocean City, New Jersey, from Italy in the 1920s, and he schooled his son in how to dress—from ascots and diamond cufflinks down to yellow silk suits and spit-shined pointed-toe loafers.

Talese and Wolfe might have seemed like competitors, especially in the New York literary and journalistic cognoscenti—in style, at least. Pundits repeatedly remarked, whether true or not, that the duo would often walk along Madison Avenue together, periodically posing, side by side, in reflecting store windows, comparing and admiring their outfits. But Wolfe was clearly second string, attire-wise, because he always seemed to look basically the same, albeit with some fresh accoutrements to his white on white. But, in contrast, Talese was and is a work of art each day, walking Madison Avenue, or summering in South Jersey, Ocean City, or Connecticut, a more recent retreat, all decked out at a supermarket, arriving, top down, in his classic yellow 1957 TR3.[11]

Wolfe, who died in 2018 at age eighty-eight, contended that his white suit "writer" costume came about by accident, although he immediately discovered its effect, which obviously delighted him and fulfilled in a perverse way his need to be noticed. "I had a white suit made that was too hot for summer," he once told an interviewer, "so I wore it in December. I found that it really irritated people – I had hit upon this harmless form of aggression!"[12]

Aggression was not exactly what I felt when I first read a long article in *Esquire* in 1963 about the hot rod and custom car craze in Southern California and the automobile "artists" like George Barris who embellished his creations with "Kandy Kolors." I was, rather, astonished and a bit puzzled. Who was this writer, a guy I had never heard of named Tom Wolfe, and what in hell did he think he was doing? But I read the whole piece in one sitting.

The article wasn't just about cars; there was a longer and much more intriguing scope to it: An emerging teenage culture in Southern California, weird new ways of dancing – the "hully-gully," "the shampoo," and "the bird" – and clothes and hairstyles. "Bouffant hairdos . . . and slacks that are, well," Wolfe wrote, "skin-tight does not get the idea across: it's more the conformation than how tight the slacks are; . . . it's as if some lecherous old tailor with a gluteus-maximus fixation designed them."[13]

More than anything, it was about the meaning of cars to these kids whose appreciation and awareness of art were focused on these four-wheel sculptures – in stark contrast to what they might have been taught in school, if they had ever listened. "I don't have to dwell on the point that cars mean more to these kids than architecture did in Europe's great formal century, say, 1750 to 1850," Wolfe commented. "They are freedom, style, sex, power, motion, colour – everything is right there."[14]

This article, nearly ten thousand words, was filled with this kind of off-the-wall information and compelling observations by Wolfe, then a thirty-three-year-old reporter for the *New York Herald Tribune*. But despite the fact that I didn't understand, as one might say today, where he was coming from, it sure did turn me on.

Not just because of his insights, but more than anything, its style. It seemed as if this guy was not reporting; he was, rather, performing on the page and, at the same time, pushing the limits of what we were then calling journalism, breaking rules and established procedures that seemed not only irreverent but downright remarkable and courageous. I had never read anything like this before — I mean, in journalism. I remember thinking: "This guy is letting it all out." As in the full title of his piece: "There Goes (Varoom! Varoom!) That Kandy-Kolored (Thphhhhh!) Tangerine-Flake Streamline Baby (Rahghhh!) Around the Bend (Brummmmmmmmmmmmmmmmm) . . . "

The piece was published two years later in a collection of Wolfe's work with the same title, along with a number of articles he had written in the early 1960s for *Esquire* or *New York* magazine in which he continued to push the limits of what was then considered journalism. Writing in the accents of his characters, making up punctuation marks (::::::::::::::::::::::), or yelling and screaming at his readers or his characters IN CAPS — mocking the people he was writing about and himself, whatever seemed to come to mind that would make his readers — listen — or read. I remember thinking (I'm not kidding!), could I write something, making up all these noises and crazy punctuation marks and send it off in a manila envelope to one of these magazines and get published? I never tried, although I am guessing that lots of other writers did, but as I was to learn as the years went by, one of Wolfe's greatest skills as a writer was making the outrageous seem natural, brilliant — and funny — even if you didn't understand everything he was doing or saying. Which was exactly the message in Kurt Vonnegut's review of *Tangerine Flake* in the *New York Times*. Vonnegut summed up Wolfe's work and style in the final paragraph of the review: "Verdict: Excellent book by a genius who will do anything to get attention."[15]

In 1968 Wolfe published *The Electric Kool-Aid Acid Test*, his account of the Merry Pranksters led by their guru, Ken Kesey, the author of the peyote-inspired novel and Broadway play *One Flew Over the Cuckoo's Nest*, a group that traveled cross country in a school bus painted yellow, orange, blue, and red while experimenting with Kool-Aid laced with LSD and other psychedelic substances. And then with his fourth book, *Radical Chic and Mau-Mauing the Flak Catchers*, Wolfe captured the action and the irony at a party at Leonard Bernstein's penthouse apartment on the Upper East Side, bringing together in one space a seemingly absurd group of guests: New York's cultural and artistic elite with the leaders of the Black Panther Party. Bernstein — Lenny to his friends — the conductor of the New York Philharmonic Orchestra and an accomplished composer and author, was a leading social figure in the New York intelligentsia. Wolfe, who had not been invited and had crashed the party, wrote a scathing take-down of the event — a scenario *Time* magazine described in a review as an "appallingly funny, cool, small, deflative two-scene social drama about America's biggest, hottest, and most perplexing problem — the confrontation between Black Rage and White Guilt."[16]

Wolfe made up the term "radical chic," which has led to such other derivations as "terrorist chic," "ashcan chic," "hippie chic," "Parisian chic," "shabby chic." Later Wolfe was responsible for another phrase, the one that characterized the 1970s: "The Me Decade."

CHAPTER 3

THE FIRST CREATIVE NONFICTIONISTS

Not everyone was proclaiming Wolfe's brilliance after *Tangerine Flake*. To the contrary. There was plenty of pushback on Wolfe and the idea of new journalism, most prominently and publicly from Dwight Macdonald, a writer, editor, and TV commentator who, in a damning critique in the *New York Review of Books* in 1966, lashed out at Wolfe and his new journalism ideas. Was it new? he asked. Was it journalism? Was it, in fact, literature? Or fiction masquerading as nonfiction? It was, Macdonald said, "parajournalism," or even more damning, "a bastard form," with writers "having it both ways, exploiting the factual authority of journalism and the atmospheric license of fiction." At the time, I guess, "having it both ways," or even writing it and employing the tools of both genres, was somehow a bad thing, mostly because journalists have been so protective of their turf. There's still a lot of this turf-warring going on today as the boundaries of nonfiction are becoming so fluid, primarily because of the popularity of memoir and other offshoots, such as the lyric essay and auto-fiction.[1]

Macdonald and many others were quick to point out, quite rightly, as I soon learned, that this journalism Wolfe was hailing was not at all new; writers and journalists have been using fictional techniques to write nonfiction for hundreds of years, including the author of *Robinson Crusoe*, Daniel Defoe, the man considered the father of English journalism.

Most critics believe that *Crusoe* was a novel, very loosely based on the story of a young sailor, Alexander Selkirk, stranded on a desert island for four years. Defoe's next book, however, *A Journal of the Plague Year,* published in 1722, might well be categorized today as new journalism or creative nonfiction. *A Journal of the Plague Year* is a story told from the first-person perspective of someone named H. F., who recounts his experience living in London during an outbreak of the plague in 1665 to 1666. But — and here was the rub — the *Plague Year* he captured so vividly took place when Defoe was only five or six years old. Which may well be why he faced such controversy and criticism soon after *A Journal of the Plague Year* was published. One critic called Defoe, generally, "a false, shuffling, prevaricating rascal." Another observed that he was a master of "forging a story and imposing it on the world as truth."[2]

Considering Defoe's work now, I can certainly understand what he was doing — trying to sell books and make a living, a challenge for all writers then, and even now, while also communicating ideas and information that would be pretty much unavailable or maybe not even of interest to readers. And although he designed a personal narrative surrounding the facts in his journal — the information he was providing was accurate, based upon the available research at the time — at least according to another biographer, Watson Nicholson, who disputed the notion that the *Journal* was a novel, a much-debated subject of contention.

Nicholson maintained that there was "overwhelming evidence of the complete authenticity of Defoe's 'masterpiece of the imagination.'" There was not, Nicholson said, "a single essential statement in the *Journal* not based on historic fact." True, Defoe had a way of embroidering, but even so, "the employment of the first person in the narrative in no sense interferes with the authenticity of the facts recorded."[3]

Too bad, I think, as I am writing part of this book while in isolation during the Covid-19 pandemic, that Defoe is not around to receive the accolades today that he may have deserved centuries ago from this "masterpiece of imagination." Writing in the *New York Times,* Orhan Pamuk, recipient of the Nobel Prize in literature, author of the then forthcoming novel *Nights of the Plague,* describes *A Journal of the Plague Year* as "the single most illuminating work of literature ever written on contagion and human behavior."

Defoe, Pamuk said, recaptured in many respects exactly the lives we were leading in 2020 and 2021 in Covid-land (people keeping their distance when they meet on the street, sharing the intensity of their suffering and their fear of death, or wasting away in overcrowded hospitals). His work, using the plague as a vehicle, "shows us that behind the endless remonstrances and boundless rage there also lies an anger against fate, against a divine will that witnesses and perhaps even condones all this death and human suffering." There was, Pamuk wrote, "rage against the institutions of organized religion that seem unsure of how to deal with any of it." Not unlike the rage we recently experienced against our leaders in health care who were unprepared for the pandemic and against the White House cabal that had tried repeatedly to brush it away, as if it hardly had happened.[4]

Defoe was not an outlier. A long line of writers famous today for novels that are and will be read and admired for centuries were writing journalism to pay their bills by using the narrative techniques, employed in their fiction. Charles Dickens's first book, *Sketches by Boz, Illustrative of Every-Day Life and Every-Day People,* which describes life in London in the mid-1830s, would likely be referred to as a work of creative nonfiction today. "Nothing," a reviewer of *Boz* said, "escapes Dickens' street-smart eye and ear, as he visits the pleasure gardens of Vauxhall, the second-hand clothes shops of Monmouth Street, the city's pawnshops and theaters and gin joints."[5]

Mark Twain, of *Tom Sawyer* and *Huckleberry Finn* fame, made his living through most of his life as a public speaker and an essayist and from what we would call today "travel writing," with books like *The Innocents Abroad* and *Life on the Mississippi. Roughing It,* perhaps his most popular nonfiction book today, provides a dramatic and often hilarious account of Twain's overland stagecoach journey to Nevada, his experiences as a silver miner and a cub newspaper reporter. Twain, in contrast to Dickens, was a master of embellishment. "Twain," Richard Russo writes in his introduction to *Mark Twain's Collected Nonfiction: Volume 2,* "didn't lose much sleep over the idiosyncratic demands of fiction versus nonfiction. Both offered numerous and varied opportunities to an inspired, indeed unparalleled, bullshitter." Are the events in *Roughing It* true? "Once asked that same question about one of his own stories," Russo writes, "David Sedaris replied, 'They're true enough,' and it's easy to imagine

Twain saying the same thing about his youthful adventures in the American West."[6]

Their novels may have provided a more lasting fame, but nonfiction—encountering real life—was sometimes more fulfilling, and for Jack London, forever haunting. London's *The Call of the Wild* was published in 1902 and *The Sea Wolf,* the year after—perhaps his two most successful novels. But in 1903, after having lost a commission to write an article about the coronation of King Edward VII from the perspective of the working class, he stayed in London, and posed as a stranded and impoverished sailor, living in the Whitechapel district of the East End of London, sleeping in flop houses, begging for work, and often nearly starving.

What he observed and lived through there eventually led to his nonfiction book *People of the Abyss* in 1903, which he considered the most important book he ever wrote. "No other book of mine took so much of my young heart and tears as that study of the economic degradation of the poor." His friend and fellow writer Upton Sinclair once wrote that London, for many years after his book was published, was "haunted beyond all peace" by his immersive research experience.[7]

Sinclair, like London a novelist, may have also been haunted by what he learned in researching his own book around the same time. Sinclair's *The Jungle* revealed the scandal of the meatpacking industry—the most dangerous job for the working man and woman in America at the turn of the twentieth century, and perhaps even now as well. The book tells the story of the fictional character Jurgis Rudkus, who escapes the hard life of a peasant in Lithuania and journeys with his family to Chicago in pursuit of the American dream. Jurgis and his family confront horrific conditions, "wage slavery," and no matter how hard he works, he is defeated and humiliated and beaten down at every step along the way. He is laid off from the plant repeatedly and is eventually jailed for fighting, for vagrancy, and for not paying his debts. His suffering is relentless. His house is repossessed, his wife is raped and later dies in childbirth. His toddler son drowns in a flood on a street.[8]

Although *The Jungle* is a novel, Sinclair researched the book much like a reporter would today—like Talese now or Defoe three hundred years before him. Sinclair embedded himself in stockyards and slaughterhouses in Chicago

—

and conducted in-depth interviews not just with workers but with bartenders, clergymen, politicians—anyone who would talk with him who might have a story to tell. Roaming the neighborhoods around the stockyards, Sinclair happened upon the wedding of a Lithuanian laborer and his fifteen-year-old bride, who become the protagonists of this story—Ona and Jurgis. The first chapter of his book, a long wedding scene, introduces most of the main characters and prepares the reader for their horrific life journeys. *The Jungle* was serialized in installments in a highly popular socialist newspaper called *Appeal to Reason* in 1905 before Doubleday, Page & Company published the book the following year. It has not been out of print since.[9]

Writing in *Slate* in 2006, in a review of the book on the hundredth anniversary of its publication, Karen Olsson connects *The Jungle* to the work of writers practicing new journalism or creative nonfiction today. "Once the opening chapter's long wedding scene is over," she writes, "the narrative rarely lingers in any one setting for long, instead surging from one miserable place to the next, offering a dark, brutal picture of the city based on the sort of reportorial research practiced nowadays by Tom Wolfe and Richard Price. The writing is often sentimental, but its pace and panoramic quality keep the pages turning."[10]

Despite its literary success, Sinclair had hoped that *The Jungle* would improve the plight of American immigrant workers, but President Theodore Roosevelt and others in government at the time, along with reform-oriented activists, paid much more attention to the scandalous conditions in the meatpacking industry, from rotten meat to rat droppings, mixed with sawdust and dirt. Sinclair's revelations led to a series of legislative initiatives, including the Pure Food and Drug Act and the Meat Inspection Act—initiatives that pioneered a steady onslaught of legislation protecting the consumer on many fronts from illicit industry practices. Sinclair should have been delighted, but he was more than a little disappointed. He once remarked: "I aimed at the public's heart and by accident I hit it in the stomach."

Three decades after those books by London and Sinclair, George Orwell used his skills as a fiction writer to craft two masterful immersion books of what we can call today creative nonfiction. For the first, *Down and Out in Paris and London,* he, like London, lived the life of near destitution in Paris as a laborer in restaurant kitchens and, similarly, as a tramp in London. *The Road to Wigan Pier* is his account of the hardships of working-class life in Yorkshire and Lancashire. Nonfiction — mostly. Later he wrote his most famous and recognizable books, the novels *Nineteen Eighty-Four* and *Animal Farm.*[11]

Orwell's fellow dystopian visionary, Aldous Huxley, who was a fan and once a teacher of Orwell, is probably best known today for his novel *Brave New World*. Huxley was a formidable literary figure — literally, at about six feet four inches tall, and intellectually; many theorized that he had memorized the encyclopedia, to explain his expansive knowledge. Despite having severely impaired vision due to an infection early in life, he read and absorbed absolutely everything he could. "His intellectual memory was phenomenal," said his brother Julian Huxley (a controversial figure himself as an advocate for eugenics); Aldous was "doubtless trained by a tenacious will to surmount the original horror of threatened blindness."[12]

Huxley's fiction was based on his real-life experiences, often satirizing elements of high society, but he was also an accomplished writer of nonfiction as an essayist, travel writer, and journalist. One biographer assesses Huxley's *Along the Road* as one of the best modern works of travel writing. A *New Yorker* profiler of the author asserts, after reading his essay "Hyperion to a Satyr," a piece about the impact of the Hyperion Activated Sludge Plant on a Los Angeles beach, that Huxley "might have invented the New Journalism all on his own, had he realized the potential."[13] His nonfiction legacy even lives on in pop culture — the Doors took their name from his book *The Doors of Perception,* published in 1954, in which he wrote about an experience using the hallucinogenic drug mescaline.[14]

Ernest Hemingway was at first a journalist, working in 1917 and 1918 for the *Kansas City Star,* when he was barely eighteen years old, and then later for three years beginning in 1920 for the *Toronto Daily Star.* Throughout his life, he filed stories for many other newspapers, magazines, and wire services. Reviewing his nonfiction work now, his scene setting techniques, use of realistic dialogue, dramatic detailing of character and place, all with his distinctive voice, you could easily say that he was writing what would be called new journalism or creative nonfiction today, much like Talese and Wolfe.

When I first started teaching in the early 1970s, I assigned a lot of Hem-

—

ingway's nonfiction to my students, excerpts from *Death in the Afternoon*, his bullfighting book, and pieces from his war reporting. Many of my students were studying news writing then. This was at a time when there were jobs and opportunities for journalists, unlike today. Creative nonfiction or even the new journalism was not an option – not in English departments like the one in which I was teaching or in journalism schools, which, despite Wolfe and his many followers, pretty much sloughed off new journalism and its message.

During those years, I would impress upon my students the importance of learning the basics of journalism. I would say to them that wherever their future paths as writers might take them, just learning interviewing techniques, the basics of research, and the who-what-when-where and why of things was a terrific foundation to launch their careers. And then I would point to all of the Hemingway readings I had assigned. "Look what he achieved," I would say, "starting out as a journalist: And then a Nobel Prize in Literature!"

Was I right about learning the basics? I think I was, even though there was always a caveat. You needed to know the rules in order to know when and why to break them, which I was encouraging them to do. But would Hemingway agree with me? Of course, he would, I thought. But, as I was to learn later, maybe not. Hemingway's appreciation of his years in journalism was not at all clear cut. Depending on his mood at any given moment, he would embrace what he learned as a journalist – or totally discount it. He was, as many of his biographies have made clear, a complicated fellow.

When he began working at the *Kansas City Star*, his editor immediately pressed a style sheet in his hands that stated the four basic rules he would be expected to follow: "Use short sentences. Use short paragraphs. Use vigorous English. Be positive, not negative." With perhaps the exception of the fourth, these rules, let's call them guidelines, pretty much summed up his very distinctive and memorable style as a fiction writer. For a long time, or so people thought, Hemingway embraced those rules passed on to him when he was eighteen years old, as he told a reporter in an interview in 1940: "Those were the best rules I ever learned for the business of writing. I've never forgotten them. No man with any talent, who feels and writes truly about the thing he is trying to say, can fail to write well if he abides by them."[15]

And yet, years before he made those remarks, he wrote his bibliographer,

Louis Henry Cohn, saying: "The newspaper stuff I have written . . . has nothing to do with the other writing which is entirely apart. If you have made your living as a newspaper man, learning your trade, writing against deadlines, writing to make stuff timely rather than permanent, no one has any right to dig this stuff up and use it against the stuff you have written to write the best you can." Like I said, he was a complicated fellow.[16]

You can find the best retrospective on Hemingway's nonfiction in *By-Line: Ernest Hemingway,* an anthology edited by William White, published in 1967. White, a professor of journalism and American history at Wayne State University, owned what was thought to be the largest collection of books written by Hemingway. In *By-Line,* he reprinted or excerpted nearly a hundred examples — only a third of the nonfiction Hemingway had produced in his lifetime. Despite his obvious respect and appreciation of Hemingway's genius, White puzzled over Hemingway's periodic indifference to the genre he was writing, a "blurring of the distinction between his news writing and his imaginative writing."

In his introduction, White offers a number of examples, including "Italy, 1927," a piece Hemingway wrote for the *New Republic* as journalism, then published as a short story with a new title in *Men Without Women,* a collection of his short stories, and then again in an anthology of his writing; "On the Quai at Smyrna," written as nonfiction for the *Toronto Star,* also later published as fiction in the same anthology; and a news dispatch he wrote for the North American Newspaper Alliance that he later included as fiction in an anthology he edited, *Men at War: The Best War Stories of All Time.* White eventually asks rhetorically, "What did he mean by stories?" Hemingway, he concludes, "no matter what he wrote or why he was writing, or for whom, was always the creative writer: he used his material to suit his imaginative purposes."[17]

Even knowing that Hemingway was a complicated fellow, to be kind to him and his work, "complicated" was a great understatement. Throughout his career he was perceived by many, especially in the press, as an adventurous rogue and macho-man — hunting big game in Africa, risking his life repeatedly in various areas of combat to gather the material for his stories, fiction or nonfiction (or both) — no matter the danger. He played this macho game for his admiring public, posing with his hunting trophies, his battlefront dress, his shirtless manly physique, often baring his fists, ready to fight — virtually anybody. But few ever saw the real behind-the-scenes Hemingway until a young writer for the *New Yorker* persuaded him to allow her to immerse herself in his private life and become an integral part of it.

She was Lillian Ross, who had been writing for the magazine since 1945 and, eventually, wrote more personal narrative profiles than any other long-form writer in the world. Ross trained her profiling eye on too many people to even list here, including Ira Gershwin, J. D. Salinger, Clint Eastwood, Adlai Stevenson, Charlie Chaplin, John Huston . . . I could go on. But perhaps her most famous profile — or the one that triggered the most attention and controversy — was of Ernest Hemingway, after Ross spent two days with him in 1950 when the author visited New York. The piece was titled "How Do You Like It Now, Gentlemen?"[18]

Getting to Hemingway was not easy for Ross. It was a process. She did not work through a book publicist, send him an e-mail, or call him on the telephone to make an appointment, as we might do today. Ross traveled to Ketchum, Idaho, in the middle of the winter in 1948 — it was ten degrees below zero, and Hemingway made her wait for hours — to interview him about a profile she was writing about bullfighting, a subject that she found in many ways distasteful. Hemingway, she thought, gave a good interview, finally, and Ross followed up with a number of questions in letters and phone calls over the next few months until her article was published. In the process of their correspondence, they began writing long letters to each other. Hemingway began calling her "daughter," an obvious endearment.[19]

I remember reading this Hemingway profile sometime in the early 1970s, a dozen years after Hemingway had died, and feeling both amazed and enlightened. Ross captured the legendary Papa in a way no one had ever come close to, revealing his eccentric personality. Was this really the bizarre man, the great Hemingway, or had she made this stuff up? Lots of things happened during the two days Ross spent with Hemingway and his third wife, Mary, shopping for a winter coat and comfortable felt slippers, touring museums, visiting with a few friends, including Hemingway's favorite, the woman he called "The Kraut," who was the celebrated actress Marlene Dietrich. And wherever they went, Papa was always drinking, mostly champagne, even for breakfast, or sipping secretly from a flask on their many outings.

31

All of his actions were kind of spontaneous and unpredictable; you had to be there, on the scene, watching and waiting, being involved and at a distance at the same time to observe. And the way he talked, as Ross documented — like Indian talk was portrayed in western B-movies from the 1940s and 1950s — was weird and, looking at it now, out of context, obviously disrespectful. Today, the liberties and insensitivities writers then often milked for the sake of their stories would lead to rejection and inevitable litigation.[20]

Like when Ross met Hemingway and his wife Mary at the airport — he was coming from Havana. And he had somehow kidnapped or charmed his seat-mate, a short wiry guy named Myers, who was being held captive in a one-arm Hemingway embrace and perspiring like crazy. Hemingway's other arm clutched a scuffed, dilapidated briefcase pasted up with travel stickers.

Ross describes Hemingway before we find out what's going on with Myers: "Hemingway was wearing a red plaid wool shirt, a figured wool necktie, a tan wool sweater-vest, a brown tweed jacket tight across the back and with sleeves too short for his arms, gray flannel slacks, Argyle socks, and loafers, and he looked bearish, cordial, and constricted. His hair, which was very long in back, was gray, except at the temples, where it was white; his mustache was white, and he had a ragged, half-inch full white beard. There was a bump about the size of a walnut over his left eye. He was wearing steel-rimmed spectacles, with a piece of paper under the nosepiece."

Ross's descriptions of her subjects were long and legendary. She accumulated details, often mundane, and she continued to build on the visual portrait she was painting throughout her profiles. Like the little piece of paper Hemingway, she had noticed, had tucked under the nosepiece of his eyeglasses. Later in the story, Mary says to Ross, "He's had that same piece of paper under the nosepiece for weeks. When he really wants to get cleaned up, he changes the paper." Which pretty much said a lot about Hemingway without any further commentary.

At the airport, Hemingway told Ross that his briefcase contained the unfinished manuscript of his new book, *Across the River and into the Trees*. He explained that he had persuaded Myers, his seat companion on the flight, to read it. "He read book all way up on plane," Hemingway said in his Indian talk. "He like book, I think." Myers, trapped in Hemingway's bear-like grasp as they talked

—

in the airport, was mystified. All he could say to Ross was, "Whew!" To which Hemingway replied: "Book too much for him. Book start slow, then increase in pace till it becomes impossible to stand. . . . Book is like engine. We have to slack her off gradually."[21]

Ross's profile of Hemingway created quite a stir, with some criticizing her for making fun of America's greatest novelist. But Hemingway not only read Ross's piece before it was published, and approved it, he cooperated later when Ross expanded the piece into a book-length work, *Portrait of Hemingway.*

There were other writers who were also profiling Hemingway, including the critic Malcolm Cowley on assignment for *Life* magazine as early as 1948. But no one had ever captured the real Hemingway as Lillian Ross did. Writing in *Medium* in May 2021, soon after Ross's death at ninety-nine, the historian Steve Newman wrote: "If you've not read anything about Hemingway, start with Ross's insightful portrait; a portrait that is honest, never fawning, and above all else beautifully written. Her style was the forerunner of what we now know as the new journalism."[22]

Ross published ten books in her lifetime, but her first and most admired was *Picture,* published in 1952, after she went to Hollywood and stayed for a year and a half to observe the creation of John Huston's movie *The Red Badge of Courage.* The piece first appeared in a five-part series in the *New Yorker.* Ross, by the way, had been inspired by John Hersey's narrative *Hiroshima,* which was published in full in the *New Yorker* in 1946. She had an idea that she presented to her editor, William Shawn, in a very memorable and telling way: "I don't see why I shouldn't try to do a fact piece in novel form, or maybe a novel in fact form."[23]

In *Hiroshima,* Hersey profiled six victims of the horrific atomic bombing in Japan and told their stories in intimate and often minute-by-minute detail. *Hiroshima* was hailed as a revolutionary tour de force of journalism written in a story-oriented narrative style — like a novel. It was, many have said, the first genuine true-life novel. And it singlehandedly over the next few months seemed to make the world aware of the threat of nuclear power. And perhaps actually curbed the desire for other countries to develop and employ such tools of potential devastation.

By the time *Hiroshima* was published, Hersey had already been awarded the Pulitzer Prize for the novel *A Bell for Adano* (1945), and throughout his very fruitful career he published more than twenty books, jumping back and forth from fiction to nonfiction. As productive as he was in both genres, and as influential and impactful as *Hiroshima* was, Hersey seemed confused and somewhat angered about the nonfiction-fiction form that came later and the way it was practiced.

He claimed that writers like Tom Wolfe, Truman Capote, and Norman Mailer were inventing information used in their nonfiction pieces for personal and commercial gain without respect for the purity of journalism or, for that matter, their readers or the subjects they were writing about. Nicholas Lemann, in a *New Yorker* review of a new biography of Hersey, *Mr. Straight Arrow* by Jeremy Treglown, speculated: "Hersey thought of himself as a literary artist who experimented with various forms to create work that was guided by a high moral purpose; now one of those forms was being used by people who had no moral purpose that made sense to him."[24]

I can't say that I ever speak to my students in terms of moral purpose — a bit too pie-in-the-sky and jargonish, especially for those in their early twenties. But I do talk with them about the idea of not just writing for the sake of writing a good story, but to write also with a point of focus or a mission in mind. Even if the mission is simply to reveal Frank Sinatra's egocentricity which is worse when he has a cold. Or customized cars in the early 1960s as a way of saying something about the youth of America.

I should point out that sometimes the mission or point of focus will not come to a writer immediately. Talese did not know that Sinatra would refuse to see him or that he had a cold until he showed up in Hollywood; Wolfe had no idea what he would find when he went to his first custom car show in Southern California. The mission — the reason for writing what you are writing — will invariably come clear at some point during the researching or the writing process, if you look for it. You want your writing to be out-of-sight terrific, but also you want the piece as a whole to have a message. There are writers — many — mostly in nonfiction, who write with a mission, a moral purpose in mind, right from the beginning. Writers who want to illuminate something that is wrong or misunderstood and utilize narrative to suggest or cause change. I think Defoe did that by capturing the pandemic in the seventeenth century, as did Sinclair with the meatpacking industry even though his work caused a change that he had not intended. Jack London, and Orwell in *Down and Out in Paris and London,* highlighted the hopelessness of poverty.

A perfect example of a writer with a mission in mind and a story to tell who caused a change and created a worldwide and enlightened movement is Rachel Carson. *Silent Spring,* her book demonstrating the negative effects of pesticides on the environment, paved the way for many other narrative writers to embrace the environmental movement, precipitated by Carson: Michael Pollan, E. O. Wilson, Elizabeth Kolbert, Bill McKibben, to name a few. Although she is best known for *Silent Spring,* published in 1962, most of her early writing focused on the oceans, the subject of her first major publication. Carson originally wrote "Undersea" for a publication of the U.S. Bureau of Fisheries, where she was working at the time, but her department head told her it was too good to live in a government document. Her career was launched when she submitted it to the *Atlantic,* which published it in 1937. The essay led to her first book, *Under the Sea Wind,* published in 1941, but it was mostly paid little attention during the war and the aftermath years. She tried again with a similarly themed book, published in 1951, *The Sea Around Us.*[25]

She had initially submitted an excerpt from *The Sea Around Us* to the *Atlantic,* for obvious reasons, but the editors turned it down for being too "poetic." And maybe that was true for the *Atlantic,* but not for her readers—or for the *New Yorker,* which published "The Sea Around Us" in three parts, the magazine's first ever profile that wasn't about a person or persons. *The Sea Around Us* won the National Book Award for nonfiction in 1952 and stayed on the *New York Times* best-seller list for eighty-six weeks. The "poetic prose" rejected by the *Atlantic* distinguished her work and touched readers in a way that was unforgettably heart-rending and three-dimensional.

Silent Spring was her last book, and certainly her most significant and lasting. Although not as artful in its entirety as *The Sea Around Us,* it begins in the same imaginative—and poetic—way that makes her work so memorable and profound: "There was once a town in the heart of America where all life seemed to be in harmony with its surroundings. The town lay in the midst of a checker-

---

board of prosperous farms, with fields of grain and hillsides of orchards, where white clouds of bloom drifted above the green land. In autumn, oak and maple and birch set up a blaze of color that flamed and flickered across a backdrop of pines."[26]

She goes on to describe the irreplaceable beauty of this panoramic place — an array of wildflowers, foxes barking in the hills, deer roaming freely, and the people who came to see them and enjoy what was their perfect natural world. Until it wasn't. "Then, one spring, a strange blight crept over the area, and everything began to change. Some evil spell had settled on the community; mysterious maladies swept the flocks of chickens, and the cattle and sheep sickened and died. Everywhere was the shadow of death."[27]

At the end of this passage, she explains, suddenly and startlingly:

> No witchcraft, no enemy action had snuffed out life in this stricken world. The people had done it themselves.
>
> This town does not actually exist; I know of no community that has experienced all the misfortunes I describe. Yet every one of them has actually happened somewhere in the world, and many communities have already suffered a substantial number of them. A grim spectre has crept upon us almost unnoticed, and soon my imaginary town may have thousands of real counterparts. What is silencing the voices of spring in countless towns in America? I shall make an attempt to explain.[28]

Carson wrote most of *Silent Spring* while suffering from breast cancer. Her writing, along with a nationally televised CBS interview and testimony in front of Congress (both of which she did while incredibly weak and in pain), precipitated the passage of the Clean Air Act of 1963, the Clean Water Act of 1972, the National Environmental Protection Act of 1969, the Endangered Species Act of 1972, the Wilderness Act of 1964, and the formation of the Environmental Protection Agency in 1972. Carson died soon after her book was published.[29]

The focus on narrative and the use of techniques from fiction in writing nonfiction led to the debatable label that Wolfe and others gave to the new journalism — but it was Carson's poetic interpretation and presentation of fact and information that, perhaps more than any other writer, pushed the change in terminology to what we now call creative nonfiction.

Jill Lepore summarized the impact of *Silent Spring* in the *New Yorker* in 2018: "The number of books that have done as much good in the world can be counted on the arms of a starfish."[30]

CHAPTER 4

A STATUE OF A WOMAN IN THE PITTSBURGH AIRPORT AND ALL SHE REPRESENTS

I don't think it is a coincidence or an exaggeration to say that down through time and certainly over the past century women writers, such as Rachel Carson, have produced an overwhelming number of change-making stories told through narrative, more perhaps than men. Women who wanted to be journalists during the time that London, Sinclair, Hemingway, Orwell, and others were publishing and enjoying attention and praise always had two missions in mind. There was the story they wanted to write that might create change, and an even more challenging mission: to penetrate the white male journalist fortress that was dead-set against offering them opportunities to write their stories, because they were women.

Until very recently, women journalists were not considered worthy of writing serious stories. Even in the 1960s, as Wolfe and Talese were beginning to pioneer their new journalism, it was not new enough to include women. Gail Sheehy's book *Passages,* about the predictable crises people experience as they age, published in 1977, was on the *New York Times* best-seller list for three consecutive years, and the Library of Congress named it one of the ten most influential books of our time. Writing in *The Cut* a few years before she died in 2020, Sheehy remembered the struggle and the challenge for women journalists in the 1960s and 1970s: the atmosphere of forced division, the lack of acknowledgment of the work they produced, where they were positioned in the news-room.

"When I was a news chick at the *New York Herald Tribune*," she wrote, "se-questered in the flamingo pink Women's Department (as were all the paper's female journalists in the '60s), the male reporters I might encounter in the elevator looked straight through me, probably assuming I was somebody's stenographer."

One specific elevator ride, however, led to an opportunity to write, after she asked the tall sandy-haired reporter: "Mr. Wolfe, what's it like, writing for Clay Felker?" Felker was the editor of *New York* and later became the editor of *Esquire* and later yet of the *Village Voice*. Wolfe, to his credit, encouraged her to find out from the source – Felker himself.

"I crossed the DMZ into the City Room, all bobbing heads of white men with crew cuts (except for Bad Boy [Jimmy] Breslin and his tangle of black curls) and tapped on the door of the editor-in-chief. Clay Felker's booming voice came back: 'Where did you come from? The estrogen zone?'"[1]

Even ten years later, in the *New Journalism* anthology of the twenty writers selected as the best new journalists of the era, edited by Wolfe and E. W. John-son, only two women were included: Joan Didion and Barbara Goldsmith, who wrote many books in her long career, including the classic best seller *Little Gloria . . . Happy at Last,* about Gloria Vanderbilt's difficult coming of age, which be-came both a movie and a TV series.

But long before Sheehy was confined to the "estrogen zone," women jour-nalists were persona non grata in newsrooms, not included on mastheads and not legitimately acknowledged in bylines. But women managed, through force of will and ingenuity, to do good in the world or for the world by hiding who they were, often assuming a male identity – or disguising themselves as some-one else. And not only were they writing narrative, employing the techniques of fiction writers, as Wolfe had described, but daringly and courageously in-volving themselves in their stories, diving into unknown territory in situations that men could not or would not confront. And they worked really hard at it because they were, in many cases, not wanted and certainly not appreciated as women. But they not only made history; they changed history. And in order to do that, they often changed their names.

——

There are three statues at the Pittsburgh International Airport, through which I mostly travel from home to wherever and back. Two are heroic examples of the city's history. First, George Washington, the father of our country, who initiated the French and Indian War near Pittsburgh and helped build Fort Necessity and Fort Duquesne; second, the famed Pittsburgh Steelers running back Franco Harris, making his incredible immaculate reception in a divisional playoff game against the Oakland Raiders. If you are a Pittsburgher or an NFL fan, you will know the exact details of this improbable catch he made and the thirty seconds that followed, leading the Steelers to their first of four Super Bowl victories. If you've never heard of the immaculate reception, you ought to look it up, unless you want to be perceived as a fool while visiting the town.

The third statue is quite a contrast to George and Franco and somewhat of a surprise and maybe a bit misleading: A young woman, twenty-four years old, with short brown hair, wearing a neat, tailored plaid coat and black leather gloves, with a small woolen hat on the back of her head. She is carrying at her side a small leather satchel. She was a journalist who early in her career worked as a reporter for two local newspapers, but achieved greatness after she left Pittsburgh in 1887 to work for the *New York World*.[2]

Her name, when she began her journalistic career in Pittsburgh, was Elizabeth Jane Cochrane. But by the time she left the area where she had grown up, she was known as Nellie Bly. It was a name chosen by her editor, taken from a Stephen Foster song. So, a man was able to name her and forge her identity. Women were not allowed to write under their own names at that time, because — according to their publishers and editors — being weak and helpless, they would be much too vulnerable to the wrath of the men who were subjects of the undercover stories they wrote.[3]

Bly — or Cochrane — became famous worldwide by circling the globe in a record-breaking seventy-two days, leaving the fictional character Phileas Fogg, the protagonist in Jules Verne's novel *Around the World in Eighty Days,* published in 1873, in the dust. The statue in Pittsburgh depicts her outfit on the day of her departure, on November 14, 1889. The satchel she carried, the size of a small toaster oven, held everything she needed for those seventy-two days of

———

journeying by ship, train, and horseback, including her writing materials and a small flask with a drinking cup. Bly had confronted a great deal of resistance when she proposed her around-the-world plan to her editor, who told her, "No one but a man can do this," to which she replied: "Very well, start the man, and I'll start the same day for some other newspaper and beat him."[4]

She won the assignment and the race against Fogg. Her editor was well aware that Bly could do anything she set her mind to, not despite the fact that she was a woman, but because of it.[5]

For her first big story for the *New York World* the previous year she exposed the horrific living conditions of the patients of what was then known as an "insane asylum" on Blackwell's Island, now Roosevelt Island, in New York. Her plan was to get herself committed to Blackwell's by convincing officials that she was insane, a performance that might have earned an Academy Award if she had been making a movie.[6]

In preparation, Bly rented a room in a tenement boarding house, the Temporary Home for Females, on Second Avenue in the East Village in New York. In her room, she practiced how to look and act insane, as she would later describe in the first of ten articles for the *World*: "I flew to the mirror and examined my face. I remembered all I had read of the doings of crazy people, how first of all they have staring eyes, and so I opened mine as wide as possible and stared unblinkingly at my own reflection. . . . I read snatches of improbable and impossible ghost stories, so that when the dawn came to chase away the night, I felt that I was in a fit mood for my mission."[7]

When she was satisfied that she was well-prepared to prove herself insane, she had momentary second thoughts. "Who could tell but that the strain of playing crazy and being shut up with a crowd of mad people, might turn my own brain, and I would never get back. But not once did I think of shirking my mission. Calmly, outwardly at least, I went out to my crazy business."

Her story, the first in a ten-part series, begins that way—from acting out in the boarding house to being taken by police to the Essex Market Police Courtroom and acting out again so that a sympathetic Judge Duffy allowed her to move one more step forward—to be admitted to Bellevue Hospital's "pavilion for the insane." And then finally, after another day of examination and acting out, sent where she wanted to be all along, Blackwell's—the focus of her stories

—

about the city's treatment of the mentally ill—where she was immediately un-dressed and prepared for confinement. She wrote:

> The water was ice-cold, and a crazy woman began to scrub me. I can find no other word that will express it but scrubbing. From a small tin pan, she took some soft soap and rubbed it all over me, even all over my face and my pretty hair. I was at last past seeing or speaking, although I had begged that my hair be left untouched. Rub, rub, rub, went the old woman, chattering to herself. My teeth chattered and my limbs were goose-fleshed and blue with cold. Suddenly I got, one after the other, three buckets of water over my head—ice-cold water, too—into my eyes, my ears, my nose and my mouth. I think I experienced some of the sensations of a drowning person as they dragged me, gasping, shivering and quaking, from the tub. For once I did look insane . . . They put me, dripping wet, into a short canton flannel slip, labeled across the extreme end in large black letters, "Lunatic Asylum, B. I., H. 6." The letters meant Blackwell's Island, Hall 6.[8]

Nellie Bly's "Ten Days in a Mad-House," capturing her experiences at Blackwell's Island, immediately made a difference, as she wrote in the introduction to her series: "I am happy to be able to state as a result of my visit to the asylum and the exposures consequent thereon, that the City of New York has appropriated $1,000,000 more per annum than ever before for the care of the insane. So, I have at least the satisfaction of knowing that the poor unfortunates will be the better cared for because of my work." Like Rachel Carson, a fellow Pittsburgher, her mission forced change. Although not enough change to allow women to write as women under their own given names.

Picture a scene two years after Bly's sensational exposé: A helpless young girl in old tattered clothes staggers and stumbles across a busy street in San Francisco's Mission District and suddenly faints in front of a moving carriage, which nearly runs her down. The police are called to move her out of the street, but when she resists, they club her with wooden batons, throw her on the hard floor of a horse-drawn buggy, and transport her to the emergency room of a nearby hospital. The staff at the hospital, men and women both, are dismissive and annoyed, and pepper her with lewd and insulting remarks. She is treated coldly and quickly, no real examination provided, medicated with a concoction of mustard and hot water to precipitate vomiting—and soon thereafter released.[9]

Two weeks later, the *San Francisco Examiner*, owned by William Randolph Hearst, published a five-part series of stories capturing and documenting the brutal and insensitive treatment of women in hospital emergency rooms. Like Bly's work, this dramatic account of treatment led to the establishment of a well-trained ambulance service in the city—for men and women. Later, this writer—identified as Annie Laurie—was to become the first woman journalist to cover a prize fight. Later still, disguised as a boy, she was the first reporter on the scene to cover the horrific Galveston hurricane of 1900 in Texas.[10]

And then in July 1888, Nell Nelson, a young schoolteacher in Chicago, wearing a brown veil and a tattered coat, began taking a number of jobs in factories, stitching coats, shoe linings, and shirts at the Excelsior Underwear Company for eighty cents a dozen. It was hard work, to say the least—a lack of ventilation, poor lighting—and it was bloody hot. And as it turned out, the first dozen shirts she sewed were free—at least to her employer. For, she learned: Rent for the sewing machine she was using was fifty cents. And the thread for the shirts she sewed? An additional charge of thirty-five cents. But if that wasn't bad enough, Nelson and her fellow employees were insulted and berated. And not just at Excelsior; it was no different wherever she went. Her series of stories ran for nineteen straight weeks, doubling circulation for the *Chicago Times*. And then there was Eva Gay, who, in disguise, infiltrated an industrial laundry to document the unhealthy conditions for the women who labored there.

These writers made an impact; they changed lives because of their personal narratives, but despite their bylines, few readers knew who they really were. But as Kim Todd wrote, the names these women used, their bylines, "were often fake. Stunt reporters relied on pseudonyms, which offered protection as they waded deep into unladylike territory to poke sticks at powerful men. Annie Laurie was really Winifred Sweet; Gay was Eva Valesh; Marks was Eleanor Stackhouse. . . . 'Many of the brightest women frequently disguise their identity, not under one nom de plume, but under half a dozen,' wrote a male editor for the trade publication *The Journalist* in 1889. 'This renders anything like a solid reputation almost impossible.'"

—

All of these boundary-breaking reporters were forced into a similar identity deception. And the treatment of some of these stories, as serious as they were, was often trivialized with inappropriate illustrations of billowing skirts and wild wind-whipped hair, depicting the helplessness of the "opposite" sex. Even the ways in which women writers were referred to and labeled were often demeaning. Laurie, Bly, and their ilk were treated as novelty writers, performing tricks to get access to their stories. In fact, they were called as a group, as Todd reports, the "stunt girls."[11]

There was another label, which was most ironic, especially since it wasn't actually the "stunt" that captivated readers and motivated political and social action, but the voices, observations, and feelings—the deep-seated personal observations of the writers and the descriptions of the characters they captured. When the stories were especially poignant, critics and colleagues referred to the women who wrote these stories as the "sob sisters."[12]

The personalization, the confessional aspects of these stories, would, nearly a century later, become a flashpoint of the creative nonfiction debate and movement, when writers like James Wolcott demeaned them in *Vanity Fair*, characterizing their emotional honesty and intensity as "navel gazing." But at the time, the confessional aspects of their work weren't seen as worth debating—or criticizing. This whining and wailing about the ills of the world, the man's world, was to be expected coming from women. Journalists generally did not take the "girls" seriously. They were simply a means to the end. They used a woman to get a story that would not be possible for a man to get, a story that would sell papers and advertising and attract attention and praise—perhaps until Ida Tarbell.

Ida Tarbell, an investigative journalist and lecturer, became as famous and as influential as Upton Sinclair and others of what Theodore Roosevelt had labeled as the "muckraking" crowd. *The History of the Standard Oil Company* by Tarbell was first published as a nineteen-part series in *McClure's Magazine* and then in 1904 as a two-volume book. As one critic described her reporting, Tarbell "fed the antitrust frenzy by verifying what many had suspected for years: the pattern of deceit, secrecy and unregulated concentration of power that characterized Gilded Age business practice with its 'commercial Machiavellianism.'"[13] Tarbell was prolific, to say the least, and most enjoyed digging deep into her subjects for long periods of time, as in her series of articles for *McClure's* about the life of Napoleon and an eye-opening twenty-part series on Abraham Lincoln to which she dedicated four years of her life.

Tarbell's success and celebrity were due, not so much to the impact and drama of her prose, but more so to her dogged dedication to truth and accuracy and to uncovering heretofore undiscovered information and sources that led to deeper and richer stories. Liza Mundy, writing in the *Atlantic,* observed that "a half century before the *New Yorker's* Joseph Mitchell went to the waterfront to write about clammers and fishermen, before John McPhee started hanging out with greengrocers, Tarbell was visiting out-of-the-way sectors and practicing immersive journalism. . . . Today," Mundy concluded, "Robert Caro is lionized for his exhaustive gumshoe method, but Tarbell was there before him, reading pamphlets and the opinion columns of local papers. 'There is nothing about which everything has been done and said' became her core insight."[14]

Even after Tarbell and the work of the stunt girls had produced such serious and game-changing work, it remained a struggle for women to be considered equals in the journalistic world. Even when they succeeded, broke through the barriers, their work was often discounted or ignored. As it was for Martha Gellhorn, who was on the scene in Madrid in the heat of the Spanish Civil War.

Here's the opening of a dispatch from Madrid filed by Gellhorn in July 1937, which appeared in *Collier's* magazine:

At first the shells went over: you could hear the thud as they left the Fascists' guns, a sort of groaning cough; then you heard them fluttering toward you. As they came closer the sound went faster and straighter and sharper and then, very fast, you heard the great booming noise when they hit.

But now, for I don't know how long—because time didn't mean much—they had been hitting on the street in front of the hotel, and on the corner, and to the left in the side street. When the shells hit that close, it was a different sound. The shells whistled toward you—it was as if they whirled at you—faster than you could imagine speed, and, spinning that way, they whined: the whine rose higher and quicker and was a close scream—and then they hit and it was like granite thunder. There wasn't anything to do, or anywhere to go: you could only wait. But waiting alone in a room that got dustier and dustier as the powdered cobblestones of the street floated into it was pretty bad.

—

I went downstairs into the lobby, practicing on the way how to breathe. You couldn't help breathing strangely, just taking the air into your throat and not being able to inhale it.[15]

Later, despite her accomplishments, Gellhorn had to fight or trick her way into reporting on World War II. Women journalists could not be trusted to report the news accurately, or so it was believed, and they were much too vulnerable to be let loose in a war zone like their male colleagues. But Gellhorn ignored the warnings and the arbitrary rules excluding women. She was one of the very few correspondents to make it ashore during the D-Day invasion, male or female. She did this by hiding in a bathroom of a hospital ship to be part of the landing, and once ashore disguised herself as an orderly, carrying a stretcher. She was discovered on the beach a few days later while conducting interviews with the soldiers who had safely landed, and she was stripped of her press credentials. She was not, however, deterred. A year later she was part of the first wave of reporters at the Dachau concentration camp when it was liberated.[16]

I think it is really terrific every time I pass through the Pittsburgh airport that Nellie Bly has been so deservedly honored, side by side with Franco and George, but I do wonder if travelers really understand the significance of her statue and what it should mean to them and the world—not only the amazing trip around the world in seventy-two days, but the beginning of the liberation of women from a bastion of white men who had demeaned and disregarded them simply because of their gender. This liberation would, however, not be quick or easy.

CHAPTER 5

WHAT WHITE PUBLISHERS WON'T PRINT

Woman journalists faced barriers to their inclusion, but the barriers Black women writers faced could seem nearly insurmountable. Gradually, however, Black women were beginning to find a voice through newspapers and magazines — although not in the journalistic mainstream, but rather through out-of-the-way publications like the very leftist, very radical *New York Daily Compass,* published from 1949 through 1952. The *Daily Compass* was best known for its featured columnist, I. F. Stone, who, after the *Daily Compass* folded, published his influential newsletter, *I. F. Stone's Weekly.*

Marvel Cooke's lead article in the *Compass,* a long investigative series published in early January 1950 and reprinted in many creative nonfiction anthologies today, begins dramatically. After the first sentence, a reader can hardly not be compelled to move forward:

> I was a slave. I was part of the "paper bag brigade" waiting patiently in front of Woolworth's on 170th Street, between Jones and Walton Avenues, for someone to "buy" me for an hour or two or, if I were lucky, for a day. That is The Bronx Slave Market, where Negro women wait, in rain or shine, in bitter cold or under broiling sun, to be hired by local housewives looking for bargains in human labor.[1]

Later, Cooke continues:

> My first job netted me absolutely nothing. My employer on this occasion was a slave boss and I quit cold soon after I started.
>
> My second job netted me $3.40 for a full day of the hardest kind of domestic work. My "Madam" — that is how the "slaves" describe those who hire them — on this occasion was a gentle Mrs. Simon Legree who fed me three crackers, a sliver of cream cheese, jelly and a glass of coffee while she ate a savory stew.[2]

Before her work at the *Daily Compass,* Cooke was a columnist for the NAACP magazine *The Crisis,* then edited by W. E. B. Du Bois. Not long after, she became the first woman reporter for the *Amsterdam News,* New York's leading Black newspaper. When the *Compass* folded, Cooke shifted her focus to the political and art world. She was appointed New York director for the Council of Arts, Sciences, and Professions, and national vice chairman of the National Council for Soviet-American Friendship. She was a longtime member of the Communist party and became a target during Joseph McCarthy's witch hunt for spies and defectors. Questioned about where she was born while testifying at a congressional hearing, she put McCarthy in his place: "I was born in Minnesota, across the St. Croix River from where Sen. McCarthy comes," she said, "but we're not all the same out that way." That remark ended the questioning.[3]

For Cooke, activism took precedence over her passion for the written word. Kathleen Currie, who interviewed Cooke in 1989, noted all of the memorabilia on the walls of her apartment from friends and colleagues, mostly writers and artists, including Richard Wright, Paul Robeson, Langston Hughes, and Elizabeth Catlett. But no evidence of Cooke's journalistic work. When asked, Cooke replied that her work as a journalist was "not important."[4]

But historians have disagreed, noting her impact and influence, beginning with her narrative voice and involvement in the stories she wrote. Michigan State University historian LaShawn Harris writes: "Cooke's ability to unravel and depict New Yorkers' everyday politics was made possible by her unique style of collecting and gathering information. Like Zora Neale Hurston and many African American writers and cultural anthropologists, Cooke immersed herself in the lives of her subjects and embraced radical methods of producing social knowledge."[5]

Although a few newspapers and magazines supported and published Cooke's work, Ida B. Wells, born a slave in Mississippi in 1862, chose self-publishing as the best way—and probably the only way—to document the atrocities of lynching in the Jim Crow South. (The *New York Times* once referred to her as "a slanderous and nasty-minded mulattress.") Much of her work was published in the *Memphis Free Speech and Headlight,* which she co-owned and edited from 1888 to 1892, until a white mob burned the newspaper's office. Warned not to return to Memphis, she eventually settled in Chicago.[6]

Wells's writing was laced with vivid detail, intensely, graphically, penetratingly powerful. And it was not just the atrocities leveled against the Black population in the South; she spoke out forcefully against the inhumane treatment of the mentally ill, which was invariably more brutal for those who were Black. Here, from her self-published book *The Red Record: Tabulating Statistics and Alleged Causes of Lynching in the United States* (1895), she describes how one "insane" Black man, an alleged murderer, was put to death by an infuriated mob in Paris, Arkansas.

Arriving here at 12 o'clock the train was met by a surging mass of humanity 10,000 strong. The negro was placed upon a carnival float in mockery of a king upon his throne, and, followed by an immense crowd, was escorted through the city so that all might see the most inhuman monster known in current history. The line of march was up Main Street to the square, around the square down Clarksville street to Church Street, thence to the open prairies about 300 yards from the Texas & Pacific depot. Here Smith was placed upon a scaffold, six feet square and ten feet high, securely bound, within the view of all beholders. Here the victim was tortured for fifty minutes by red-hot iron brands thrust against his quivering body. Commencing at the feet the brands were placed against him inch by inch until they were thrust against the face. Then, being apparently dead, kerosene was poured upon him, cottonseed hulls placed beneath him and set on fire. In less time than it takes to relate it, the tortured man was wafted beyond the grave to another fire, hotter and more terrible than the one just experienced.[7]

As in Paris, watching and reporting, Wells was fearless. She roamed the Deep South, documenting ongoing brutality. "She went," David Smith wrote in 2018 in the *Guardian,* "where people had been hanged, shot, beaten, burned alive, drowned or mutilated. She examined photos of victims hanging from trees as mobs looked on, pored over local newspaper accounts, took sworn statements from eyewitnesses and, on occasion, even hired private investigators." Smith interviewed Nikole Hannah-Jones, the creator and co-editor of *The 1619 Project,* who replied, when asked about Wells's in-your-face on-the-scene reporting: "One has to ask, 'Would I have the courage to do that?' There was no help that was going to come for you. There was no protection from the law. Black folks didn't even have a lot of legal rights and they certainly didn't have much protection from law enforcement."[8]

Smith also quoted a passage from Wells's autobiography, *Crusade for Justice,* in which she wrote of the danger and possible peril of her work: "I had already determined to sell my life as dearly as possible if attacked. If I could take one lyncher with me, this would even up the score a little bit."[9]

Zora Neale Hurston's life may not have been in danger when she began writing in the early 1930s, at least not to the extent of Wells's constant vulnerability. But Hurston's very existence, her inability to support herself for her remarkable work, in contrast to many other white writers at the time, would eventually drag her down.

Hurston's essays, short stories, novels, and journalism were published around the same time as Orwell's, Hemingway's, and Huxley's. She too was an immersionist, but of a different sort; her background and training were in anthropology, which she had studied at Barnard College, where she was its first Black student and first Black graduate, in 1928. For her first nonfiction book, *Mules and Men,* she returned to her birthplace, Eatonville, Florida, to dig into the roots of slavery, collecting oral histories, sermons, and songs that had been passed down through generations. *Tell My Horse,* published in 1938, was a study of voodoo in Haiti and Jamaica in which she participated as an initiate; she actually lived the life, at first-hand.[10]

Hurston also wrote novels. Her first, *Their Eyes Were Watching God,* was published in 1937; it was followed by *Moses, Man of the Mountain* in 1939. Her memoir, *Dust Tracks on a Road*, was reviewed quite favorably in the *New York Times*. Many of her other books were reviewed equally well over the years, but unlike the works of Orwell or Huxley, they attracted few readers, undoubtedly because of who she was — a Black woman trying to break into a white reading world by describing, no matter how vividly, the legacy and culture rooted in slavery in the American South. She suffered ongoing resistance from publishers because of the content of her books.

In an essay in 1950 for *Negro Digest,* "What White Publishers Won't Print," Hurston wrote: "I have been amazed by the Anglo-Saxon's lack of curiosity about the internal lives and emotions of the Negroes and for that matter, any non-Anglo-Saxon peoples within our borders, above the class of unskilled labor."[11]

A Hurston biographer, Valerie Boyd, recently observed that Hurston never received the financial awards she deserved. The largest royalty she ever received for any of her books was $943.75.[12]

Later in her life, always living on the edge financially, she took an assignment for a Black newspaper, the *Pittsburgh Courier,* to cover the trial of Ruby McCollum, a Black woman who had shot and killed her white lover, Dr. Leroy Adams, a well-known physician in north central Florida. She contributed sixteen articles in all. McCollum pleaded self-defense, maintaining that Adams had forced her to have sex and insisted that they have a child together. The trial went on for many weeks. But the verdict was clear even before the trial began. The jury was made up entirely of white men. Judge Adams, who presided over the trail, was Dr. Adams's cousin.[13]

A review in the *New Yorker* by Lauren Michele Jackson of *You Don't Know Us Negroes,* a recently published volume of fifty of Hurston's prose pieces, captures her skill as a reporter and her ability to go beyond the headlines and the obvious stories to capture the essence of the individuals, especially the colored observers in the courtroom, who were restricted to second-class seating in the balcony and, most important, a wronged Black woman, helpless and resigned to her fate.

"The woman," Jackson writes, "gives so little. . . . The woman sits so motionless in the courtroom that the writer must fixate on the tiniest details, like a flexing of the fingers on the hand that allegedly wielded the gun." And then, quoting Hurston: "The undiscerning could gain the impression that this Ruby McCollum was indifferent to her fate."

"At one point," Jackson continues, "McCollum sighs and looks up. 'In this one gesture, one glimpsed the pattern of her whole life,' Hurston wrote. And Hurston, Jackson concludes, "was there to see it."[14]

Hurston died in 1960 totally destitute. She was buried in Pierce, Florida, where she had been living, in an unmarked grave. In 1973, another Black woman writer, a poet, novelist, and creative nonfiction writer, Alice Walker, who went on to win the Pulitzer Prize for fiction in 1984 for *The Color Purple*, went to Pierce to search out Hurston's burial site. Walker later played a crucial role in rescuing Hurston's legacy by encouraging publishers to rediscover (or begin to discover) her.[15]

In a scene describing Walker's visit in 1973, Valerie Boyd writes: "Walker bravely entered the snake-infested cemetery where Hurston's remains had been laid to rest. Wading through waist-high weeds, she soon stumbled upon a sunken rectangular patch of ground that she determined to be Hurston's grave. Unable to afford the marker she wanted—a tall majestic black stone called 'Ebony Mist'—Walker chose a plain gray headstone instead. Borrowing from a Jean Toomer poem, she dressed the marker up with a fitting epigraph: 'Zora Neale Hurston: A genius of the South.'"[16]

Hurston was not the kind of genius that Vonnegut had concluded Wolfe was in his review of *Tangerine Flake*. Wolfe's genius was rooted in his ability to call attention to himself and, later, as he continued to write and publish, to a literary genre, the new journalism. Not that this was a bad or useless endeavor. He inspired a movement and a significant and lasting attitude of change and respect that opened the doors for journalists—all writers—to maximize and expand their work into an art form. But he had always been in a privileged position, white, well-educated and connected, able to influence what would be heard and embraced by those in the know who, essentially, controlled what was being published as journalism or nonfiction at the time. Hurston and the other women writers here, Black or white, were never in the position to wield their influence in such a persuasive way. The genius of Hurston, Wells, Bly, and others, in addition to their brave storytelling, was in their dedication to their work and their persistence to be heard and survive while confronting an ongoing atmosphere of resistance and at times humiliating ridicule. Their genius, if it can be called that, was to never give up their own personal missions despite the forces that had been wielded against them.

Even as women in journalism were systematically barred from opportunities and advancement and often unacknowledged for their work, women essayists had been similarly, though not so forcefully, pretty much disregarded or marginalized long before Nellie Bly and Annie Laurie. And long after.

Women were writing essays for as long as Defoe had been pouring out his adventurous and appealing nonfiction/fiction histories, but most of the essays written by women in the eighteenth and nineteenth centuries focused on issues that mostly concerned women, in which men had no interest. In a *New Yorker* essay in 2008, Jill Lepore quoted the philosopher David Hume saying that women suffered from an "aversion to matter of fact" and an "appetite for falsehood," which, ironically, was a pretty accurate description of the beliefs of a frighteningly large minority of Americans in Hume's time or perhaps even at the time Lepore wrote her article.[17]

In 1994, the essayist, memoirist, and film critic Phillip Lopate published a well-regarded anthology, *The Art of the Personal Essay,* the goal of which was to develop a canon for the personal essay, which he felt, quite rightly, had been neglected in literary arenas. This volume, the first of a series of essay anthologies he was to produce over the next quarter century, helped transform the essay out of the dark ages and reestablish its literary status and relevance.[18]

But very few women were included in his collection, especially from earlier centuries. Lopate then explained that he was much more interested in simply calling attention to and starting a conversation about the essay form. And, in fact, thirty years ago diversity was not much of an interest or focus, especially in the academy, which is where the essay had been sustained over the years. Essayists were a tight-knit group; they wrote a lot about literature, and they wrote a lot about themselves and each other. Perhaps it seemed as if they didn't much care that readers and editors paid them little attention, but maybe also their indifference to "outsiders" was a shield of protection.

There were many panels and discussions after the publication of *The Art of the Personal Essay,* although women essayists were invariably, if included at all, an afterthought. Sometimes these conversations made it seem like "essaying" was an exclusive activity of an "old boys' club," like maybe squash or polo or cigar smoking. Very insular.

I recently read a transcript of a roundtable conversation, "The History of the Essay," that took place in 1999 at Michigan State University and featured prominent essayists and critics. Here were Milton Rosenberg, Thomas Kaminski, and Robert Root, all experienced essayists and literary historians, and Joseph Epstein, compiler of *The Norton Book of Personal Essays* and the author of a dozen collections of personal essays – quite a prestigious and prominent group.[19]

I could just picture them – maybe they were smoking cigars and sipping aged bourbon – smiling and nodding at each other as they imparted their wisdom. The discussion went on for nearly two hours and all of the major essayists from Seneca the Younger to Montaigne to Samuel Johnson up to present-day practitioners like Lopate were included. In those entire two hours, only three women essayists were mentioned, all quite briefly – Annie Dillard, Joan Didion, and Agnes Repplier, along with the journalist Maureen Dowd. Never mentioned? Virginia Woolf, Alice Walker, Nora Ephron, Zadie Smith.

In 2020, Lopate published another anthology, *The Glorious American Essay: One Hundred Essays from Colonial Times to the Present,* which he followed with another volume, *The Golden Age of the American Essay: 1945–1970.* Unlike his first anthology, *Glorious* featured many more essays by women, such as Sarah Moore Grimké's "On the Condition of Women in the United States" (1837) and Margaret Fuller's "Woman in the Nineteenth Century" (1845) – writers who had long been forgotten in the literary world. Lopate also included many popular and well-known women essayists like Jane Addams, Elizabeth Cady Stanton, Zora Neale Hurston, Hannah Arendt, and Susan Sontag, to name a very few, essayists the Michigan State panelists had failed to mention.

This exclusion of and ambivalence toward women essayists, still so evident in 1999, would soon change. The evolution of creative nonfiction opened doors for women writers. Women journalists and essayists alike, struggling so long for a vehicle of free expression and literary acceptance, embraced the freedoms of style, structure, and subject matter invited by creative nonfiction.

There were many women writers responsible for this evolution in the late twentieth and twenty-first centuries – names the literary world would easily rec-

---

ognize, including Vivian Gornick, Daphne Merkin, Rebecca Solnit, Joyce Carol Oates. But then there's the mysterious and anonymous columnist for the online magazine *Rumpus*, known to readers by only one name: Sugar, who precipitated a spiritual transition.

The "Dear Sugar" column, published weekly beginning in 2010, was set up in a way similar to the older and more traditional advice columns like Dear Abby and Ann Landers. Readers wrote in with questions and problems, many related to their personal or work lives — and Abby or Ann would give their sound, common-sense replies, often helpful perhaps, and always restrained. Sugar in contrast was far from restrained; she was honest and in-your-face, often, unlike Landers and Abby, sharing personal stories about her own life and problems, especially about her insecurity as a writer. One of the early "Sugar" columns, which instantly went viral on Facebook and Twitter, immediately established a tone and spark, a rallying cry of rebellion, for all women who wanted to write and could not, because of a lack of confidence or interest from editors or peers.

The column was responding to a letter written by a twenty-six-year-old who confessed at the beginning: "I write like a girl, I write about my lady life experiences, and it usually comes out as unfiltered emotion, unrequited love, and eventual discussion of my vagina as a metaphor. . . . I am a pathetic and confused young woman of twenty-six who can't write." She went on this way for most of the letter, confessing her self-trivialization, insecurity, and depression. "I am sick with panic that I cannot — will not — override my limitations, insecurities, jealousies, and ineptitude, to write well. . . . I fear that even if I do manage to write that the stories I write — about my vagina, etc. — will be disregarded and mocked." She ended with a question: "How does a women get up and become the writer she wishes to be?"[20]

Sugar replied by first describing her own struggles and insecurities as a young writer, but soon got to her characteristic honest, no-nonsense advice.

> The most fascinating thing to me about your letter is that buried beneath all the anxiety and sorrow and fear and self-loathing, there's arrogance at its core. It presumes you *should* be successful at twenty-six, when really it takes most writers so much longer to get there. It laments that you'll never be as good as David Foster Wallace — a genius, a master of the craft — while at the same time describing

how little you write. You loathe yourself, and yet you're consumed by the grandiose ideas you have about your own importance. You're up too high and down
too low. Neither is the place where we get any work done.

This, I imagine, must have been sobering and surprising to the letter writer.
But the last line of the column struck home to this writer and to many young
women writers filled with doubt and insecurity about their work and their future as women writers: "So, write," Sugar concluded. "Not like a girl. Not like
a boy. Write like a motherfucker."

Within months, Sugar's column was reprinted in magazines and newspapers
and re-tweeted endlessly. This and other columns generated more than two
million views in the two years after it was published.[21] "Write like a motherfucker" coffee mugs, travel mugs, and posters were available for sale almost
immediately. An article in the *New Republic* called Sugar "the ultimate advice
columnist for the Internet age." She was later portrayed in a play called *Tiny
Beautiful Things* at the Public Theater in New York.[22]

Sugar's short, direct messages resonated in a way that empowered many
women writers, perhaps even Sugar herself. Sugar's identity remained mostly
unknown until a coming-out party in San Francisco in 2012: her name was
Cheryl Strayed, and her story of adventure, trauma, and self-reflection, *Wild:
From Lost to Found on the Pacific Coast Trail,* was soon to be published. The book
became an instant best seller, as well as a feature film starring Reese Wither-
spoon. Since then, Strayed has gone on to write other books and many essays
and revived her Sugar identity in an Apple podcast, "Dear Sugars." But her message to that confused woman writer in 2010 may be the most significant and
long-lasting words she ever wrote. They were especially inspiring to Elissa Bassist, who wrote the original letter to Sugar. Bassist's first book, *Hysterical,* a memoir, was published by Hachette in 2022—twelve years after Sugar's response.[23]

Over the past twenty-five years, women writers writing creative nonfiction,
Cheryl Strayed, Roxane Gay, Eula Biss, Maggie Nelson, and a host of others,
have become the heart and pulse of the genre, the force and energy sustaining
it. The boundaries that had been arbitrarily imposed for so long, mostly by white
men, have gradually faded away—if you had a good story to tell, no matter how
raw and intimate and revealing. You could even write under your own name.

CHAPTER 6

F*** THE ESTABLISHMENT

Having never heard of Wolfe or, for that matter, new journalism before I first read the "Tangerine Flake" article in 1963 certainly contributed to the surprise of the experience. I don't think I had ever read *Esquire* magazine either, or actually purchased a copy, anyway, until then. I had read a few of the writers mentioned above, Defoe, Dickens, Twain, novels assigned in my high school English classes. On my own, I read a few Hemingway novels and stories. I had always been a reader, not necessarily an enlightened one. At home, I chose books from my father's meager library in our basement, whatever titles seemed interesting. He had some good books by John Steinbeck, *Of Mice and Men* and *The Grapes of Wrath*. I had watched those movies; the books were better. James Michener's *Hawaii* was so damn long, and I was often bored, wanting to give it up. But I kept reading, turning pages, through many weeks until I finished. I was glad I did. He wasn't a great writer, but he sure could pack a lot of information into a story. I never watched that movie.

I had plenty of time to read at home; it wasn't as if I was the most popular kid in the neighborhood or in school; friends were not flocking at my door inviting me out to parties or wanting to come in and hang out. For one thing, growing up, I was Jewish and way overweight in a mostly Catholic neighborhood, and I got banged around a lot—for both transgressions. (The Jews, so they said, had killed Christ.) I did some banging back, however. It was not all one-sided. In high school, I continued my war with nearly everyone, especially my teachers. I didn't go to a lot of classes or fulfill many assignments. And my truancy and horrific grades were such that I could not, after graduation, get accepted into a college. Not that I really wanted to go to college. Besides, what upstanding college would want me, even if I tried? Like that famous Groucho Marx quote: "I don't want to belong to any club that will accept me as a member."

I didn't want to go into the military either, not really. But it seemed at the time the only choice that made sense; this was during the draft years – and the early days of our Vietnam engagement. There was no volunteer army like today. You had to serve or get a deferment to go to college (and maybe then serve and maybe not when you graduated) or leave the country or plead your case as a conscientious objector. That was not me – none of that. I enlisted in the U.S. Coast Guard.

While in boot camp at the Coast Guard Training Center in Cape May, New Jersey, there wasn't much else to do after a long day of endless forced marching, doing push-ups and sit-ups, mopping and polishing floors, memorizing the ins and outs of the M1 rifle, learning semaphore and a bunch of other seamanship stuff that we all immediately forgot. But there were always books. I galloped through the few I had brought with me, and then borrowed from anyone in my company who had packed them in their duffel bags before leaving home.

Then I was transferred to the naval station at Norfolk, Virginia, for Morse Code "radiomen" training, which meant sitting at a typewriter eight hours a day, five days a week, with fifteen other radiomen in training, listening to gobbledygook of random code piped from a loudspeaker. We were learning to synchronize our fingers to automatically and instinctively respond to the dot-dashes of the sound. At day's end, I would regularly take refuge in the base library to escape the bleep of the code and the incessant clacking of keys in my ears, to seep myself in the silence – and read.

The books I read I found on a rack in front of the librarian's desk, mostly those popular then. Leon Uris's *Exodus,* Nevil Shute's *On the Beach,* and Budd Schulberg's *What Makes Sammy Run?* But when I finished those and explored the shelves along the walls, I found books that were surprisingly inspiring and cathartic: Philip Roth's *Goodbye, Columbus,* J. D. Salinger's *Catcher in the Rye,*

James Baldwin's *Giovanni's Room,* and John Knowles's *A Separate Peace.* And I discovered Frank Slaughter, who wrote dozens of novels about physicians in every conceivable milieu. I had not read Tom Wolfe or Gay Talese, although I did find Norman Mailer's first novel, *The Naked and the Dead.* It was pretty damn good.

When I mustered out, I was in a state of life limbo, but during my tour of duty and then afterward working a few unfulfilling jobs, I had conjured up the notion of becoming a writer. A ridiculous idea at the time for me. But writing was the only thing I could think of that I wanted to do. I was twenty years old when I mustered out, had no education beyond high school — if you want to call it "education" — and much of my literary awareness and knowledge stemmed from the pleasure of reading whatever books I could find in the local library, along with my curiosity and envy about how the writers I was reading and appreciating did what so many did so remarkably.

I had no interest in becoming a fiction writer, despite the novels I had been reading. I had been very isolated in Pittsburgh; rarely did my family venture out of the city or even into other neighborhoods. Pittsburgh was then and continues to be a very siloed city. I lived near Squirrel Hill, then the mostly Jewish district. There were "Little Italy" and "Polish Hill" enclaves and the "South Side" and the "North Side"; to get to either "side" there were bridges over the Monongahela and Allegheny Rivers, which many Pittsburghers rarely, and often with reluctance, crossed. Pittsburghers liked to remain in familiar territory.

But meeting all of those kids in the military from every corner of the country, of various nationalities, listening to them talk about their families and where they were born — Alabama, Texas — how they lived their lives, intrigued me. In my company there was a Seminole Indian from the Everglades who would tell you everything you wanted to know about alligators, even if you didn't want to know it. There was a guy from a family in Georgia whose plantation had been burned to the ground during the Civil War who swore that before he died he would regain his family's heritage and do away with the Blacks and the Jews who had ruined his life. I also learned how to play poker and blackjack — I won some money sometimes — smoke cigarettes and drink beer and bourbon. What had I been missing sequestered in the Squirrel Hill area, I wondered? Why had I been so isolated, and what could I do about it? Being that great American novelist that so many writers dreamed of was not for me. I didn't want to make stuff up. Nonfiction — real life, different people, not just the Jews and the Catholics who hated Jews I had grown up with, what and who I was discovering in the military — is what appealed to me.

So, after the military and bouncing around for a while, I got a job as a traveling shoe salesman representing the J. W. Carter Boot Company of Nashville, Tennessee, and another brand, Nurse Mates. (My father owned a shoe store in a Pittsburgh suburb; he had been in the shoe business all his life — a self-described "shoe dog." He had vouched for me as an able salesman and a young potential upcoming shoe dog. His protégé.) I bought a suit, a tie, and a hat with a feather in the band and went on the road on my own. I covered three states for both of these manufacturers — and my months on the road took me into general stores, army-navy stores, shoe stores, and hospitals — meeting an array of folks I would have never come into contact with had I remained at home in Pittsburgh. Just like the military. And then at night going into diners or local bars and observing. I enjoyed doing this, sitting at a counter, nursing a coffee or a beer, listening to how the natives talked, sounded, gestured, and imagining what their lives were like or what I could learn if knew them, hung out with them, became, in a way, like them. But, to be honest, I didn't sell many shoes.

I soon realized that shoe-dogging wasn't the life for me, despite my father's hope and prediction. There had to be more to life than discussing neoprene soles, scuffed toes, and metatarsal arches. So I quit and got a job driving a beer truck, delivering beer kegs to bars and fraternity houses and sorting out empty bottles turned in for deposit back at the warehouse, a tedious and uncomfortable task, swiping away the flies and wasps buzzing around me and wishing I was somewhere else, especially at two dollars an hour. I sold soft drinks or souvenirs at Forbes Field, where the Pirates and the Steelers played. I went door to door selling magazines. I drank a lot of beer and smoked as much marijuana as I could get, which, then, was not a lot. Day-to-day, mostly I wandered around, walking and thinking in circles, wondering what the hell I was going to do and how someone, a lost soul like me (yes, I was feeling sorry for myself) could become a writer.

Eventually I went to school and tried to learn as much as I could from my professors. That in many ways didn't work out too well, and I learned a lot more about writing in the business world and by continuing to do what gave me the greatest of pleasure – reading the most intriguing writers I could find and trying to understand what they were doing on the page that made their work interesting and in most cases riveting.

And despite the fact that I really had no direction at that stage of my life, choosing what to read or, for that matter, deciding anything else about my future, that, I realize now, was the best thing to happen to me on my way to becoming a writer at that particular time in history. I don't like being as old as I am. When I am called a "boomer," I twinge. But, in retrospect, I realize that I was quite fortunate to have been a wannabe writer during the 1960s, the era that historians referred to as the "Decade of Revolution," or most memorably, "The Age of Aquarius."

The sixties were a life-changing time in America, certainly the most significant decade of the twentieth century. The perfect time for the new journalism. Even if it was not actually new, it was new to me. Everything was new in the sixties, compared with the previous decade.

The 1950s, when I was growing up, had been pretty much an uptight bore. The country and many of its leaders were a bunch of Rip Van Winkles. In my high school the expected uniform for boys was khaki pants and button-down shirts, if their families, unlike mine, could afford "the Ivy League look"; most boys had crewcuts or, if they wanted to be daring, flat-tops. Girls wore plaid skirts with white blouses. Or, if they wanted to look super-smart and fashionable, Villager sweaters and plain Capezio flats. My dad, like most dads I knew, wore ties and white shirts to work. Talk about a beige tone. Women? My mother and all the mothers I knew were homemakers. They did the family laundry, cooked our dinners, and kept the house orderly and clean. At night there was television, if you could afford a television, mostly black and white with a round eleven- or thirteen-inch screen, family friendly stuff like *Leave It to Beaver* and *I Love Lucy.* You could hardly find a show without a laugh track. Not that all was bad or boring in the 1950s. Rock and roll was hot – Chuck Berry, Fats Domino, and Buddy Holly. Chubby Checker was twisting. We were living through what historians called "the post-war boom."

All of this changed with the 1960s, when the United States launched a

---

military action in Southeast Asia that precipitated a senseless and bloody war that went on for more than the next decade. When four Black students in Greensboro, North Carolina, refused to leave a restaurant after they were told they would not be served, opening a never-ending salvo against the injustice and ignorance of Jim Crow. When President Kennedy was murdered in Dallas in 1963, and a half dozen years later when Martin Luther King and Robert Kennedy were shot and killed in 1968. When antiwar protesters invaded and occupied major universities, including Columbia in New York and the Sorbonne in Paris – despite the billy clubs and tear gas that confronted them. When four students were murdered during a protest at Kent State University in early 1970. And, all along the way, the rapid and amazing emergence of bold cultural and lifestyle changes – marijuana – pot, as we called it. And free sex! Or loose sex. Or communal sex. And long-haired filthy dirty hippies. And Woodstock. And the ongoing chant uniting the protesters, no matter what their grievances, "Fuck the establishment."

"Fuck the establishment" could be a way of describing the books being published at that time – those that took journalism or nonfiction way beyond anything I or most anyone else had imagined – that were, for me, an education in themselves. In fact, there was a period in the 1960s, three or four years, with so many groundbreaking books and essays published and being categorized as new journalism – not just by Wolfe and Talese – that it was hard to decide what to read first or what to read again and again. It seemed like every few months there was a new twist to the genre.

In 1965, the same year Wolfe published *Tangerine Flake*, the *New Yorker* serialized Truman Capote's *In Cold Blood*, the story of the murder of a family in a small town in Kansas by two desperate drifters and their complex relationship during and after the murders. I wasn't reading the *New Yorker* very much at that time, maybe because I thought it was a magazine only about New York? I was pretty naive; it wasn't as if I could consult a lot of people – or really, anybody – in the know about literature to guide me.

But Capote was on TV doing interviews, lots of late-night talk shows, and the reviews in the few newspapers I was reading were pretty amazing. Capote was made for TV. He was short, just five feet three inches tall and, as one writer

—

later described him, "a flamboyantly effeminate elf, his tiny body and sharp tongue best summarized in his own assessment: 'I'm about as tall as a shotgun, and just as noisy.'"[1] Later I learned that it wasn't enough to just write a book in the 1960s. You had to be a character, have a distinctive presence to get attention in the popular media. Wolfe and Talese had their costumes. Norman Mailer did his best to act out. He once head-butted Gore Vidal in the greenroom before an appearance on *The Dick Cavett Show.* Later he became a candidate for mayor of New York, with the journalist Jimmy Breslin as his running mate for the City Council presidency.

I bought *In Cold Blood* in 1966 as soon as it hit the newsstands and bookstores. (Yes, there were newsstands back then.) What impressed me first was that it read like a novel with three separate, engrossing, and intersecting narratives portraying the victims, the killers, and the people of the community where the crime had taken place. Capote had been a fiction writer long before he began writing nonfiction. His first novella, *Other Voices, Other Rooms,* attracted attention, not just for its fine and sensitive prose but for its homosexual theme, more than just unusual in America in 1948. *Breakfast at Tiffany's,* another novella, published ten years later, was soon made into a popular and highly praised movie starring Audrey Hepburn.

In fact, Capote, who had mixed feelings about being characterized as a journalist, even a new journalist, described his book as a "nonfiction novel." But it was filled with fact, neatly synchronized within the stories so that readers learned background, history, all the necessary journalism, perhaps without even realizing that they were learning what they needed to know. What impressed me even more than anything was the way he treated his characters, with sensitivity and detail—the victims, the killers, the people of the community. He was able to squeeze the most intimate thoughts and memories from everyone he interviewed—a skill he had developed long before *In Cold Blood.*

Capote wrote "The Duke and His Domain," a profile of Marlon Brando, for the *New Yorker* in 1957. Brando began talking about his mother's alcoholism—a subject he rarely discussed, especially with a writer. "She was there in a room, holding on to me. And I let her fall. Because I couldn't take it anymore—watching her breaking apart, like a piece of porcelain. I stepped right over her. I walked right out. I was indifferent . . ."[2]

In *The Craft of Interviewing,* John Brady, the editor of *Writer's Digest Magazine,* discussed this rare intimacy. "When puzzled friends asked Brando why he said that to a reporter, Brando said, 'well the little bastard spent half the night telling me all his problems. I figured the least I could do was tell him a few of mine.'"[3]

Despite the success of *In Cold Blood,* Capote has been criticized, not only for the way he mixed fact and imagination, but perhaps more for his process of researching the book. Critics have challenged Capote for his reliance on memory, rather than notes or transcriptions, except for those prepared by his devoted and efficient editorial assistant, Harper Lee, who had just submitted her novel *To Kill a Mockingbird* to her publisher. Setting aside criticism of Capote's seemingly irresponsible research methods, *In Cold Blood* remains a perfect example, then and now, of how a talented fiction writer, using all of the tools of his genre, can recreate a real-life event and embrace a community with cinematic beauty and precision. *In Cold Blood* is often described as the book that launched the true-crime genre, setting the tone for Vincent Bugliosi's *Helter Skelter,* John Berendt's *Midnight in the Garden of Good and Evil,* and Erik Larson's true-crime history book, *The Devil in the White City.*

Like Capote, Norman Mailer was a fiction writer first. His first book, *The Naked and the Dead,* published in 1948 when he was twenty-five years old, was immediately praised as one of the finest novels written about World War II. But the novels after that were not greeted with much enthusiasm. During that time, he was often criticized as a one-book author—until he turned to nonfiction and politics with the publication of *The Armies of the Night: History as a Novel/The Novel as History,* about the peace demonstrations in Washington, D.C., on the steps of the Pentagon in October 1967.

Armies of the Night pushed the limits of what was considered to be journalism far beyond Wolfe or Capote or any other nonfictionist I had read at that time. Using his skills as a novelist, he captured in one quick paragraph the swarm of fanatical and totally outlandish protesters amassing at the steps of the Pentagon, which was the underlying story he was telling. "The hippies were there in great number, perambulating down the hill, many dressed like the legions of Sgt. Pepper's Band, some were gotten up like Arab sheiks, or in Park Avenue doormen's greatcoats, others like Rogers and Clark of the West, Wyatt Earp,

Kit Carson, Daniel Boone in buckskin, some had grown mustaches to look like Have Gun, Will Travel – Paladin's surrogate was here! – and wild Indians with feathers, a hippie gotten up like Batman, another like Claude Rains in The Invisible Man – his face wrapped in a turban of bandages and he wore a black satin top hat."[4]

The book goes far beyond the way a journalist would cover an event, as its subtitle reflects. It is much more about the recent history of revolution in the United States and about Mailer himself and his own anxieties as a writer and, more than anything, perhaps, his flawed personality. It is not written in the first person, however, as a reader might expect, but in the third person. Mailer, through the entire book, reports and writes as if he is looking at himself as others might perceive him and, simultaneously, as he perceives himself, as "Mailer," thus being able to reveal his innermost thoughts and actions from a double personal perspective. I have written many of my books in the third person and a few in the first person. Each presents different challenges, but to achieve the first and third person seamlessly and simultaneously had never crossed my mind. If it had, I would have quickly blinked it away, not necessarily because it was impossible, just way out of my range. But Mailer did it – a tour de force – even if Mailer comes off through most of the book as a not very likable, verbose, and often drunken narrator.

In a scene early in the book he describes himself (or "Mailer") facing a group of six hundred students for a talk he had promised to give, drunken, barely able to stand: "Mumbling and spewing obscenities as he staggered around the stage – which he had commandeered by threatening to beat up the previous MC – Mailer described in detail his search for a usable privy on the premises. 'I'm here because I'm like LBJ, was one of Mailer's milder observations. He's as full of crap as I am.'"[5]

In 1968, Mailer won the National Book Award and the Pulitzer Prize for The Armies of the Night. The following year he published Miami and the Siege of Chicago, which chronicled the Republican and Democratic presidential conventions of 1968, rife with political turmoil, backbiting, anger and resentment. I read both of these books as soon as they came out and although I didn't like Mailer and the personality he revealed, I admired his boldness. How would I characterize this book, I wondered? Not exactly fiction. Not exactly new journalism. It was Mailer being Mailer—brilliant, obnoxious, single-handedly distinctive, and absolutely riveting. I knew that I could never write anything like that; it would be senseless to try. If Vonnegut had categorized Wolfe as a genius, then how in the world would he describe Mailer?

Mailer was awarded a second Pulitzer in 1980 for *The Executioner's Song,* a deep, intense, 1,072-page story of murder, obsession, and punishment, which Mailer, perhaps dueling with Capote over names, had called a "true life novel." Although it was clearly what would be called creative nonfiction today, the book was given the Pulitzer for fiction.

Essentially, *The Executioner's Song* is about the life and death of Gary Gilmore, who murdered two men in Utah in 1976 and was executed a little more than a year later, in late 1977. It was not only a brilliant book, but the event itself, the execution, had made history and, at the time, changed history. Lethal injection or what was once called "the electric chair" had been the longtime most accepted methods of execution, but Gilmore was put to death the old way, like in the military, by a firing squad. And a half century ago, when all of this took place, there had been a national moratorium on the death penalty in the United States, from 1972 to 1977. Gilmore's execution was the first immediately after the moratorium had been lifted. What made the story even more compelling was the fact that, while others sitting on death row around the country were fighting for their lives, not wanting to die, Gilmore was fighting in reverse; he had spent most of his adult life in jail and he knew what was in store for him, a lifetime of brutal incarceration, so, as far as he was concerned, he wanted to get it over with.

Although Mailer was the writer of the book, it wasn't really, mostly, his story, or even his material. Over the years, Larry Schiller, an accomplished photographer and film director and producer, had become more than a little obsessed with Gilmore and his story and had devoted hundreds of hours in Provo, Utah, interviewing Gilmore and everyone else who appears in the book, and others who never made the cut. But he knew he was not the person to write it.

So he hired Norman Mailer and relinquished his 15,000 pages of interview transcripts so that Mailer could do his thing. Who knew, I thought, when I first heard this story and later read the book, that you could actually hire Norman Mailer? Or for that matter, that a Pulitzer Prize winner would, in a way, lower

---

himself, risk his prestige, to actually, like a common ordinary freelancer, allow himself to be hired? Could I hire Mailer, I wondered? How much would he cost? Although Mailer eventually interviewed the mothers of Gilmore's victims and visited Provo to capture the Utah vibe and landscape, he never talked with, never even set eyes, personally, on Gilmore. Here again, another remarkable twist to the potential of the genre when, as Macdonald had said with derision, they wanted to have it — fiction and nonfiction — both ways. Mailer and Capote demonstrated that you could have it — write it — both ways.[6]

Even though in her long career she was to become an essayist, novelist, playwright, and screenwriter, I don't think Joan Didion had any illusions of having it both ways, or any way but her way. When I first read her work in 1968 when her first nonfiction book was published, *Slouching Towards Bethlehem*, I thought she was adding her own dimension, a new dimension, to what was being called the new journalism — a personal interiority that even Mailer, with all of his self-confession and introspection and ruminations about the anxiety of writing, had not ever achieved.

Didion not only researched and covered events in the best manner of the journalist, as did Mailer and Capote and Talese, but she shared what was happening in her own life during the time she was writing — anecdotes and information that might seem at first to a reader unnecessary or intrusive or way overboard in the context of her reporting. But they weren't, as Didion was able to write them. Reading Didion you would learn that she was constantly and incredibly nervous about almost everything. That she suffered from severe migraine headaches, that she often blunted her pain with gin and hot water, often using Dexedrine to counteract the gin. You'd learn about her fear of going blind or the dissonance in her marriage.

In "The White Album," the title piece in a collection of essays published in 1979, about her life in California in the late 1960s, she seems to write about everything that comes to mind. In one paragraph alone near the beginning of the essay she writes about visiting Honolulu, watching Robert Kennedy's funeral on TV, ordering from room service, rereading the works of George Orwell, and a story in the newspaper that day about a mother who placed her daughter, five years old, on the divider in the center of a highway and ran away — and the child's "fingers had to be pried loose from the Cyclone fence when she was rescued twelve hours later by the California Highway Patrol." We get all of this and more, peppered with stark and vivid detail, so that a reader cannot fail to be engrossed.

And then, suddenly out of nowhere, in that same essay, in what she called a "Flash Cut," is an excerpt from a transcript of a psychiatric evaluation of a woman who had alienated herself "almost entirely from the world of other human beings." The transcript goes on for about a page, describing a sheer litany of the woman's emotional disabilities. Only then, after the reader digests the transcript, does Didion reveal: "The patient to whom this psychiatric report refers is me."

The essay continues in this fashion, one seemingly unrelated topic after another. And then, a favorite part for me: We are in a studio with a band called the Doors, and then "a twenty-four year-old graduate of U.C.L.A. who wore black vinyl pants and no underwear and tended to suggest some range of the possible just beyond a suicide pact." This was Jim Morrison. How in the hell did she do this, I wondered, and make it all fit together in one overarching narrative essay of nearly 11,000 words?[7]

I always felt that characterizing Didion as a new journalist, at least in the way Wolfe had portrayed it, did not reflect the broad scope of her work and style and more than anything her intelligence and foresight. She was barely twenty-three when she first came to New York to work for *Vogue* magazine and she immediately, as a very young reporter, established a voice that was truly distinctive — reflective and personal and philosophical. Once, in 1961, a writer at *Vogue* had backed out of a story that she had been assigned about the meaning of self-respect. As the magazine was going to press, Didion, then in her middle twenties, was asked at the last minute to write something on the same subject to fill the allotted space. She jumped right in with an essay with this lead paragraph:

"Once, in a dry season, I wrote in large letters across two pages of a notebook that innocence ends when one is stripped of the delusion that one likes oneself. Although now, some years later, I marvel that a mind on the outs with itself should have nonetheless made painstaking record of its every tremor, I recall with embarrassing clarity the flavor of those particular ashes. It was a matter of misplaced self-respect." The essay, "Self-Respect: Its Source, Its Power," was republished later in 1968 in *Slouching Towards Bethlehem*.[8]

Didion, by the way, had been given specific directions related to the space available in the magazine layout—down to the character count. Her essay, written in less than a day, fit to the letter.

Didion, even in 1961 at *Vogue*, had a presence on the page—a persona and a voice that always made me think she was talking to me, intimately, one on one. "The most radical aspect of her voice when she started writing for magazines in the 1960s," Sara Davidson observed in a retrospective of Didion's work in *LitHub* soon after she died in 2021, "was that she, Joan, spoke to you, the reader, as if grabbing you by the lapels."[9]

This was evident in the first paragraph of an essay published in the *Saturday Evening Post* in 1967 that became the title of her book *Slouching Towards Bethlehem*. In one paragraph she nailed the mood and dissonance of the upcoming generation. This was far from the myth of the "Age of Aquarius."[10]

> The center was not holding. It was a country of bankruptcy notices and public-auction announcements and commonplace reports of casual killings and misplaced children and abandoned homes and vandals who misplaced even the four-letter words they scrawled. It was a country in which families routinely disappeared, trailing bad checks and repossession papers. Adolescents drifted from city to torn city, sloughing off both the past and the future as snakes shed their skins, children who were never taught and would never now learn the games that had held the society together. People were missing. Children were missing. Parents were missing. Those left behind filed desultory missing-persons reports, then moved on themselves.

Didion labored over each sentence, establishing an intimacy with her voice that would sustain her work and inspire readers and writers far longer than most of the other new journalists. Today, when I ask my creative nonfiction students (mostly women) to name the writers who first inspired them, Joan Didion, because of her thoughtfulness and complexity, because of her pristine prose and her ability to connect with readers, will often be at the top of their lists.

CHAPTER 7

THE IMPERFECT PRIMER

There were many other writers in the 1960s who were transforming journalism or nonfiction in a vivid variety of ways. That Wolfe and Johnson anthology, after Wolfe's introduction, provided a generous taste of them. It is a brilliant collection of the absolute best of the new journalism work of the 1960s, inspired by the evangelist, the Johnny Appleseed of the genre. If you were selected by Wolfe, you were obviously anointed. It was the perfect primer for my students in those early days — a master list chosen by the master. Or so I thought at the time.

Here was "The Soft Psyche of Joshua Logan," Talese's profile of the Broadway director that included the confrontation with Claudia McNeil, an excerpt from Truman Capote's *In Cold Blood*, a piece by Terry Southern about the Dixie National Baton Twirling Institute on the campus of the University of Mississippi in Oxford ("Ole Miss"), and a profile of Martin Luther King, set on the day of his funeral, by the historian Garry Wills, who twenty years later won a Pulitzer Prize in general nonfiction for his book *Lincoln at Gettysburg: The Words That Remade America*. Southern was an editor at *Esquire* at the time he wrote his twirling piece, but was then best known for his screenwriting work, most especially *Dr. Strangelove* and the Steve McQueen hit *The Cincinnati Kid*. Some of the other writers included in Wolfe's collection, not too well-known then, gained prominence later, such as John Gregory Dunne (Joan Didion's husband), Adam Smith, Joe Eszterhas, and Joe McGinniss. There were also, predictably, two pieces by Wolfe himself, from *Radical Chic* and *The Electric Kool-Aid Acid Test*.

Wolfe and Johnson also included two pieces about the Vietnam War, predictably chaotic and bloody, Nicholas Tomalin's "The General Goes Zapping Charlie Cong," and an excerpt from Michael Herr's upcoming book, *Dispatches*, "Khesanh," in which he described the plight and states of mind of our troops — the self-described "grunts." Herr captured who they were and how they felt about themselves and the war and the inevitable awareness with which they lived that if they weren't killed by the Viet Cong they'd likely be killed by the incompetence of their own leaders or by one another.

And the Grunts themselves knew: the madness, the bitterness, the horror and doom of it. They were hip to it, and more; they savored it. It was no more insane than most of what was going down, and often enough it had its refracted logic. "Eat the apple, fuck the Corps," they say, and write it up on their helmets and flak jackets for their officers to see. (One kid tattooed it on his shoulder.) And sometimes they'd look at you and laugh silently and long, the laugh on them and on you for being with them when you didn't have to be. And what could be funnier, really, given all that an 18-year-old boy could learn in a month of patrolling the Z? It was that joke at the deepest part of the blackest kernel of fear, and you could die laughing. They even wrote a song, a letter to the mother of a dead marine, that went something like, "Tough shit, tough shit, your kid got greased, but what the fuck, he was just a Grunt . . . "[1]

The other Vietnam piece, by Tomalin, a British journalist writing for the *Sunday Times*, brought home the sheer selfish, incompetent, disingenuous absurdity of the war. The lead could never have been published during World War II, or even the Korean conflict, not because it could not have happened, but mostly because it would never have been revealed: "After a light lunch last Wednesday, General James F. Hollingsworth, of Big Red One, took off in his personal helicopter and killed more Vietnamese than all the troops he commanded."[2]

The book also included two excerpts from Hunter Thompson, one at the early stages of his Gonzo transformation, "The Kentucky Derby Is Decadent and Depraved," written two years before the publication of his infamous book *Fear and Loathing in Las Vegas,* and a second piece, pre-Gonzo, an excerpt from his first book, *Hell's Angels: The Strange and Terrible Saga of the Outlaw Motorcycle Gangs,* published in 1967.

There are many ways to define "Gonzo," but basically it meant that the writer, usually part of the story, lets loose in his writing without boundaries. He could be outlandish, outrageous, and bizarre. A reporter from Louisville captured the meaning of Gonzo and Thompson quite succinctly: "It generally consists of the fusion of reality and stark fantasy in a way that amuses the author and outrages his audience. It is Point of View Run Wild."[3]

The derivation of "Gonzo" has been debated. An editor for the *Boston Globe,* in reviewing Thompson's "Kentucky Derby," said it was a South Boston Irish slang term referring to the last one standing after a bar fight. Thompson's literary executor, on the other hand, credits James Booker's instrumental jazz track of the same name, first recorded and released in 1960. I like the first explanation — very Hunter Thompson — better, but probably both are somewhat true.[4]

Thompson's Las Vegas and Kentucky Derby treatments, and they were "treatments," plus much of what he wrote before and after that, would have not fared well in any sort of journalistic fact checking. Which was of no concern to Thompson; quite the opposite, in fact. He was brash, profane, and sarcastic and pretty much wild-assed crazy in his work and life, and often under the spell of some sort of illusionary substance, and he created his own completely undocumented reality — just for the hell of it. He may well have changed the course of history in 1972 when he was covering the U.S. presidential election for *Rolling Stone* by spreading a rumor that the leading Democratic primary candidate, Senator Edmund Muskie of Maine, was an addict, hooked on an obscure root drug, Tabernanthe Iboga. "Not much has been written about the Ibogaine Effect as a serious factor in the presidential campaign," Thompson wrote, "but word leaked out that some of Muskie's top advisers called in a Brazilian doctor who was said to be treating the candidate with 'some kind of strange drug.'"

Five years later, during an interview with the CBC, Thompson admitted that the whole thing was a joke. "I couldn't believe that people took this stuff seriously," he said. "I never said he was [taking Ibogaine] . . . I said there was a rumour in Milwaukee that he was, which was true when I started the rumour in Milwaukee."[5]

Muskie lost the nomination that year to Senator George McGovern of South Dakota, who went on to be trounced by Richard Nixon in the general election.

But all of these selections by Wolfe and Johnson, as terrific as they were, did not really reflect the full scope of what was happening, what was being written as new journalism or nonfiction at the time. There were only two women highlighted in the collection. Where was Lillian Ross or Rachel Carson? Or other women writing nonfiction, Mary McCarthy, Susan Sontag, Nora Ephron, Gloria Steinem, all of whom had been writing very powerful and change-making journalism fused with narrative? And writers of color? Authors of all twenty-two pieces collected in the volume were white. People of color writing nonfiction at that time, such as James Baldwin, the Nobel Prize laureate V. S. Naipaul, and perhaps most especially Alex Haley and Malcolm X might have been obvious choices.

The Autobiography of Malcolm X wasn't exactly new journalism as Wolfe had described it, and it wasn't exactly an autobiography, as readers might have expected. It was rather, an autobiography of Malcolm X written by someone else: Alex Haley. But however you label the genre, when it was published in 1965, eight months after Malcolm X was assassinated, it immediately became one of the most celebrated and respected books, not just in the 1960s, but of all time.

Haley, a retired U.S. Coast Guardsman (a fellow "Coastie") fancied himself a writer when he mustered out, and found work quite quickly (unlike me), first at *Reader's Digest*. Soon he began working with *Playboy* magazine, where he conducted a series of interviews (for a regular feature called "The Playboy Interviews") with many prominent African American artists and thought leaders, including Miles Davis, Sammy Davis, Jr., Martin Luther King, Quincy Jones, and eventually Malcolm X. Soon after the Malcolm X interview appeared, Doubleday Publishing Company commissioned Haley to write Malcolm X's autobiography. Or whatever you wanted to call it. Over the next few years, Haley conducted at least fifty interviews, two or three hours at a time, with Malcolm

X and then turned his words into dramatic, smooth-flowing, very readable and compelling prose.[6]

This may sound like Haley was ghostwriting, and in a way he was, but the challenge for him was to breach his subject's anger — Malcolm called himself "the angriest black man in America" — a formidable task even for a fellow Black man.

"We got off to a very poor start," Haley wrote in the epilogue of the book. "To use a word he liked, I think both of us were a bit 'spooky.' Sitting right there and staring at me was the fiery Malcolm X who could be as acid toward Negroes who angered him as he was against whites in general."[7]

Haley worked to gain his subject's trust, initially a frustrating process, but he knew that unless he earned Malcolm X's confidence he would never capture the real person, whose feelings about the world he was born into actually began a few months before he was born. A party of Ku Klux Klanners on horseback, wielding torches, raided his pregnant mother's home, threatening her and shattering the windows of the house with their gun butts. This was the first scene in the first chapter of the book, called "Nightmare."

It was the subject of Malcolm's mother that eventually broke the ice for Haley. In the epilogue he recalled the moment when he knew he would be able to help Malcolm X tell his really true story, when he convinced him to think beyond hatred and resentment and remember his mother.

> Slowly, Malcolm X began to talk, now walking in a tight circle. "She was always standing over the stove, trying to stretch whatever we had to eat. We stayed so hungry that we were dizzy. I remember the color of dresses she used to wear — they were a kind of faded-out gray. . . ." And he kept on talking until dawn, so tired that the big feet would often almost stumble in their pacing. From this stream-of-consciousness reminiscing I finally got out of him the foundation for this book's beginning chapters. After that night, he never again hesitated to tell me even the most intimate details of his personal life, over the next two years. His talking about his mother triggered something.[8]

The *Autobiography* was immediately hailed as a masterpiece explaining the divide between white and Black America. It sold six million copies from 1965 to 1975, and many millions since then. It would have perfectly fit in with Wolfe's new journalism narrative framework and his anthology. But, for Wolfe, it obviously didn't.

Haley's book, *Roots: The Saga of an American Family,* based on the journey of his ancestors from Africa into slavery in the United States, was published in 1976. It was adapted into an eight-part TV series in 1977, which immediately became the most watched television event in U.S. history. The story it told changed the way African Americans conceived of themselves, having a great impact on children in grade school, their parents, and their grandparents. In a podcast on Slate.com celebrating the fiftieth anniversary of the book's publication, Josh Levin, a national editor, interviewed people who had watched the show in 1977, capturing the excitement, the terror, and the pride that they shared. (I have edited the quotations slightly for context and clarity.)

One speaker, identified in the podcast transcript as "S3," said, "I was very young, but I still will never forget it." S3 continued, "I mean, Came nightmares, I was traumatized. I mean, I was, you know, really torn up."

Another speaker, identified as "S2," recalled, "Our phone would ring. 'Did you see that? Are you watching?'"

S3 added, "And the very next day, that's all we were talking about was *Roots.* And after [another] episode it was like, no one would be missing [it]."

At another point, S3 noted, "This is the first time that I was seeing it. It's not that I didn't know about slavery, but I really didn't know about slavery."

S2 replied: "My grandmother, she would come over and she would watch it. She always had her hands busy shelling pecans or . . . beans. She wouldn't really talk, but she would be like, Mmmmm hmm. Uhhh."

"There was something beautiful about these Black folk in this struggle and their survival," S3 said. "This is where I come from. This is who I come from."

S2 agreed: "It made me start to think about blackness and what it meant to be in this black skin."[9]

Not much later, however, questions about the accuracy and authenticity of the story of the lives of seven generations of Haley's family, from his eighteenth-century ancestor in Gambia onward, set off controversy and litigation (over plagiarism issues) and, unfortunately, spiraling back to *The Autobiography,* in which Haley allegedly manipulated the facts to more smoothly shape the narrative. This was an unfair and unrelated comparison. And really, it wasn't as if Wolfe

—

and others hadn't shaped or reshaped their own narratives, as John Hersey had implied. *Roots* won the Pulitzer Prize in 1977 and remained on the *New York Times* best-seller list for twenty-two weeks.

I had not read "Notes of a Native Son," James Baldwin's essay from 1955, until sometime in the late 1960s, and I wondered then if this could be called new journalism. At the time, everything I was reading, I was trying to decide and pinpoint what was new journalism and what wasn't. This was probably a waste of time and energy, but I thought if I wanted to be a new journalist (and I did at the time), then I needed to understand the discerning lines. I am not talking about the line between fact and fiction. I would be dealing with that a few years later. I mean, rather, the genre line. When was nonfiction considered new journalism and when was it essay and when was it something else?

But that didn't matter to me when I read "Notes of a Native Son." I was absolutely flabbergasted by how brilliant and compelling it was. Baldwin was not just reporting with flair and style like Wolfe or Mailer; he was digging deep into an era of one young man's life — so deep and so intimate that reading this essay was not really what I was doing; I was, rather, living the essay, living Baldwin's life, with him. In all of the other work I had been reading, Didion, Mailer, Capote, and others, there was always a way to recognize the space between those writers and the story they were telling or the event they were describing. But in Baldwin's prose, so intimate, so honest, that space disappeared. I was not a Black man and I did not come of age in the 1940s, but as I read this piece, again and again, Baldwin's father was my father, Baldwin's teachers were my teachers, and Baldwin's quest to find himself and find a way forward in life was me.

There's a scene in that essay that for me is unforgettable. Baldwin was living and working in New Jersey at the time, in his twenties, and he quickly discovered that you didn't have to be a "Negro" in the Old South to be victimized by Jim Crow and made to feel not just unworthy, but to him, inexplicably invisible or, worse, abhorrent. Every day he would wander the streets, choosing a place to eat lunch or dinner, and very often he discovered that he was either being ignored by those who were supposed to be obliged to serve him or informed by them, sometimes politely and sometimes not, "We don't serve Negroes here."

This situation—"We don't serve Negroes here"—made him angry and crazy and he found himself out of control and acting out, sometimes even making a spectacle of himself—not just in the streets; even at work. He was fired from the same job twice. Baldwin's anger simmers and grows as the essay moves forward; as you read you can feel the frustration and fury burning inside him. Until one day he goes out with a friend to see a movie (*This Land Is Mine,* with Charles Laughton and Maureen O'Hara), and after the movie ends he and his friend want to have a hamburger and a cup of coffee, so they enter a place near the theater called the American Diner where he is told once again, "We don't serve Negroes here." This was the humiliating last straw in front of his friend, who was white.

Leaving the diner, Baldwin walks away from his friend, elbowing through the crowded streets not knowing where he is going—just escaping—until he sees an "enormous glittering restaurant in which I knew not even the intercession of the Virgin would cause me to be served."

He walks in, sits down at a table, and waits. He does not remember how long he waited, until a waitress approached the table. She did not ask him for his order; she told him pretty much what he expected to hear, was waiting to hear. "We don't serve Negroes here." She did not, he remembers, say it with hostility; she seemed apologetic. He recognized fear in her face. He pretends not to have understood or heard what she had said to him and he motions her to come closer and she repeats that phrase that had haunted him, "We don't serve Negroes here."

With the repetition of that phrase, "I realized she would never come any closer," Baldwin suddenly explodes. There was nothing on the table except for a pitcher of water, and he hurled it at her. It missed and shattered against a mirror behind the bar. "And with that sound, my frozen blood abruptly thawed, I returned from wherever I had been, I saw for the first time, the restaurant, the people with their mouths open, already it seemed to me, rising as one man, and I realized what I had done and where I was, and I was frightened." He does not escape easily. "A round, pot-bellied man grabbed me by the nape of the neck just as I reached the doors and began to beat me about the face." In the end, Baldwin got away, streaking blindly down the street with nowhere to go.[10]

The scene he describes is breathtaking. I felt the relief and confusion that

---

Baldwin had obviously felt as he fled. And then Baldwin did what so many writers have such difficulty in doing. He provides a bigger picture, a point of self-realization, telling his readers what the scene had meant both when it happened and the wisdom and realization that it later provided. "I could not get over two facts, both equally difficult for the imagination to grasp, and one was that I could have been murdered. But the other was that I had been ready to commit murder. I saw nothing very clearly, but I did see this: that my life, my real life, was in danger, and not from anything other people might do but from the hatred I carried in my own heart."[11]

I've read this essay and this scene quite often over the years; I frequently assign the essay to my students. And every time I read the essay, I recognize a little bit more its brilliance, the way it is constructed, in scenes that provide self-reflection and movement, and the way the scenes build to a crescendo of realization. And then he begins again, building and leading the reader into another series of stories or scenes that provide another facet of meaning and realization. When you finish reading this essay, many of Baldwin's essays, you feel penetrated as if you have lived someone else's life, as if another dimension has been added to your own life. I can't explain, simply by studying his style, how Baldwin achieves this connection with his readers. But I knew after reading this essay that I could never achieve the intimacy and wisdom that Baldwin instills in his readers.

But to get back to the beginning, where I started this chapter: I could see why Wolfe would not have included Baldwin in his anthology. Not because he was Black, but more so he was not part of Wolfe's old boy network. (Although that was mostly because he was Black.) I don't think it would be unfair to say that Wolfe didn't care a whit about being inclusive; it probably never entered his mind. Diversity today is on everyone's mind, as it should be. But clearly, based on what was being published then, it was a side issue, if it was an issue at all. But also, maybe, "Notes of a Native Son" and many of Baldwin's other essays were just too damn good. It would show, alongside the many writers Wolfe included in that collection, what was missing in the new journalism. And what would inevitably come next: creative nonfiction.

PART 2

CHAPTER 8

THE SHOE DOG GOES TO COLLEGE

In 1964, I enrolled in the School of General Studies at the University of Pittsburgh where, my first semester, I took a number of courses, philosophy, political science, and the required freshman English. I remember those courses that first year not so much because of what I learned, but more because of the excitement and the attraction of this new and learned milieu I had entered. Unlike the cacophony of the highways as I traveled selling shoes or the robotic rigor of serving in the Coast Guard, this was to me a sacred temple of learning about those who had devoted their lives to scholarship. Master's degrees and Ph.D.s. Incredible achievements. I honestly had no idea what a Ph.D. was, but I knew it took a long time of study to get it, and you called those who had earned it "Doctor." I have, over these many years, recognized the fallacy, reality, and value of these letters and degrees, but at that time I found those scholars—professors who were doctors—most intimidating. Even their place of work and study was intimidating—not a temple, but a genuine cathedral.

The CL—the Cathedral of Learning—was the main classroom building on the campus at the University of Pittsburgh. A gothic structure forty-two stories high, commissioned in 1921 and finished ten years later (the first class there was held in 1931), it was then and continues to be the tallest educational building in the Western Hemisphere and the second tallest in the world, behind only

———

the main building at Moscow State University in Russia. Scattered throughout most of the offices and classrooms in the CL are thirty-one carefully designed rooms reflecting the traditions and the heritage of the many nationalities enriching the city, helping it to become the steel capital of the world: the Polish, the Hungarians, the Lithuanians, and many others who arrived near the beginning of the twentieth century to keep the furnace fires burning, not just for steel but for glass and aluminum, and made a home there. And the many other nationalities, Irish, Scottish, English, who had established the city at the confluence of three rivers in the eighteenth century to build a fort to fight the French in 1750 and the British in 1777, and a town that would grow into an industrial powerhouse of a city, which in 1972 had a population of nearly 800,000 people.[1]

You went into one of these Nationality Rooms—you can still go on tours today—and you were thrust back in time to a church or cathedral or museum or chapel from centuries past. Hand-chiseled wood carvings, stained glass, wooden chandeliers, bronze sculptures, rare books and portraits that depicted the heroes and scholars of a forgotten past. It was magnificent and mindboggling for these very young men and women, mostly then from the neighborhoods and heritages the rooms represented or the small towns surrounding the city and the county of Allegheny, who attended Pitt at that time. Including me.

My freshman English "professor," let's call him Bill Miller, was a teaching assistant working on a Ph.D. in literature, a tall pockmarked string bean of a guy with unruly greasy hair and a paunchy belly. Freshman English, often called "composition 101," was a basic writing course to prepare students to write papers that were readable and organized as they progressed through their undergraduate years and chose a major—geography or history or philosophy or political science. Miller was a good teacher, and effectively outlined the basics of the five-paragraph essay—an introduction, three body paragraphs that support and develop ideas, and then a summary or concluding paragraph. Not as simple as it sounds, but doable if you took the time to think about it and squeeze it out.

But it was frustrating and limiting and not what real writing was all about. Not that I professed to know what real writing was all about, but it was not like the stuff I had been reading at the time and not really what I wanted to do. I couldn't help embellishing, figuring a way to satisfy my weekly assignments while writing some kind of a story and adding a bit of colorful observations, some pizazz. But Miller caught on to what I was doing right away—the first class, in fact. He had asked us to start off by writing something about our lives; it didn't have to be five paragraphs. And I had written something about the time I spent sorting empty bottles and driving a beer truck for a few months after shoe-dogging. It was, I guessed, an essay, and hopefully amusing. I handed in my story and walked back to my desk to gather my books and notes, and I was the last student to leave the room; it took me a couple of moments to pack up; I was always carrying a load of books wherever I went. Out of the corner of my eye, I could tell that he was reading what I had written. As I opened the door to depart, he said, "Wait." I walked back to his desk. "This is pretty good." He was nodding down at my composition, or whatever you wanted to call it, hand-written on blue-lined tablet paper. "What do you do?" he asked. "I mean, in life. Or what do you want to do?"

I told him this was why I had decided to go to college: to find a profession. I was lost, I admitted, looking for answers.

"Well," he motioned at my essay, pausing to nod and purse his lips, "this is pretty good. Well-written. You ought to think about being a writer."

I had, of course, fantasized about being a writer before, and at the time I was just beginning to read all of those books that were really turning me on, but that was the first time anyone posed the idea out loud to me or acknowl-edged the possibility that I might have what it takes. Whatever what it takes was, I didn't know. Miller and I didn't talk about this again, and at the end of the term he had earned his Ph.D. and got a job teaching somewhere in the Midwest. But he had provided the spark I needed, been waiting for—the approbation—to push me in a direction that I was to follow for the rest of my life. I think about this now, as I have been teaching for more than half a century, how crucial a teacher can be in the life journeys of their students, even sometimes with one remark at the right moment. Especially when they want to do something dif-ferent, out of the ordinary and the mainstream. Like creative nonfiction was then and to a certain extent is today.

Over the years I have frequently tried to reach out to Bill Miller and thank him for his encouragement. Without his off-the-cuff remark so early in my college career, I often wonder if I would have pursued the writing life. I have tried to connect with him a half dozen times, but he has never answered. Perhaps, I initially thought, this was because my letters and e-mails were way too overboard in appreciation and praise and made him uncomfortable. But once, years later, sitting in a coffee shop, I spotted him through the front window, walking up the street, and I rushed outside and pursued him, calling his name quite loudly to get his attention. When I caught up with him and told him how he had been instrumental in launching my writing life—I had by then published my first two books—I realized why he had never replied. I knew as he looked at me and nodded politely as I talked that he had no idea who in the hell I was. But it honestly didn't matter. I knew who in the hell he was—the source of one of those moments in a teacher's work that resonated and made a difference.

Back in the 1960s there were very few creative writing programs in the United States, unlike the many hundreds you can find at colleges and universities and even high schools today. And MFA programs in creative writing were nearly nonexistent. It's hard to imagine now, but there was a time when most writers were not affiliated with universities. Writers were much more a part of the world—driving taxis, selling insurance, teaching high school, thinking, knowing, that you had to experience life in order to write about it. Writers were like painters and composers; they followed their muse and created literature— poems, stories, plays. Hemingway, Fitzgerald, Welty, Capote, and all the others, the immortal masters, did not learn craft from a tweedy pipe-puffing professor; they went out and lived life and poured their souls into their poetry and prose. There were apprenticeships and mentoring for artists and writers, of course. But courses in creative writing? Who needed courses?

To put this in perspective, teaching or studying creative writing in a university setting in the 1960s was pretty damn unusual. Maybe even nearly impossible. The Association of Writers and Writing Programs (AWP) was established in 1967 with twelve member colleges and universities. It has grown substantially, to more than five hundred colleges and universities as members. AWP today publishes a magazine, *The Writer's Chronicle*, with tens of thousands of readers, and hosts conferences, including the Annual Conference and Book Fair, which brings many thousands of attendees. In the early 1970s, a half dozen years

—

after I graduated, there were fifty-two creative writing programs and only fifteen MFA programs – none in nonfiction; now there are more than two hundred.[2]

But most of these programs in the early days were small – more in name and in spirit than in fact. There were a few major programs, however, like the famed Iowa Writers' Workshop, founded in 1936. And there was kind of a boom right after the Second World War, with veterans supported by the G.I. Bill. The benefit money from the G.I. Bill could only be used for degree or certificate programs, which behooved university administrators to establish something "official." The "Writing Seminars" at Johns Hopkins University were founded in 1947, the same year the Stegner Fellowships were introduced at Stanford. Cornell University started a creative writing program in 1948. But none of these and the other programs available offered nonfiction as an option. It was strictly poetry and fiction. Even Iowa – even today. Technically the Iowa Writers' Workshop continues to not offer nonfiction, but a separate program was established in 1976 to accommodate nonfictionists; it's a terrific program, which has produced many great writers, but here again nonfictionists didn't fit in with the mainstream, "the artists" – not even and maybe especially not in the premier creative writing program in the world.[3]

At that time, there was a very small creative writing program at Pitt, mostly for fiction writers; and the university did not have a journalism department. So what to do if I wanted to be a nonfiction writer? There were two faculty members I had heard about. I went to the library and looked them up. The first, Myron Taube, taught short story writing periodically, but mostly he taught literature courses. He had published a few stories in literary – little – journals I had never heard of. And then I barely knew what a literary journal was, and I assumed quite correctly that hardly anyone read them. But there was another guy, Montgomery "Monty" Culver, who taught most of the courses oriented toward creative writing and who was obviously the real deal. His short stories had appeared in *Esquire* and the *Saturday Evening Post*. As a student in 1951, he had won an *Atlantic Monthly* "first" award, his first publication in a major magazine, and an O. Henry Short Story Award. This was the guy I wanted to study with.[4]

But I couldn't just register for a Culver course, like most other students, because I wasn't like most other students. I was what you would call today a "nontraditional" student or, then, a "night school" general studies student. Most of the writing courses that Professor Culver was teaching were off-limits to me. Today in almost all universities you can take courses anytime, no matter what school you are a part of—General Studies or Arts and Sciences. But Arts and Sciences then meant day school primarily and had higher scholastic requirements. Basically, you had to take the dreaded SAT (then an abbreviation for Scholastic Aptitude Test) to be accepted into Arts and Sciences. And I was pretty certain, based on my high school years, I would not pass it. You also had to be vetted with letters of recommendation, transcripts; whereas night school students, assuming they were high school graduates and had the cold cash to pay tuition, could simply register for classes and work their way to a degree. But mostly taking only the courses offered in the evening and designated "General Studies."

There were a couple of writing courses I could take, and I did—descriptive writing, expository writing—and they were interesting, but pretty generic, mostly offered to students seeking a liberal arts degree or those in other fields seeking easy electives. They were fine, I guess, as I worked my way toward an undergraduate degree. If this had been ten years later, considering the rapid growth of creative writing programs, my journey toward the writing life might have been different. My hope and expectation to learn to be a writer as a university student did not really pan out. But, as it turned out, I became much more prepared to write and to learn about writing and the writing life outside of the academy and in a different kind of classroom—an office building that had a beer tap.

Like many nontraditional night students, I had a day job. I'd work all day, nine to five-ish in downtown Pittsburgh, and then drive to the Oakland section, dominated by the university campus. After parking, I'd head down to the basement cafeteria at the CL, then called the Tuck Shop, get a coffee or something to eat, with the other "second-class" citizens on the same schedule or grind. "Second class" is how we "night school" students jokingly referred to ourselves. We weren't like those young kids living cushy lives in dorm rooms and fraternity and sorority houses, partying weekends, all on their parents' bankbooks. We were in the working world – and maybe we would be way ahead of them when they finally ventured out on their own, degree in hand, with scarce experience in the real world. At least that's what we hoped.

I met a lot of interesting people during that period, folks I would have never encountered had I not been so second class, and we would trade school and life stories. I remember Patsy, the nurse who attended classes three nights a week, from 6:30 to 9:15, and then studied in the library until it was time for her hospital shift at midnight. George, a "shop" teacher at a vocational school, trapped in the same job for years because he lacked a degree, commuted an hour each night from his hometown outside Pittsburgh. And Lloyd, a postal worker who wanted to be an engineer. Lloyd had a family, a wife and three kids, and in order to study in peace and quiet he would get up early, take the first bus from his neighborhood, find a quiet corner in the back and read and do home-work as the bus traveled its circuit back and forth between where he lived and his workplace. He had it timed so that he could study through three circuits until he had to report to work when his bus pulled in at the right stop.

These were all very diverse people leading, it seemed, ordinary lives compli-cated with challenges and experiences that I would not have encountered, or so I thought, had I been taking classes with the arts and sciences undergrads a few years younger than me. I didn't realize then that these were some of the folks I would be thinking about not too many years later when I began campaigning for this new or different writing genre now called creative nonfiction.

My nine-to-five full-time job was at a communications agency – advertising and public relations. It was a big firm – the second largest in the city – and busy, servicing various industries then alive and thriving in Pittsburgh – steel, coal, oil, glass. Outside of New York, Pittsburgh had more corporate headquarters offices than any other city in the United States. I started as a go-fer (these days you would call me an intern), and I gradually worked my way up as an assistant and then a full-fledged account executive. I learned how to write news releases about products or events with snappy leads. I wrote catalogue copy and put to-gether brochures. I worked with printers and typesetters and designers. I would have never gotten such opportunities and experiences in the classroom. Maybe you won't want to call the work I was doing literature, but it was real world

—

stuff, often shared with large and diverse audiences – readers. I liked this work, because what I did counted. No practice and waiting a week for a professor's evaluation and verdict. You got a day to write something, or maybe just a couple of hours. You gave your work to a copy editor, and he slashed it with a big black pen and handed it back to you, sometimes without a word, and you went back at it, learning fast on the job.

The agency I worked for had a beer client, a big money-maker, so it set up a beer tap in the lobby opposite the reception desk in our building; you could pour yourself a tall glass – whenever. And we did – even sometimes for break-fast. After work, at five o'clock, many of us gathered to talk over the day or decide, after a few beer rounds, where we would go for cocktails and dinner. Sometimes I didn't make it to class. Believe me, whatever you might have seen on *Mad Men* played out in Pittsburgh.

One day I did a *Mad Men* thing; I mean, I took a chance with a wild idea. I wrote Johnny Carson a letter. *The Tonight Show Starring Johnny Carson* was the biggest thing on late-night TV from the early 1960s and for thirty years there-after. The show was the model for all of the late-night talk shows that followed it over the years, even up to present day – an opening monologue, guest inter-views, along with a house band and periodic performances by rock stars or comedians. It seemed like everybody who stayed up late watched Johnny before falling asleep. Or while falling asleep. Invariably, the next morning, wherever you were – diners, gas stations, supermarkets, dry cleaners – there'd be "Did you see Johnny last night" conversations. Which was the essence of the little story I wrote in the opening paragraph of my letter. "Did you see Johnny last night – quacking like Donald Duck?"

The letter was for the agency's new big deal client, the United States De-partment of the Interior, which had hired us, supported by a number of large corporations, mostly in the natural gas industry, to promote the hundredth anniversary of the discovery of helium. Or to put it another way, the Helium Centennial. Talk about boring. How to get people to pay attention to helium – a chemical element, a gas, no one cared or knew anything about? But I knew something, one of the few things I had learned in science classes in high school, that if you breathed in helium your voice would change – you quacked, like a

duck. And my letter started with a little scene capturing Johnny's opening monologue in which he quacked like Donald Duck.

I didn't tell anyone in the agency that I wrote the letter. I just sent it off,
figuring it was a dumb idea and no one at NBC would even read it. Or that by
the time they read the letter, they must have received so many every day, the
centennial would be over. But to make a long story short, I got a phone call
within a week from one of the *Tonight Show* producers; Johnny, he said, was
intrigued by the idea of talking like Donald Duck. Months later what I had fantasized actually happened. Which was hilarious, Johnny making a show of suck-
ing in the gas and then followed by quip after funny quip. Or should I say "quack
after quack"? Even now, when I mention my helium adventures to old-time
Tonight Show aficionados, they remember this episode.

I took part or led the way in many Helium Centennial events — or let's say
stunts. With industry money, a monument was constructed in Amarillo, Texas,
where helium was first discovered — a time capsule called the Helium Centennial
Time Columns, three stainless-steel time capsules, narrow cylinders that came
together like a tripod, supporting a fourth cylinder shooting straight up six
stories into the sky — a dramatic, erect shaft, like a majestic silver penis glittering
in the relentless Texas sun. The cylinders simulated the containers in which
helium was stored and shipped in a liquefied state.

The unveiling ceremony of the Time Columns was over-the-top dramatic.
The entire monument was covered by a gigantic canvas, which was lifted by a
helicopter at the peak of the ceremony, right before the dedication of the monument when Vice President Hubert Humphrey was scheduled to speak. I had,
in fact, written Humphrey's remarks, although he totally discarded my text and
spoke spontaneously. He did a better job than I did, I admit. We also sponsored
and promoted a contest for high school students, asking them to pick an item
that would go into the time capsule that would not be opened for a thousand
years. The winner would get an all-expenses-paid trip to Amarillo — not much
of a selling point, I know, but with it a ride in the helium-filled Goodyear Blimp.

The winning item — I was one of the judges — was a Sears, Roebuck catalogue, which was, sort of, the Amazon.com of its day. Not many people under
the age of forty have ever seen or heard of a Sears, Roebuck catalogue, or even

Sears, Roebuck and Company, but I do wonder what in the world folks will think or imagine 950 years from now when the capsule is opened and they leaf through this 600-page hunk of paper revealing ringer washer machines, hubcaps and petticoats, and houses for sale. If there are people remaining on earth 950 years from now in Amarillo or anywhere else. The monument remains in Amarillo today—a minor tourist attraction.

You may be thinking that was all too silly and wasteful—of money and time, and you'd be right—sort of. But these stunts did do what they were supposed to do: to make people, the general public, more aware of helium, not that this was its hundredth anniversary—who cared about that?—but what it was and why it was, this element, important, essential, in our daily lives. My letter to Johnny Carson had done exactly that, for after he entertained his audience with quacks, he interviewed a helium expert—Jon Lindbergh, the son of Charles Lindbergh, one of the world's first aquanauts, who, during the deepest of dives, breathed a mixture of oxygen, nitrogen, and helium to stay alive. So helium, and the importance of its conservation, was discussed on the Johnny Carson show for millions of viewers to pay attention to, at least for a minute.

My "Dear Johnny" letter was a triumph for the agency that would lead to new clients seeking similar publicity miracles. I had a big future in store for me in the advertising and public relations game, my bosses told me. I could make it big in New York. But I knew all along that this agency and my involvement in the corporate world was just a stop for me on the way to somewhere else. Although where somewhere else was, I had no idea.

But I had learned a creative nonfiction lesson—or a number of lessons—that would make a significant difference in my writing and publishing journeys much later on. One was to be bold and take risks. If I hadn't taken a chance on writing to Johnny Carson then maybe the entire course of my career would have not played out in the same way; hitting pay dirt with Johnny was reinforcing and confidence building. Another was to respect the power of narrative to attract, intrigue, and inform readers. The story I told about Johnny inhaling was a snapshot of what could be real life; it made what I had written seem possible. It was a picture to spark a reader's imagination. Even more important and long-lasting, my agency experience helped me realize that the literary and the business worlds are not so far apart and are often dependent on each other. I was too young at the time to understand the interconnectivity of the two, but it was to resonate later as I became more involved in the academy and then in publishing. Creative writing was as much a business as it was an art form, a way-out concept in a much more idealistic world of the 1960s and 1970s, and a reality, like it or not, today.

CHAPTER 9

A MENTOR, A MOUNTAIN MAN, AND THE BEGINNING OF THE WRITING LIFE

During my time at the agency and in between schoolwork assignments, I had been writing every day, pounding away on my Adler typewriter late at night, or getting up before dawn and putting in a few hours before work in the morning. Just like boot camp. I had started this regimen almost immediately after first registering at Pitt and meeting Bill Miller and kept it going pretty regularly. But I had no idea what I was doing. I was just writing, mostly scenes, stuff I remembered that had happened to me or that I had observed happening to others.

I loved my early morning and late-night schedule. It was therapeutic and sometimes downright exciting when I wrote something that worked. Although what worked for me maybe wouldn't work for anybody else. Soon I had graduated—I got my degree—and soon after that quit the agency. But who, I wondered, could help me now that I was on my own? How did I know that all those pages on yellow newsprint I had written laid out in tiny stacks everywhere in my bedroom were any good? I was fully aware that going on like this for untold years was part of the reality of writing, but I was much too practical and an obvious type-A personality to just sit and type, waiting for lightning to strike.

—

The only writer I knew — or sort of knew — was that guy Monty Culver. I had taken an intro writing course with Monty a few years back; unlike his colleagues, he seemed to enjoy teaching at night or maybe teaching adults. But I had never talked with him; he was kind of an odd duck, idiosyncratic, not at all, it seemed to me then, approachable. But I really had nowhere else to go if I wanted help. Culver was the only person I knew of who was actually teaching and publishing real writing.

Eventually I wrote him a letter, explaining my passion, my commitment to writing. It was sincere, emotional, and overwritten, and after I mailed it I could imagine him reading what I went on and on about and laughing out loud. I had no faith that he would remember me from his class, and maybe it was better if he didn't remember me, I thought. The work I had turned in received passing grades, but I had obviously not dazzled him. But I got a short note back right away, saying essentially that there were others like me who had graduated and felt the urge — the calling — to write. He said he had organized an informal writers' group for those folks that met every week after one of his evening classes in the CL — at 9:15. I could sit in. The next meeting was the following day. A Wednesday.

As long as I would know him, which was for a very long time, I could never tell how tall a man Monty was. He wasn't exactly stoop-shouldered; he was just kind of oddly shaped, slightly curved from feet to head. I often imagined putting my right hand on his back and my left hand on his chest, applying pressure and straightening him out. And because of his odd posture, his trousers never seemed to fit; baggy in the back and tight in the front, primarily because of ample paunch, too much beer and a shrunken butt, especially noticeable because of his upper body, narrow shoulders and nearly caved-in chest. He looked like a character from a Charles Dickens novel, trapped at a darkened sunless desk for hours on end stooped over a book of accounts. And he had his peculiarities — or "tics" you could call them; ceaselessly combing his hands — very narrow fingers tipped yellow with nicotine from his chain-smoking — through his brown gray-speckled greasy-looking hair. He made noises; he was relentlessly clearing his throat during any class or conversation. And he mumbled, so that his students were often raising their hands and asking him to repeat what he had just said. Not really a typical Mr. Chips professor but a guy who, maybe like me, never seemed to quite fit in.

But the way he talked, when he finally got around to talking, his rich, deep baritone, which he drew out almost like a musical chant, would command complete and instant attention. And as I think back, maybe it wasn't the voice alone; maybe it was the pregnant pause before he chose to speak that commanded such attention. His tics would stop, and he would slowly and slightly straighten out his frame, mostly by lifting his head, and you could feel in the air that something was coming — probably brief, but to the point and profound. Or at the very least definitive.

That Wednesday evening, I joined Monty and maybe six or eight people from, say, mid-thirties to mid-fifties sitting around an old conference table in one of the CL nationality rooms; I was by far the youngest. There was an elementary school teacher — and two women who described themselves as suburban housewives who had evidently taken courses from Monty as undergrads. The teacher and the other two women came and went from the group, attending for a while and disappearing and sometimes returning. And others, men and women, appeared and disappeared as the weeks went on. It seemed, they realized, that it was a lot easier to talk about writing, or about what you wanted to write, than to really write. Which has always been and will always be true.

There were two men who attended regularly. One fellow who was writing a series of stories for what seemed to be a book about a wire service editor in touch with a bunch of spelunkers trapped in a landslide in a cave, precipitated by a fierce storm. The editor, his protagonist, at his teletype was somehow, through his regular updated reports, the only communications link between the folks who were trapped and their potential rescuers. And although interesting, the story got kind of boring and repetitious after a while, the rescue party never seeming to get any closer to the trapped group in the cave, and the editor protagonist continuing to write news flashes reported on radio and TV. Monty was encouraging. He wasn't someone who praised easily, but he could always find a positive spin.

The other guy was a Korean War veteran who had had a head wound — shrapnel — and was living on disability and trying to write his way through the

———

"demons of combat," as he once put it, or his inability to work or think clearly or, in some cases, control his erratic behaviors. This was long before anyone acknowledged what we now know as PTSD. He was kind of unpredictable. He would, on some weeks, talk nonstop about what he was writing. He would go on and on until Monty had to curtail his comments. Or he would sit through the session totally mute, stewing and glaring at the rest of us. I had no idea how he and Monty had met. Maybe the same way Monty and I had connected, through a letter or phone call. Or in a bar. Both of these guys were trying to write fiction, but what might have been more fitting for both of them, and for most of the members of our makeshift class, was creative nonfiction, allowing them to recast their lives in an authentic and dramatic fashion. Had this been today and not fifty years ago, they might have found more success and satisfaction from their work. And the freedom to reveal themselves, as so many creative nonfictionists are doing today.

But back to that first Wednesday and Monty.

After the members of our informal writing group sat around and introduced ourselves, Monty asked if anyone had any work to discuss. There was no e-mail back then and no way of getting manuscripts to one another in advance. It was all unplanned and spontaneous, almost but not quite a workshop as we know it today. No one seemed to have work to discuss that night; I said I had a story that I had just written. It was quite autobiographical, about a kid I knew in grade school who would eventually die from leukemia. And it was about my struggle to pretend I did not care about him, just so I wouldn't be upset when he died. It was a serious subject although the way I had written it was funny — or supposed to be funny — and very sad at the same time. I dug it out of my brief-case and handed it over.

The way the group worked was that we would sit around the table and Monty would read over the piece quickly, and if he thought it was ready to share, he'd read it aloud and then we'd talk about it. There was a long silence as he looked at my story, pretty much skimming through the pages, though I noticed that he made little marks in the margins as he read. Maybe twenty minutes had passed as we all just sat there and stared at him, waiting for some sort of acknowledgment or response. We were afraid to speak so as not to distract him. I could hardly breathe, I was so nervous; I had never had a "literary expert" look at my work; I had been, like so many writers then and even now, laboring in the darkness of doubt and insecurity.

Monty had been running his hands through his hair and clearing his throat as he read, but when he looked up, the tics disappeared, and we all just stared and waited. And then suddenly Monty began to laugh and laugh and shake his head up and down. This was clearly his sign of approval, or so I hoped. And then he read the entire story to the group that night. We all laughed—even the Korean War guy—and a couple of the women actually cried when my friend died. It was a triumphant evening for me, the first legitimate highlight of my writing career.

Whether he knew it or not, that night Monty became what all inexperienced writers need, then and now, a mentor. Maybe my only real mentor. And when he handed my manuscript back to me, I discovered that the marks he had made throughout the piece in the margins were little, very pristine stars: "*****."

I visited Monty's office any time he had hours, and we had many talks about the ways in which personal experience and research were intertwined with narrative. We spent hours discussing Orwell's "Shooting the Elephant" and Hersey's *Hiroshima,* Kerouac's *On the Road* and Capote's *In Cold Blood.* And eventually we went out for beers together, just smoking and talking, mostly about writing and what we were reading. Monty had an affinity for dive bars, so it was not too difficult, assuming I had a spare half hour to roam the campus and peek into the more unsavory spots, to find him. I can still picture him today, a lone figure hunched over the bar in a dark corner, chain smoking and sipping a Bud from the bottle and feverishly marking up student manuscripts. Despite his obvious desire to lose himself, he always seemed genuinely pleased when I found him. This turned out to be very important to me, just hanging out and talking. Or just sitting there, side by side, and not talking, which sometimes happened. Made me feel more like a writer. A real writer. Not just a pretender, trying to write, even though I was just at the beginning of a quest to write.

Later I came to realize that one of the reasons—perhaps the main reason—that it took so long for creative nonfiction to emerge as a genre on the same level as poetry and fiction was this lack of connection with other writers and the understanding and empathy that togetherness might nurture and foster. Maybe we were doing something different and maybe we were a very tiny minority, or so it might have seemed, but what we were writing or trying to write deserved acknowledgment and respect and the legitimacy that went with it. I think this is one of the reasons that creative writing programs have become ubiquitous. It's not just what you might learn about the craft, but the intimacy and camaraderie, the very oneness of the group that keeps you going. This was certainly not what I was thinking about in the early 1970s; the realization and the work I did to make this happen — my efforts to gather and link the creative nonfiction community — slowly evolved years later.

Fueled by Monty's support and my own obsessive ambition, I began writing — and publishing — at first for any publication that would take my work. My experience in the shoe world led to assignments from trade magazines like *Boot and Shoe Recorder*, a slick magazine, and *The Footwear News*, a weekly tabloid. (Like I said, I took advantage of all opportunities; Wolcott had correctly described me as a "human octopus.") I wrote for *Women's Wear Daily*, *The Kiwanis Magazine*, the *Rotarian* and even *Presbyterian Life* and *The Jewish Chronicle;* when it came to publishing, I was nondenominational.

The idea of writing like a madman and publishing anywhere and everywhere was to get what we called "clips" — a body of work we could duplicate and send to editors whom we queried, asking for assignments. A much more laborious process than sending links and Word docs to editors interested in our work today, although the competition then was less overwhelming and frenetic. Unlike today, with blogs and self-published books, not everyone thought they could be a writer. I did a lot of experimenting with different material and approaches, not for any special reason but just, quite simply, to do it and to practice what I was learning while reading Talese and Wolfe and Mailer; I wrote down, verbatim, conversations I overheard that were interesting or amusing or even silly; I noted the way these folks talked, heads shaking, hands waving or finger pointing, whatever seemed significant — or weird. I jotted down descriptions of landscapes or storefronts. I wrote short scenes and long scenes and figured out how to knit them together so there was an arc, a structure just like John McPhee did in *The Pine Barrens* and later in his masterpiece essay "Travels in Georgia" in 1972. Every morning my writing schedule began with a story that captured what I had observed the day before.

All the while, whenever possible, obsessed, or shall I say, committed, as I was, I continued to have self-made adventures for more experiences. I rode cross-country, back and forth, with transcontinental truckers. I performed as a clown for a week with Ringling Brothers. I wrote a story about that and how my personality changed when I put on makeup and wore a crazy costume; this story was published. I hung out in the backwoods of West Virginia and western Pennsylvania with various characters I would run into and befriend. A one-armed blacksmith, Caulkey Walmer, who had forged his new arm after his brother accidentally shot his off, with scrap from a junkyard. And a cooper who practiced his trade with the schnitzelbank, or "shaving horse," brought to this country by his grandfather. I hung out with Baldy E. Lee, a champion snake sacker — a competition that charges the participant to jump into a pit of venomous rattlesnakes and copperheads, grab them bare-handed, and toss them into a canvas bag in thirty seconds. There were penalties if you were bitten in the process, including loss of life.

Harry ("Mountain Man") McCool took me rattlesnake and bear hunting and introduced me to chaw — Mail Pouch — and coonskin caps. McCool was a giant, way above six feet, 220 pounds or more, and seemingly fearless in the backwoods, although he had never been more than fifty miles from his house in his entire life. When his wife was sent to Pittsburgh for emergency surgery, he asked me to take care of her in his place. The city simply scared him silly. I laughed and made fun of him but did what he asked. He once scared me silly, payback, when I opened his refrigerator for a couple of beers and was confronted with a rattlesnake coiled to strike, and I screamed and jumped back. It was his turn to laugh and make fun. The snake was frozen solid. Years later, I wrote a book about these guys (*The People of Penn's Woods West*) and produced my first and only documentary movie, *A Place Just Right*, featuring McCool, Caulkey, and others I met during that time. The film won a major award and was featured at festivals internationally.

As time passed, I made progress with substantial publications. I sold a piece to *Sports Illustrated* about a famous — or maybe infamous — Pittsburgher, Bruno

Sammartino, a world champion in professional wrestling. Some say that professional wrestling has changed over the years and that now it is legitimate, but back then it was a fake and a sham. I think I made Bruno come off quite well in my piece. As a human specimen, he was a block of head-to-toe muscle. I met him face-to-face in my gym shorts in the ring at a local athletic club. First thing he said was that professional wrestling was no joke, as many believed, and that wrestlers were as fit and competitive as any others in football or baseball or hockey, more so in fact because wrestling was authentic combat; you could get hurt—"real bad." Then he grabbed me in a big bear hug, lifted me over his head and spun me around until I was dizzy, and he whispered to me: "If you were an opponent I could break you in pieces."

I was hoping, as I hung there in space, that he didn't intend to prove his point. "But I won't," he said. He laid me down on the canvas like a baby.

That same year, I immersed myself with a weird evangelistic clan in the back hills of Kentucky, "Judo and Karate for Christ," another *Sports Illustrated* story, where members chopped, kicked, flipped, and hurled their fellow disciples in the name of the Lord Jesus, and I was downright scared for my life. The leader of the group, an evangelistic preacher named Mike Crain, sliced a watermelon in half, which I had placed on my bare chest and stomach, with one massive chop of a gigantic, menacing Samurai sword. This was the way all followers of the group demonstrated their faith and trust in the Lord Jesus and in Crain's divine mission. I had observed Crain demonstrating this feat on disciples before I volunteered, so I knew—or hoped—he could pull it off without slicing his victim—me—in two, but I couldn't help wondering if Crain's oneness with God would work for me. After all, I was Jewish.

In the late 1960s, I had become a motorcycle fanatic. If I was meeting such interesting people as Baldy, Caulkey, and McCool a hundred miles from where I lived, I could only imagine who I would meet and what I would discover on the road from Pittsburgh thousands of miles and in any direction from home on two wheels. My first book, *Bike Fever*, about the motorcycle subculture and roaming the country on my big black BMW motorcycle—my Beemer—was published in 1971. The motorcycle seemed to fit my second-class status—or, as I came to think of myself—my outsider image, which I played to the hilt, acting, strutting around like the black-leather-clad black-booted Jewish wannabe thug that I wasn't. Didn't Wolfe say that writers should call attention to themselves? Maybe even irritating the hell out of other people? On my motorcycle, I imagined I was living the writing life. And sometimes, especially in the English department, pissing people off.

I thought then, with my first book published, that I had finally found my life's work, having as many new experiences as possible, experimenting with the techniques that the new journalists had pioneered, going all out; pushing the envelope — no limits. But then my next book, *The Best Seat in Baseball, But You Have to Stand! The Game as Umpires See It,* opened my eyes to some of the ethical pitfalls and moral complexities of the new journalism/creative nonfiction genre.

CHAPTER 10

INNOCENT VICTIMS

There are two scenes in that book that I especially remember so many years later. The first was when I captured a heated late-night conversation in a hotel room between Harry Wendelstedt, a member of the four-man umpiring crew I had been following through most of the season, and two other National League umpires who were passing through town heading for other game assignments. I wrote what they said—word-for-word dialogue—and described in detail their gestures and facial expressions and even the excessive amounts of alcohol they were consuming. I noted what they were drinking: scotch and German brandy.

It was a powerful scene and reflected a great deal about what they were feeling deep down about their work and their colleagues and one particular member of the crew I was following, Art Williams, who was the first Black umpire in the league. The two other members of the crew were Nick Colosi and Doug Harvey.

But I was not in on the conversation that night at all. I had been listening—eavesdropping—and frantically scribbling notes while sitting on a step outside and not far from their hotel room door. Those scene-setting details I included, what was going on in the room behind that closed door, were imagined, although not totally without reasonable substance. I saw them carry the bottles into the room. I knew the room; mine was identical. And, more important to me then, the conversation itself, which periodically grew heated – they were often shouting at one another – reflected and solidified one of the major themes in my book: racism in baseball, and Art Williams's struggle to adjust and fit in twenty-five years after the first Black player, Jackie Robinson, had been allowed, not necessarily welcomed, into the major leagues.

To put it mildly, these umpires were not happy to be working with Williams, either as crew members or league colleagues, and they resented the circumstances under which he had been hired because he was Black – what we would call today a diversity hire – and because he had not worked his way up through the system, paying his dues as they had. Some umpires in the league might have waited ten years before being promoted from the minor leagues to the majors; Williams had made it to the bigs in less than three, and because of his lack of experience, they agreed, his work did not measure up to major league umpiring standards. Or was there something else underlying their resentment? The conversation had included a bit of soul-searching. Were they racist, they asked each other? They didn't, they admitted, really know.

As it turned out, that scene in the hotel room, what was said and the tension and frustration it reflected, led to an even more powerful scene that I did witness – a confrontation the following evening among Wendelstedt and Harvey and Williams that was mean and vitriolic. It began on the field during a game they were officiating when one of the players, allegedly, insulted Williams with a racist remark after he made a controversial call. "Allegedly," because Williams insisted that the incident had not happened, while Harvey and Wendelstedt asserted that they heard the remark ("Half the players on the field heard it," they maintained), and that Williams should have ejected the player from the game, as any other qualified major league umpire would immediately have done.

In the locker room after the game they began to berate Williams for lying about what the player said or did not say and that – bottom line – he was "gutless" for not taking appropriate action. The conversation grew more heated; it was actually no longer a conversation; it became an argument that grew in intensity with mean and insulting slurs by Harvey and Wendelstedt that I will not repeat here. Through most of the scene Williams held his temper, but eventually he and Wendelstedt were standing face-to-face inches apart. Neither man backed down; the scene ended that way in a cold silence. That was the second-to-last chapter of the book. The last chapter summed up the season; the men moved on and finished the season together. But the end of the season – the end of the book – was to become the beginning of the end of Art Williams's major league umpiring career.

Let me give you some back story here to put in context and explain why the umpires so vehemently attacked Williams and what made writing those two scenes so challenging. The umps were actually a good bunch of guys to hang out with and interesting in their own right. Doug Harvey, the crew chief, was eventually inducted into the Baseball Hall of Fame, one of only ten umpires to be so honored. Harry Wendelstedt, after retiring, went on to establish a successful umpire school; his son, Hunter, eventually became a major league umpire as well. And Nick Colosi during the off-season was a maître d' at the chic Copacabana night club in New York. I enjoyed their company, and it was clear that they were proud and protective of their role as authority figures, the final arbiters of every play in every game. Because I had been getting along so well with the crew, writing those scenes made me uncomfortable. This happens when you do this "hanging out" work. As hard as you try to maintain an objective distance, you invariably become attached to the people you write about, even though you might disapprove of some of their ideas and actions, even when their motivations, in context, are understandable.

As in the case of Art Williams: the three men, his fellow crew members, had met early in the season to decide how to prepare Williams to deal with the resistance and the insults he might be subjected to from players. Not just because he was Black in a white man's game, but also because of his inexperience. They had decided, as a way of preparing and steeling Williams against any racial onslaught, to "jokingly" direct as many insulting and prejudicial remarks at him as possible, in the privacy of their locker room, or during the dinners they shared. And to make it seem acceptable, they would fling similar joking insults at each other. Colosi was Italian, so they called him a "dumb dago." Harvey was part Native American; he became a wild Indian or a crazy red man, or Chief. Wendelstedt was German – a fat dumb Kraut. That was their carefully thought out plan, lame and insensitive, and, to put it mildly, downright ridiculous. So when the player allegedly insulted Williams in that game, they were furious, not so much at the player, it seemed, but at Williams, who had obviously let them down after all their efforts to prepare him. And thus the confrontation in the locker room.

For my part, I labored over those scenes, first because of the way I wrote them. In the first scene, I took liberties—the most obvious and inappropriate was that I was knowingly spying on them. I hadn't accidentally overheard this conversation; this was a purposeful act. Had they been aware that I was sitting outside the door listening, they would never have spoken the way they did. Even more to the point, I was being downright reckless. Had they opened the door and discovered me scribbling in my notebook, the access I had enjoyed, the key element enabling me to tell this story, would have ended quite abruptly.

Looking back and evaluating, I am comfortable with the way I wrote the scene, despite my imaginative liberties, but I realize now that I might not have written it at all. I might have referred to it, generally, as a lead-in to the second scene, but I was carried away with the whole idea of new journalism and the freedom to be dramatic and to surprise or even shock the reader. What they were saying was very revealing; they were equally critical of Doug Harvey, Wendelstedt's partner.

But this was different from Gay Talese hanging out and waiting for characters to reveal themselves. Or Tom Wolfe observing and reporting and making fun at Leonard Bernstein's radical chic party. In my classes, or in the workshops or presentations I now give to colleagues, we will debate endlessly about the always blurry line between fiction and nonfiction. But there is always another line, often not discussed, between what is appropriate to write and dramatize and what is out of bounds. This becomes even more critical and difficult for memoirists who are relying on memory while writing their scenes, especially when the characters they are writing about are still alive and feel wronged by them.

In that second scene, even though I was a witness to it, the insults hurled at Williams were horrific and awful. I, however, not only repeated them but wrote them in capital letters, ostensibly to reflect and punctuate the anger that burned through the room. Ethically, legally, I did nothing wrong; I just wrote what I had heard and observed, but when I read that scene now, I shudder. The entire scene was very much slanted in Williams's favor, but I cannot help thinking that when he read those words, he too shuddered with renewed anger and humiliation. I could have, in retrospect, written the scene more delicately, with restraint, and still retained the power and passion of the moment.

Of course, we all go over in our minds, repeatedly, things that we write or do in life, that we wish we could do over or take back. But writers, especially those who write true stories about real people, sometimes don't realize that the words we put on a page are the words we are forever stuck with. There's no going back and rethinking and amending. The freedom that new journalism then and creative nonfiction now offer has limits and very often repercussions. I am not saying that I no longer dramatize events I observe for my books and essays. I am always waiting for revealing scenes and I write them as vividly as possible, but I have also learned to weigh what I have written, not just how I have depicted the scene, but also the potential consequences of my story for the people I have written about. Even though I was driven by what had become my own mission for my book, to reveal the racism in baseball, I wonder now if I was carried away with my ambitions. This is a question that all writers of creative nonfiction must ask themselves. There's often a lot more at stake than just the writing of a good story, even to prove a very relevant point.

But I was very young then. This was my second book. And I had a lot to prove to myself—and to editors and readers. In those days, even though the new journalism had established somewhat of a foothold, the standards and rules of the nonfiction road were still set by the traditional journalism community. Despite Capote and Mailer and Wolfe, you were considered an outlier as a new journalist—kind of illegitimate. As I went from ballpark to ballpark with the umpires, I was often banned by the beat reporters from sitting in the press box during the game. I was not considered trustworthy; not one of the old boys who had worked with one another for decades. All the while I was covering the umpires, I felt kind of insecure. Being turned away by writers I identified with, some whose work I had read and admired for years, was, at least as I viewed it then, embarrassing and diminishing. And when my book was published, most of the criticism I received, the negative reviews (there were many positive reviews!), came from those very sportswriters who had evidently suspected right from the beginning that I was up to no good.

Mostly I was accused of trashing the game—our coveted national pastime. But I suspected more than a bit of jealousy; it wasn't as if I had revealed some secret truth; the deep roots of racism were evident, especially for those veteran sportswriters who had covered the game for decades. How could they not be, if Art Williams was the first Black umpire in the league a quarter century after Jackie Robinson had been allowed to become the first Black player? These reporters—there were few women covering baseball then to my knowledge—could have written the same or a similar story as I did, perhaps not with such an intimate and in-your-face perspective. But the results would have been the same, maybe even accepted more readily from someone who wasn't one of those "newbies."

I was also very naive and maybe kind of stupid. There was a lawsuit threatened after my book was published—not from the umpires or the National League, although they were very angry, but from a sportswriter for the *New York Daily News*. In the book, I had quoted Wendelstedt making some very critical and unsubstantiated remarks about this reporter. Wendelstedt denied what I reported, and I did not have my notes to back up my quotations. My publisher took the easy way out and settled, and I was bound by my contract to share in the payment of the penalty. It cost me a lot of money I could hardly afford to lose. I subsequently received a phone call from my publisher, lecturing me about ethics and morals and warning me that maybe I had taken this whole new journalism idea a bit too far. That I ought to back off in my next book. And why hadn't I kept my notes? He was right in that respect, which made me feel even more like a loser.

But this happened in 1975, when the book was published, not long after the Watergate scandal and Richard Nixon's resignation as president. Most of the damning evidence against Nixon and his cronies was on the Watergate tapes, which, for some reason, Nixon did not destroy, despite how threatening they were to his political survival. At the time, many journalists were advising writers, especially those dealing with controversial subjects, to destroy their notes, just so there'd be no evidence against you in case of litigation. So that's what I did, and it cost me.

Today I get up every morning and write, as always, often imagining and theorizing—without many limits. I push the envelope. But then I sit back and reconsider what I have written, looking through the eyes of the people I have written about and weighing what it all might mean to them or how it might affect their personal lives and influence those who would read about them. And then I adjust or eliminate what I suspect is out of bounds. I am very careful. Other writers may have different boundaries. That was, unfortunately, not part of my process in 1974 and 1975.

I can't help thinking and rethinking now, many years later, that maybe I went too far. That I was too heavy-handed – or too freewheeling in my attempts to prove my point in a cinematic and dramatic and hard-hitting way. And that maybe, more than anything else, in the end I actually hurt the man I was trying to help, considering what happened to him after my book was published.

Two years later, Williams was fired by the National League, allegedly for his poor performance as an umpire. To be fair to the National League, there were polls in 1974 and 1975 from players and managers that were not at all helpful to Williams; he was, they said, one of the worst umpires in baseball. Williams was not buying it, arguing that he had worked in the majors for five years and then they suddenly decided to fire him; it didn't add up. He theorized that another Black umpire had been selected for advancement to the league, and that the league did not want to have two Black umpires officiating at the same time. He subsequently lodged a complaint with the Equal Employment Opportunity Commission over the racism he confronted. But the suit was never really examined or resolved. Tragically, he died during brain surgery in 1979 to remove a tumor from his pituitary gland. He was unheralded for breaking the color barrier in umpiring as Jackie Robinson had done for players.[1]

Williams being fired shook me up. I wouldn't say we had become "friends" in 1974, because writers and their subjects rarely achieve true trust and intimacy; there are obvious and often unspoken barriers. No matter how close you get, there's still that notebook or recorder, and most important, that obsession for story and attention-getting controversy that keeps you at least one measure apart.

But then I heard from mutual friends that he blamed me and my book for some of his troubles. I am not sure whether that's true; the information came second- and third-hand. Besides, I thought, wouldn't my book have helped his cause? This didn't make sense. And he had umpired for another year after my book was published. I realized, though, that after he was fired he might have been so hurt and angry that he struck back in as many directions as possible.

I — my book — was an obvious target. I wish now that I had reached out to Williams after his firing, but to be honest, the lawsuit, the general pushback by critics and my publisher, had shaken me up and I just wanted it all to go away.

After all these years, however, I can't quite get out of my head the notion that Williams might have, inadvertently, been one of those innocent victims of the narratives that we nonfictionists must work hard to protect. I wonder now, as I think back to all the books I have written or edited, maybe thirty-five in all, so far, and many articles and essays: Have I possibly left some other innocent victims in my wake? I have certainly taken advantage of other people and their real-life stories I have sometimes had to squeeze out of them, and that for good or bad is how I view my job. The writing is part of my job, for sure, but it is the materials writers have at their disposal that make the writing compassionate, compelling, and sometimes profound. You do what you can with what you've got to work with. Even if you have to stretch your boundaries, there are always boundaries to be aware of. Never underestimate the power of your pen — and the power of narrative — the story you are composing and recreating and sharing with an unknowing and unaware public.

In 1985 I was asked to be part of a panel at the Association of Writers and Writing Programs conference. The annual AWP event is really big now. At the last conference before the pandemic, in Tampa, Florida, in 2019, there were more than thirteen thousand students, editors, and creative writing faculty from across the country and abroad and slews of job seekers parading their MFA degrees and new writers desperate to publish. But in 1985 creative writing programs were not as ubiquitous and there weren't nearly as many literary presses and little "literary" magazines setting up booths and promoting their products. That year the conference took place in San Diego, and there were fewer than five thousand attendees. Unlike today, you could easily get a seat at the headquarters hotel bar.

The panel was pitched as a discussion of what was then referred to as the "imaginative essay." Because new journalism was . . . journalism . . . it was not paid much attention in the academy. Nonfiction had been on the AWP radar over the previous couple of years, although most writers in the academy were struggling with how nonfiction or creative nonfiction fit into the bigger literary picture and obviously with terminology—how to label or describe it. Thus, the imaginative essay, although it would be hard to imagine a well-written essay that was not in its very essence imaginative.

Anyway, I gave a lot of thought to the subject from a new journalistic or creative nonfiction point of view—something I really hadn't done before to a great extent and especially my own ongoing discomfort about the Art Williams situation. And I was kind of nervous. I was then, and still am, one of these "just do it" guys, reacting spontaneously and sometimes even thoughtlessly to situations and events, sometimes even just because I wanted to be contrary. But I took my time here and thought it all out and gave my ten-minute spiel, which emphasized the nonfiction writer's moral responsibility and mission to tell the truth. I broke down the concept of writing and truth into categories: factual and objective truth, imaginative and subjective truth, and what I termed the "innocent party's truth." In my presentation, I pretty much skipped over the objective truth, which was traditional journalism. And I threw in imaginative or subjective truth because we were supposed to be discussing the imaginative essay, so I was going along with the program.

What I really wanted to talk about, what I really felt strongly about, was that latter truth I had named: the innocent victim truth. What I meant by that was, the person being interviewed or written about deserves accurate representation, so they aren't harmed in any way because of the writer's imaginative efforts. A writer, I said, can distort factual truth while portraying his or her imaginative truth only if it does not misrepresent or harm others. There ought to be some sort of reason or rationale to color facts with fantasy, whether for the sake of the composition or, for that matter, the protection of innocent victims who are part of the story.

As I look at this now, thirty-five years later, my first real effort to actually think about what I had been doing spontaneously in my work and writing over the previous fifteen years, I can pretty much over time stand with it. But the debate over the boundaries of new journalism and creative nonfiction is ongoing.

CHAPTER 11

MANIPULATING MATERIAL—AND THE PEOPLE YOU ARE WRITING ABOUT

Tom Wolfe had not ventured into the ethics and morals of new journalism in the introduction to his anthology. The lines between fact and fiction, style and substance, hardly seemed to concern the boldest new journalists, perhaps like me, so enthralled with the liberties and options opening up to them.

There were some ethical "scandals" during those early days and they made pretty big news. Clifford Irving, for example, a novelist and investigative reporter, was named "Con Man of the Year" for 1972 by *Time* magazine after writing a fake autobiography of the reclusive billionaire Howard Hughes. Irving went to prison for seventeen months.[1]

But this was pretty much clear cut; Irving was a charlatan, he took money, a rather sizable advance, from his publisher based on a lie. A lot of the background material about Howard Hughes in the book may have been interesting and accurate, but the story part—or the creative part, the idea that Hughes was cooperating and being interviewed and revealing—was all made up.

The title of a book I wrote about the genre in 2012 pretty much captures the essence of the operating approach and principles behind creative nonfiction: *You Can't Make This Stuff Up!* Although my meaning and message in choosing this title is clear and obvious, that real life stories are just as good or even better than those that are conjured and imagined, the title can be misleading. Because the fact is, depending on circumstances and intentions, you can make stuff up. And in the process even make the work better or at the very least more readable and seemingly authentic — truer to the subject. Defoe's *Journal of the Plague Year*, written in first-person perspective by a man named H. F., is a great example.

I have no idea what went through Defoe's mind when he decided to recount the plague years through the eyes of someone named H. F., but had he written the book as a journalist, putting together all available facts about the pandemic — the who, what, when, and where of it all — it would not have attracted as much attention, or any, and would certainly not have been revived and lauded during the current Covid era. Making up the narrator and letting him loose in the first person added a feeling of authenticity and made a connection to the general reader. And that was in 1722, when it was published. If Defoe had published the book in 1972, it would have been easily classified as new journalism or today as creative nonfiction.

It took a long while, incidentally, for Defoe to reveal himself as the author of *A Journal of the Plague Year*; for years readers believed that H. F. was a real person. Maybe today, his publisher would have urged Defoe to include some sort of explanation about why he had made up his narrator — yes, in order to tell the story better and to add personal insight that would help readers understand and relate. And, obviously, for transparency; it would be the right thing to do.[2]

As time passed in the 1970s and more and more writers were experimenting and taking advantage of what seemed like the elasticity of the genre, the debates over what can and cannot be made up or altered became more serious and controversial — not necessarily among readers who were and continue to be pretty much unaware of the ways in which writers can and will manipulate and enhance material, as I did in my umpire book. Or push the basic facts into an imaginary realm in which fact is nearly irrelevant. That would become the main point of contention between the new journalists and those traditionalists who held on to the stricter standards of reporting and writing. The question always came down to — then, and to a certain extent it is still debated today — where is the line between the creative and the nonfiction, the style versus the substance? How far can one push the boundaries — where is the point, that foggy blurred line, that goes beyond any notion of nonfiction and turns the work into fiction?

Given the freedom and flexibility allowed in the new journalism and later in creative nonfiction, the writer may get carried away by stretching the boundaries too far, either knowingly or unknowingly. And maybe even a bigger question: What is the intention, the motives, of the writer? What's at stake for the writer? Given all the techniques at the writer's disposal, the scope for creativity, writers will invariably devote more time and effort to their stories, which means they have a lot to lose if the story is not published in some way. Or if it is published and ends up being hurtful to the people it is written about. Writing in the old 5W way was easy and safe. But writing new journalism or creative nonfiction can turn into a quagmire of controversy, disappointment, embarrassment, regret, and, under certain circumstances, contentious and seemingly never ending litigation, as the *New Yorker* writer Janet Malcolm was to discover.

It is 1979, four years after my umpire book was published. Jeffrey Moussaieff Masson, a psychoanalyst, was fired as project director of the Sigmund Freud Archives in Paris after serving a little less than two years. During that time, Masson oversaw the publication of Freud's letters, and it was, in part, his handling of those letters and the publication of the collection that led to his firing.

Janet Malcolm, whose book *Psychoanalysis: The Impossible Profession* had been published the previous year, was intrigued—in a way, this was her turf—and she conducted a series of interviews with Masson off and on over a number of months. Eventually she published a two-part article in the *New Yorker* in 1983 about the letters and Masson's role in the publication. Alfred Knopf later published an expanded version of these articles in a book, *In the Freud Archives*.

Masson was incensed by the articles and the book and sued Malcolm, the magazine, and the publisher, for $10 million. Not only, or at least not at first, for Malcolm's stylistic portrayal of his actions and personality; his suit initially focused on his belief that he had been misquoted. On the surface, this may sound easy to resolve one way or the other. But "misquoted" to Masson meant that not only had he not said what was quoted, but that the quotes had been altered so that, even if he did say, in context, what was reported, he had not said it in the way in which it was reported. As an example: he admitted that he had called himself an "intellectual gigolo," but meant it kind of off-handedly and as part of a larger conversation. The articles and the book, said Masson, "ended my academic careers. People read me saying about myself, 'I'm an intellectual gigolo,' and they say, 'We can't hire him.'" His reputation and his future were at stake, he insisted.[3]

The Malcolm-Masson case was not quickly settled; it dragged on for years, since Malcolm, supported by the *New Yorker* and Knopf, fought back. She was, however, obliged to turn over all of her research materials, including tapes and notes she had accumulated in the process of writing the articles and the book.[4]

Over the years that followed, Masson's legal representatives identified twelve passages from Malcolm's materials that they considered in one way or another libelous. Many legal scholars weighed in with varying opinions about the practice of altering quotations, and there seemed to be some agreement that this would be allowed if there was no material difference in the content. The courts eventually determined that four of the twelve were "substantially true" and not libelous, and after a few more years of back-and-forth litigation related to the remaining passages, the court determined that there was not clear and convincing evidence of actual malice, and that the quotes were either "rational interpretations" of what Masson had said, substantially true, or at the very least nondefamatory.[5]

From beginning to end, the Malcolm versus Masson saga went on for more than ten years. But it did bring to light a surprising and more significant issue that was in some regard at the very essence of the nonfiction writer's bag of technique tricks—much more complicated than changing wording. Or even imagining. Malcolm had spoken to Masson dozens of times over a period of many months at various venues and on the telephone, but the challenge when she sat down to finally write the story was how to put all of the pieces of those conversations together, so that it read smoothly from start to finish in a narrative style.

Malcolm's initial meeting with Masson had occurred at the Chez Panisse restaurant in Berkeley, California. In the first installment of her article, Malcolm used the restaurant and its ambiance as her primary setting, linking parts of many conversations that did not actually take place there into what read like a long Masson monologue in which he seemed at once rash, narcissistic, and voluble. It was perhaps the most revealing and damning segment of the entire two-part series and the book that followed and undoubtedly the primary reason Masson decided to sue.[6]

What Malcolm had done in piecing together this long set piece in Chez Panisse was to manipulate or alter the chronology of her story, a technique writers refer to as "compression," which, as it turned out, eventually became part of the case. Although the initial lawsuit focused on the validity of twelve quotations, the practice of compression—the ethics and morality of altering chronology—became a major focus of the trial. She was not sued for her use of compression per se, but Malcolm did acknowledge that she had combined a large number of interviews into one, and Masson's attorneys attempted to use this fact to undermine her credibility. As a result, when compression was brought up while she was on the stand during the second trial, Malcolm was forced to defend the technique, testifying that compressing the pieces of her interviews into one monologue was necessary, explaining that Masson's "speaking style is an essential part of his character." And this concern, she said, motivated her treatment of Masson. "I needed to present [his monologue] in a logical, rational order so he would sound like a logical, rational person."[7]

Malcolm's defense goes straight to the heart of one of the ethical and artistic problems raised by this technique: What should a writer do when an exact adherence to chronology will leave the reader bewildered—or ruin the fluidity of the narrative? Where does one draw the line? Had Janet Malcolm crossed it?

Testimony during the trials revealed that the book depicted Masson as "a grandiose egotist—mean-spirited, self-serving, full of braggadocio, impossibly arrogant and, in the end, a self-destructive fool," as a reviewer in the *Boston Globe* put it. He did not sound very much like someone Malcolm or anyone else would want to spend time with. And Masson, perhaps a braggart and a narcissist, should have been wary of Malcolm's intentions and not spoken so freely. But there was a balancing factor—Malcolm's two-faced approach to gathering material for her story.[8]

During the months when Malcolm was researching and writing the story, collecting all of the damning quotations and facts, she had worked hard to befriend her subject. Masson and his girlfriend were guests at Malcolm's house for four days, and Malcolm arranged a party for him to meet her friends. She subsequently took him and his girlfriend on a tour of the *New Yorker* offices, introducing them all around.

What was Malcolm thinking, you might ask? But the answer is pretty clear. She was thinking this was how she could gain Masson's trust, so that he could further shoot himself in the foot by continuing to confide in her. Was this common practice for an essayist or a new journalist? Or had she crossed an ethical and moral line? Are we manipulating not only texts but also our subjects — the people we are writing about?

In 1991, in an article published in the *New Yorker* that became a controversial book, *The Journalist and the Murderer,* Malcolm answered this question in her lead — a revealing statement that would become one of the most debated, discussed, and quoted in the history of journalism.

> Every journalist who is not too stupid or too full of himself to notice what is going on knows that what he does is morally indefensible. He is a kind of confidence man, preying on people's vanity, ignorance or loneliness, gaining their trust and betraying them without remorse. Like the credulous widow who wakes up one day to find the charming young man and all her savings gone, so the consenting subject of a piece of nonfiction learns — when the article or book appears — *his* hard lesson. Journalists justify their treachery in various ways according to their temperaments. The more pompous talk about freedom of speech and "the public's right to know," the least talented talk about Art; the seemliest murmur about earning a living.[9]

The Journalist and the Murderer focused on the ethical and moral lines crossed by another writer, Joe McGinniss, in *Fatal Vision,* his best-selling book about Dr. Jeffrey MacDonald, who had been twice convicted of killing his wife and two children. For his third and final trial, MacDonald desperately wanted someone to write what he insisted was the real truth of his predicament — and his innocence. McGinniss, sensing a best seller to buoy his flagging career, equally desperately wanted to write the book. So they entered into a bizarre agreement, one that even the most reckless writer might have avoided. Essentially, McGinniss would be included as part of the MacDonald legal defense team for his upcoming trial, gaining access to every intimate moment of the struggle to save

MacDonald's career and freedom. In return, MacDonald was to share a percentage of the proceeds of the book, and he agreed to not sue McGinniss for libel just in case the agreement went awry. This was a very unusual relationship.

McGinniss befriended his subject, not just with a party and a guest house visit as Malcolm did; the two men fell into a macho bonding relationship, sharing apartments, double dating, and running together each afternoon on the beach. For that period and for the next few years after the trial, as McGinniss wrote this book, they were best friends—a friendship cemented by his constant assurances that he believed MacDonald was innocent. But McGinniss was the supreme confidence man, for *Fatal Vision*, when published in 1983, revealed his real belief—that his "friend" and financial partner was guilty as sin. MacDonald has since insisted repeatedly that it was McGinniss's book that sealed his life-in-prison fate.[10]

Malcolm's access to McGinniss was limited for *The Journalist and the Murderer*—just one five-hour interview—but it was enough to frame an entire book about the writer's betrayal of his subject. Malcolm wrote the story in two parts for the *New Yorker* without once mentioning her ongoing conflict with Masson, despite numerous similarities, even though both cases were going on at the same time. She had even hired the lawyer who defended MacDonald, Gary Bostwick, as part of her own defense team.

When the articles were published as a book, the afterword did acknowledge the similarities and her conflict, but mostly served to address the criticism she had received for not initially mentioning her situation with Masson, and she denied that she was wrong for not having done so. Although the afterword itself contradicted her denials.

The Journalist and the Murderer is undoubtedly Malcolm's most lasting literary achievement of the many books and *New Yorker* articles she published in her lifetime (she died in 2021). Modern Library has included it in its list of 100 Best Nonfiction books along with such classics as *Notes of a Native Son* (James Baldwin), *A Room of One's Own* (Virginia Woolf), *Why We Can't Wait* (Martin Luther King, Jr.), and *The Right Stuff* (Tom Wolfe). The book is used in many creative writing classrooms, and in the controversy after it was published, Gore Vidal, Nora Ephron, Jessica Mitford, and many others praised its insights and honesty. But among many writers and journalists, there have been disagreements.

Writing in the *Washington Post,* Victor Navasky pinpointed two main issues with Malcolm's book.

> The first has to do with her apparently irresistible impulse to the hasty general-ization, the self-serving universalization. It is not merely that all journalists (including the weatherman, the obituary writer, the nightly newsreader?) are morally indefensible. All defense lawyers are "haters." "People who have never sued anyone or been sued have missed a narcissistic pleasure that is not quite like any other." "Before the invention of the tape recorder, no quotation could be verbatim." Or, my favorite, "The 'I' character in journalism is almost pure invention."[11]

The other, more significant problem that Navasky found in Malcolm's book is that she is not actually criticizing a typical journalist-subject relationship. Most journalists do not have a business contract with their subjects as Mc-Ginniss did with MacDonald, one that created "unique ethical conundrums and compromises." Therefore, according to Navasky, the McGinniss v. Mac-Donald case is not a good example for Malcolm to have chosen to investigate the journalist-subject relationship.

Other writers were much more direct and downright nasty. In a review of *The Journalist and the Murderer* in the *New York Times* in 1989, Albert Scardino wrote: "She attacks the ethics of all journalists, including herself, and then fails to disclose just how far she has gone in the past in acting the role of the journalistic confidence man."[12]

In response to an observation published in the *Paris Review,* that Malcolm was the "conscience" of the profession, Tom Junod wrote in an article in *Esquire:* "I will argue, however, that the journalistic internalization of Janet Malcolm as 'journalistic conscience' constitutes a scandal in its own right, if only because for all the undeniable power of her rhetoric and 'the nice sting' of her one-liners (she is the Henny Youngman of self-hating journalists), she's utterly full of shit."[13]

PART 2

The Malcolm case, on its face a seemingly straightforward issue of practice and technique (that is, changing quotations and compressing events), had revealed that once you start closely examining these questions, you are liable to find beneath the surface a quagmire of complicated ethical concerns about the very nature and intent of journalism and creative nonfiction. Very soon other prominent writers would stumble into related and complicated conundrums that would be difficult and sometimes embarrassing to deal with.

CHAPTER 12

A LARGER REALITY? OR THE UNTRUE TRUTH?

Compression was not the only issue that came to light during the late 1970s and early 1980s that began to shape the dialogue and ongoing debate over what can and cannot or should not be done while researching and writing true stories.

Six months after Malcolm's Masson articles appeared, the *New Yorker* writer Alastair Reid faced criticism for a different but equally challenging issue – the compositing of characters, meaning combining characteristics, actions, and words of many people into one, and in the process, often inventing or imagining events that had not happened.

In an article written in 1984, Reid, an accomplished and well-regarded poet who had been a *New Yorker* correspondent for a number of years, described a conversation that happened in a bar in Spain with the bartender and some of the regular patrons. In reality, however, the conversation as Reid recounted it took place at the home of the bartender of that club three years after the bar had closed. If there was a conversation at all. The reported conversation was actually Reid's version of what would have ensued if the bar's regular patrons, who had been composited, had been present and in the bar.[1]

A couple of years earlier, Reid had written a story about a "friend" who had attended the graduation of his "grandniece" from Yale, but the graduate in question had been Reid's own son. And the friend had been Reid. Reid had revealed his methods while speaking at a seminar at Yale in 1982. There was a student in the audience, Joanne Lipman, who later became a reporter for the *Wall Street Journal* — and thus her front-page story revealing Reid's methods — two years later.

In defending or explaining his actions, Reid said that he was in search of a "larger reality," that his articles were truthful in spirit if not in total detail. "At times," he said, "we have to go further than the strict factual. Facts are part of the perceived whole." The *New Yorker* editor William Shawn at first defended Reid and his magazine. "We don't have a single fact presented as a fact that isn't one," he told a reporter from the *New York Times,* adding to the confusion and his own perhaps purposeful lack of clarity. "It doesn't mean one should discard facts or shouldn't respect facts, but the truth has to include something that goes beyond facts."[2]

As it turned out, though, *New Yorker* writers did do exactly what Shawn said they could not and should not do — quite often. Joseph Mitchell, one of the most influential personal journalism writers in the first half of the twentieth century, had published a series of articles in the *New Yorker* capturing the pulse of life and the remarkable characters who worked or hung out at the Fulton Fish Market. These were magnificent pieces that every writer I met and talked with in the 1970s and 1980s, as I explored and searched out my own voice and direction as a writer, described and praised with admiration and genuine glee. I remember once visiting the *New Yorker* offices to talk with editors and writers who pointed almost awestruck at a closed door in a dank hallway, where Mitchell was supposed to be writing. I say "supposed to be" because since those brilliant Fulton Fish portraits, Mitchell had seemingly been blocked, and had not produced a piece for the *New Yorker,* or any other magazine, for nearly twenty years. You had to give those *New Yorker* editors a lot of credit for supporting Mitchell through all of that literary drought, but in retrospect, in a biography of Mitchell by Thomas Kunkel (*Man in Profile*), his work was outed. It turned out that some of Mitchell's seemingly brilliant work had been composed — or made up.[3]

The fact that even the *New Yorker,* the pinnacle of publication for writers, especially of nonfiction, the Mecca of all long-form reportage, could not figure out the rules of writing the "true story" demonstrates the real quandary of the genre—the balance between what we might honestly imagine based on fact—and the facts themselves.

Reid's idea—or defense for his actions—of a "larger reality" did not play well with journalists, but it did have kind of a nice ring to it, and there were many in the academy, poets, essayists, and fiction writers, who began to use it in the classroom. I admit that I, too, briefly used "larger reality" with my students as I urged them to be daring, go beyond what they learned in journalism classes about the necessity of objectivity and sticking exclusively to the factual line.

"Larger reality" was a handy and glib way to justify the reasons for pushing the limits in their narratives. Which was often difficult for them to do, having been indoctrinated by their "writing the news" professors. Similarly, I also came up with the phrase "three-dimensional truth" to urge them to try to be cinematic, and I thought that was more to the point and an idea that I could live with in the context of setting and capturing the scene and of adding the dimension of their own voice and observations. I have also heard the term "emotional truth" being used in this context, but that seemed to me more apt to be used for romance novels or perhaps on a therapist's sofa.

But "larger reality," I eventually concluded, was really a bullshit term that would in essence justify writing fiction and calling it nonfiction and offered a slim excuse for laziness and not doing the legwork or the creative brainwork that could result in a story that would be just as compelling and provocative as one conceived in thin air. There was a difference between what I had written in my umpire scenes and what Reid had done. Despite the liberties I had taken, my scenes had actually happened; the characters were real and the conversation—the confrontation—was accurate. There was nothing real or true in Reid's essay, with a place that did not exist and characters who may or may not have existed, all based on a conversation that had not occurred.

There were other similar phrases of justification or explanation that would come up over the years quite similar to "larger reality." The novelist Tim O'Brien, referring to his book *The Things They Carried*, differentiated between "happening truth," the kind of factual truth a journalist would be required to employ, and "story truth," when stories might be conjured up to provide a more cinematic picture of what an experience might actually be like. O'Brien caught a lot of heat from readers and fellow writers who felt betrayed when they learned that a lot of what he wrote was not real. But in a way, that's to O'Brien's credit. *The Things They Carried* was so vivid and believable, so downright brilliant and beautiful and so damn realistic that readers were totally captivated and involved; all that he described seemed so authentic. So it was a disappointment when readers woke up from the trance of his book and came to terms with the reality of what it was — a novel.[4]

Tom Bissell, who writes mostly creative nonfiction about travel, once provided an intriguing example of the challenges of the nonfiction writer who tries to do the legwork necessary to be a responsible gatherer of information and piece together all the facts and make the work creative, even when the final product is to the best of the writer's ability and in their own hearts true and honest, may not, as written, be exactly, upon examination, literally true. For these instances, he came up with another phrase: "untrue truth."

In his essay "Truth in Oxiana," which has been published and republished in many venues, including *World Hum: The Best Travel Stories on the Internet*, Bissell begins by discussing his favorite work of nonfiction and travel writing, Robert Byron's book *The Road to Oxiana* (1937), which he describes as the perfect example of how a writer can write about what happened while "refusing to be *limited* by what happened."[5]

The Road to Oxiana follows Byron's explorations of Persia and Afghanistan; Oxiana was his name for the northern Afghani border region. Bissell provides examples of a number of beautifully written comedic dialogues that run through the book, all of which capture vivid moments of Byron's explorations and the personalities of the characters he encountered. Bissell was to discover later that these entries, much as he admired them, were often exaggerated and sometimes literally "made up." But, he admits, after exploring the same region on his own decades later, they were "perfectly representative of certain aspects of Afghani character . . . that could have never been achieved in a "straight remembered transcription" of Byron's adventures. Byron, he says, navigates "the slippery notion of the untrue truth."

Inspired by Byron, Bissell then describes a "playlet" he created in *Chasing the Sea,* his book published in 2004. The playlet, which takes place during a tour of a fortress in the Uzbek city of Bukhara, features four characters: Bissell, Rustam, a translator, Rick, a Peace Corps volunteer, and Faruza, a guide leading them on a tour of the fortress. The tour, and his descriptions of the characters, were, in a certain sense, like Byron's dialogues, also made up. Or sort of.

Bissell explains how he constructed the playlet by piecing together, in a puzzle-like fashion, notes and phrases he had scribbled during the tour, un-grammatical sentences from his Bukhara English-language tourist guide, and memories of his conversations with Rick, Rustam, and Faruza. This was, to complicate matters, all written a year after the tour had taken place. Yes, the playlet was made up, he says, "but is also, in every important sense, true, and I stand by it with clear conscience." Later in the essay, Bissell pinpoints the chal-lenge of writing nonfiction in which creativity is blended with a writer's desire to capture more than just fact — and thus the "untrue truth."[6]

"What I would argue is this: representing the truth in nonfiction is not an issue of conveyor-belt simplicity, where widgets of identical consequence float mechanically by. It is a case-by-case matter in which the heart figures as much as the brain."[7]

I remember thinking after reading this essay, three decades after the publi-cation of my book about umpires, that maybe I had unnecessarily berated myself too harshly about the liberties I had taken. Or maybe not. I have continued to go around and around about this, and in my other books, seeking some sort of formula or blueprint, an effort that, in so many cases, ends without a clear, wholly defined answer. In creative nonfiction there are many lines and bound-aries to consider, including, as Bissell eloquently stated: how the heart and soul of the story can be bonded with veracity. As Bissell says, it's a slippery notion or slope — literally. It's like trying to maintain your balance and footing while walking a sheet of ice.

The slippery notion — or in this case what was to become an ongoing controversy — had ignited a seemingly never ending uproar, a real literary hul-labaloo, nearly three years before Bissell's essay. I am calling this a hullabaloo not to make light of the situation, but only to illustrate how adamant and over the top nonfictionists can be about these issues. To the average reader, they may make very little difference; but to the practitioners, we writers of true stories, they are the very essence of the work we do. For many, the notion of melding brain and heart in a way that Bissell describes might be contradictory and perhaps unresolvable, as it happened at a workshop at Goucher College in 2003 between the faculty and students of the creative nonfiction MFA program and the esteemed journalist and memoirist Vivian Gornick.

Gornick was and is a respected, and in some ways historic, figure in the writing world. Her memoir *Fierce Attachments* from 1987 was praised in a *New York Times* review as a "fine, unflinchingly honest book." (In 2019, the *Times* selected *Fierce Attachments* as the best memoir written over the past fifty years.) She was also the author, at the time, of three other memoirs. She was an outspoken feminist even before Betty Friedan and Gloria Steinem; an essay she had published in the *Village Voice,* titled "The Next Great Moment in History Is Theirs," was influential in the foundation of the New York Radical Feminists.

By the time she spoke at Goucher, one might have thought (I did!) that the disagreements over the genre and the ethical and moral parameters — what you can and can't do while being creative with nonfiction — would have been at least partially resolved. The genre by that time was getting to be more established in the academy. It seemed that journalists, essayists, memoirists, had or would soon come to terms with one another and reluctantly accept — or at least tolerate — the different ways in which they could navigate the genre. So it was surprising that what happened at Goucher that day, although it did not actually go viral, became a national news story that surfaced off and on in literary circles for the next ten years. In fact, even now, some writers and editors can't seem to let go.

For the first hour of her appearance at Goucher, Gornick discussed her textbook *The Situation and the Story: The Art of Personal Narrative,* which had quickly become recommended or assigned reading in many creative writing programs since its publication in 2001. After a short break, Gornick read a section from *Fierce Attachments,* which recreates her recollections of a series of walks around New York City over many years with her mother, exchanging confidences, misunderstandings, grievances, gossip, presenting in many respects the stories of their lives. Gornick, then fifty-eight, knew how to read dramatically, as well as write and teach, and the effect on the audience was breathtaking. But then,

---

during the question-and-answer session that followed, Gornick's remarks were also breathtaking, but in a different context entirely.

Gornick casually and off-handedly remarked that parts of her memoir had been altered from what had actually happened in real life. She had, for one thing, from time to time, shifted or rearranged the chronology of the events she had described.

The students were surprised. This was not what they had expected to hear, so contrary to what their teachers had told them — that you had to be truthful and accurate and never make stuff up — and they and the faculty responded with a flurry of questions and objections.

Generally, I think it is best that your readers are unaware of how you have pieced together or composed your narrative. Most readers wouldn't be interested in a detailed accounting of the techniques you employed to shape your story; such an accounting would be distracting and certainly take away the mystery, power, and beauty of the story itself. But when you reveal your creative secrets to other writers, who are in a way, competitors, or flat-out jealous, you can find yourself in a tangled mess. And you never know who might be listening, as Alastair Reid had found out. In this case, it was Terry Sterling, a student and freelance writer, who was taking notes.

Gornick also revealed, during that Q and A, that she had "compressed" some of the walks and conversations with her mother in the memoir, and had also invented entirely a scene that involved a street person in a confrontation with her mother. She had also, she said as the questions continued and grew more heated, used composite characters for some of her pieces that ran early in her career in the *Village Voice*. She gave two examples — participants in a conversation at a dinner party in New York, and a man who had allegedly lived in a high-rise near her own apartment who robbed local retail stores at night. In both cases the characters were made up or a combination of a number of characters she had encountered over the years.

She said this all matter-of-factly, as Sterling reported in an article in *Salon*. (Gornick has since denied saying this.) Gornick's revelations and her nonchalance about what she had done, according to Sterling, "left some students scratching their heads afterward, trying to understand when fabricated information is acceptable in nonfiction – and when does it make you Jayson Blair?" Blair had been a reporter who fabricated and plagiarized many of the stories he wrote for the *New York Times*. He had resigned, in disgrace, in May of that year.[8]

"Tom French, a Pulitzer Prize winner from the *St. Petersburg Times*, a member of the Goucher MFA faculty," Sterling's story continued,

> politely asked Gornick how she would feel if the tables had been turned, if Gornick's mother had invented stories about her daughter and had written about them as though they were true.
>
> The question, Gornick replied, was "unanswerable."
>
> Another member of the audience asked Gornick whether she had alerted readers to the inventions of certain scenes and dialogue with, say, a prefatory note?
>
> "No," she replied, her readers were "willfully ignorant."[9]

Sterling's article in *Salon* was published a few days later, and three days after that, Maureen Corrigan, a National Public Radio book reviewer who had read the article and was clearly astonished by it, appeared on *Fresh Air* to comment – or to attack. Corrigan, who taught at George Washington University and regularly assigned Gornick's books for her classes, made it clear that Gornick's admissions had, to say the least, disappointed and disheartened her. Yes, she understood that memory can be flawed, but it was an autobiographer's pledge to tell the truth – or at least try to – and Gornick, obviously, had not held up her end of the bargain. For a book that was described by reviewers as unflinchingly honest, Gornick obviously had misled her readers and made them in the end, with this revelation, feel like "rubes."

Gornick responded and defended herself both in *Salon* and on NPR and in other venues that soon took up the dispute. "My idea of a memoir is obviously not the idea of people like the woman at Goucher who ran off to announce that I was a liar. I wasn't admitting to anything in that talk. I was describing what I thought was perfectly legitimate usage, which was the composition of a scene delivering narrative drive rather than factuality. . . . I don't think of that as lying."[10]

During the weeks after Corrigan and NPR, others weighed in with criticism of Gornick—including the *Washington Post*. Off and on in the months and years thereafter, the incident at Goucher and Gornick's revelations would be revisited during interviews and in literary panels and conferences. As late as 2015, fellow memoirist Mary Karr, in an interview in *Slate*, compared Gornick's manipulation and inventions to a deli guy who announces, "I put just a teaspoon of catshit in your sandwich, but you didn't notice it at all." Which meant, to Karr, "A small bit of catshit equals a catshit sandwich, unless I know where the catshit is and can eat around it."[11]

In 2006, an interviewer, Stephanie Farber, asked Gornick in an obviously leading way: "A literary flap of sorts erupted when you mentioned at a talk to writing students at Goucher College that you had—*gasp*—composed some scenes in *Fierce Attachments*, and that other scenes were composites of two or more incidents. Why do you think your acknowledgment raised such hackles?" And Gornick replied:

> The people at Goucher weren't educated readers of memoir. They were literalists in a journalistic tradition, and confused newspaper reporting with memoir writing. They didn't understand that memoir is composition, not reporting, not transcription. It is extremely silly to look upon the composition of scenes in a memoir as lies, or as something not the truth. Their notion of literalism and factuality was a foolish yardstick for what is true or not in a memoir. The memoir is a genre that needs educated readers, not people who are reading for all the wrong things, in all the wrong ways.[12]

Gornick was obviously being condescending. And if she meant, as she suggested to Farber that day, that she was tired of talking about what had happened at Goucher and would rather just move on, she was not doing herself much good by attacking the intelligence of journalists, at Goucher or anywhere else. In an article in response to the Farber interview, Roy Peter Clark, a faculty member at Poynter, the prestigious journalism institute, not only rebutted Gornick's opinion of "those grunts" at Goucher who "had the gall" to question her standards, but also challenged her use of the term "composition." Clark provided the dictionary definition of composing as "the aesthetic or artistic arrangement of pieces into a coherent whole." Under this definition, he argued, "works of journalism are also 'composed.' . . . The issue is not whether scenes in memoir can be composed – of course they can – but whether in the process they veer, for whatever reason – from what the author knows happened in real life."[13]

But this muddied the waters to a certain extent. When writers "write" or journalists "report" they are all composing – blending research, interviews, ideas, observations, and manipulations into a composition, no matter what it is called, that is informative and, hopefully, compelling. They should not – maybe – include in the composition content that is not, let us say, verifiable. My "maybe" here is what made all of the dialogue and debate interesting and unanswerable – the real hot point, in fact: Truth is very personal and may not always be verifiable, as Tom Bissell mentioned in the essay discussed above.

Bissell, in fact, had referred to the Gornick-Goucher controversy and, unsurprisingly, sided with Gornick: "Do these members of the Goucher College audience imagine that memoirists walk around wiring for conversation capture like snitching mobsters? Do they believe that everything in nonfiction has be exactly documented to be emotionally true? Do they not understand the huge difference between literary memoir and a newspaper article entitled 'Property Sale Raises Questions Amid Ethic Inquiry?'" Bissell noted that Thucydides, a very early writer of nonfiction, made up everything he wrote.[14]

What happened at Goucher was so memorable and seemed so significant – the real reason for the ongoing conflict – not exactly because of what Gornick said or admitted about her writing; it was her outright criticism of the journalists in the room that day and journalists generally. She implied that they were uneducated, that they did not know how to read memoir, and that there was a distinct difference between those who reported and those who composed nonfiction that they valued and believed in. That, judging by how they were responding to her remarks, they were looking at the distinction, if indeed there was a distinction, with a very narrow lens. She implied that literature – referring to her work and that of other "personal" nonfiction writers – belonged in a more hallowed and artistic atmosphere than those who simply "recorded and transcribed." Journalism was not literature in a classic sense, journalism was not artful.

Such a statement may not be earth shattering; it's been said or implied before. But few writers of Gornick's status have ever stated this as bluntly as she did. One faculty member, Leslie Rubinkowski, an experienced reporter and author, was sitting in the front row that day and she remembers the tension, the hurt and anger of both students and faculty that made the incident feel "electrified." Here was a writer with whom they thought they connected, were born of the same cloth and shared the same values, and suddenly they were being told that in some ways their work was of lesser value and accomplishment. They were on a different level, a lower level. Minor leagues compared to major leagues, and if they continued doing what they were doing, they would never make it to the big time.

Rubinkowski recognized from her perch in the front of the room that Gornick was feeling trapped and ambushed, both because she initially did not understand why her remarks had upset people in the room, and from her own rising realization that she was being questioned for something that for her was a core belief. Rubinkowski approached Gornick right after the session ended to thank her for her comments and her wonderful books. Gornick, she remembers, seemed kind of flummoxed and glassy-eyed. She said to Rubinkowski: "What just happened? What was that all about?" But she must have known exactly what it was all about, for she soon left the room and immediately departed the campus, skipping the faculty dinner she had been scheduled to attend that evening!

Gornick obviously did not expect that the reverberations of that incident would continue for the next dozen years and beyond. But what she said so bluntly to the writers in that room that day was once again at the heart of a controversy over when and how to be "creative," how to bridge the gap between what connects creativity and imagination with reportage and history and fact. I had thought that the disagreements over those issues had been reconciled, but every now and then it seemed there invariably would be another angry feud. And the controversy with the back-and-forth defenses and explanations and insults would rage again.

I think all of us in the academy or in the literary or journalistic communities, then and now, despite all of our disagreements as to the nonfiction-fiction line, and the heated fist-fighting like what happened to Gornick at Goucher, believed that there were basic standards of honesty that we all, in our own way, took

—

seriously. You might not have agreed with Gornick (or Bissell), but you accepted the idea that she had certain beliefs about her work and a moral compass that guided her and kept her true to those beliefs. You might think she did not portray her mother and their walks through the city with accuracy, but you also knew—or at least I did—that she felt in her heart that her story, even with those liberties, was told without purposeful dishonesty. In one way or the other, we would all agree that despite our disagreements we were all attempting to write our true stories honorably and without malice. At least until one of our own, John D'Agata, the director of the nonfiction program at the University of Iowa, was allowed to blatantly defy, for his own ends, all of what most of us believed in.

In his book from 2012, *The Lifespan of a Fact,* D'Agata battles with a young student intern fact-checker, Jim Fingal, over an essay D'Agata wrote about a suicide that had taken place in Las Vegas that was to be published in *The Believer.* (This book was purportedly a record of the actual exchanges between them.) Fingal, striving to do his job, repeatedly questions D'Agata about the information—the truth and accuracy—he is imparting to his reader, which the author invariably and repeatedly and arrogantly disregards.[15]

When Fingal proves that there are thirty-one strip clubs in Las Vegas and not thirty-four as D'Agata claimed, the author tells him: "The rhythm of 'thirty-four' was better in the sentence than the rhythm of 'thirty-one,' so I changed it." He swaps the name of a bar from "Boston Saloon" to "Bucket of Blood," because "'Bucket of Blood' is more interesting." And when Fingal demonstrates that D'Agata's information about how many heart attacks took place during a certain time period in Las Vegas is wrong—there were eight, not four—and asks if the text should be changed, D'Agata replies: "I like the effect of these numbers scaling down in the sentence from five to four to three, etc. So I'd like to leave it as is." This debate goes on through the 123 pages of the book, which I remember being astounded to discover was reviewed on the front page of the *New York Times Book Review.*

The essay D'Agata and Fingal are debating, titled "What Happens There," is crammed with rambling distractions featuring D'Agata as the heroic fact-finding writer he is not. His intent, if there is any intent at all other than to feature himself, is to tell a story about suicide in Las Vegas—more suicides there than

---

anywhere else in the country – glued together by the narrative re-creation of the last few moments of the life of Levi Presley, a sixteen-year-old who leaped 1,200 feet from the roof of the Stratosphere, a Las Vegas hotel and casino. D'Agata's blatant and ongoing dishonesty, what he might call "poetic truths," is not limited to what he writes; the way he goes about gathering his information is often sheer deceit. In order to obtain an interview with Presley's parents, he claims to have been the last person to have spoken to their son before his suicidal leap, as a volunteer on a suicide hotline. Later, he admits that he was mistaken. But only after the interview.[16]

The book took many of us in the creative nonfiction community by surprise. After fighting for the legitimacy of the genre for so long, we were embarrassed and angry – not just about the contents of the book itself, but the fact that *The Believer,* a respected literary journal, would have endorsed and published the essay D'Agata and Fingal were working on. (*Harper's* had previously rejected the piece.) And why would the *Times* publish a review of a book that mocked the way the newspaper protected the accuracy and integrity of its own stories? To be fair, the *Times* review was not particularly complimentary, and most of the others that followed were blisteringly critical.[17] Hannah Goldfield, a former fact checker at the *New Yorker,* in weighing the consequences of D'Agata's manipulations, pulled no punches.

"What D'Agata fails to realize," she wrote, "is that not only are these liberties indeed harmful – even if only to the reader, who is trusting the writer to be accurate in his or her description of what exists or took place in reality – they are also completely unnecessary to creating a piece of great nonfiction. The conceit that one must choose facts *or* beauty – even if it's beauty in the name of 'Truth' or a true 'idea' – is preposterous. A good writer – with the help of a fact-checker and an editor, perhaps – should be able to marry the two, and a writer who refuses to even try is, simply, a hack. If I've learned one thing at this job, it's that facts can be quite astonishing."[18]

As the discussion and debate continued over many months, D'Agata eventually revealed to Weston Cutter in the *Kenyon Review* that his conflict with Fingal had also been mostly fabricated, calling the hostility and dialogue an "exaggerated farce." Maybe this whole ruse seemed clever to the D'Agata fan

---

club; he does have many admirers. But there's really nothing funny or farcical about suicide, especially when you are telling the story of a lost and desperate sixteen-year-old.[19]

When one looks back at it now, considering all that has happened in the world since 2012, *Lifespan of a Fact* didn't really make a lot of difference. The genre survived, and D'Agata more than survived, feasting on and benefiting from the attention. The book was adapted for a Broadway play of the same name, with the lead character, D'Agata, played by Bobby Cannavale. And D'Agata's reputation as an essayist and anthologist with three collections of essays published over ten years was significantly enhanced, mostly by D'Agata himself. In a review in the *Atlantic* in 2017, William Deresiewicz lambasted D'Agata for a similar disregard of fact in all three collections while inflating or outright imagining his own expertise and insight. At the end of the review, he lamented D'Agata's self-made success.

"I fear D'Agata now commands the field, if only by dint of claiming it. No doubt one or more of his anthologies are being used as college texts, imposed on students who, in many cases, are bereft of other sources of cultural information. It kills me to think that there are going to be people walking around who believe that Socrates was an essayist because a self-important ignoramus named D'Agata told them so. Honestly, can't we do better than this?"[20]

The D'Agata situation reminds me of the prevalence of the notions of fake news and alternative facts during the Trump administration, and the misled troops of 2020 election deniers who are trying to cripple our democracy, but these were politically motivated phrases and actions in a world where integrity and fact did not seem to really matter. I like to believe that a nonfiction writer's integrity—despite Malcolm's historic and accusatory summation of the writer's soul or lack thereof in *The Journalist and the Murderer*—did and does matter and that we should be much more noble and righteous than the narcissism that D'Agata and Trump continue to display.

CHAPTER 13

DISSING THE MEMOIR

It wasn't fact versus fiction or dishonesty or deceit or even questionable ethics and morals that James Wolcott so vehemently attacked in his *Vanity Fair* roasting of creative nonfiction in 1997. His essay, titled "Me, Myself, and I," criticized the genre in another direction entirely. For Wolcott, it wasn't lying that was the problem; his objection was about how much of what was being written that was nonfiction should be written — or revealed. Especially about ourselves.

In his article, Wolcott took to task writers responsible for "an avalanche of needy, self-parodic memoirs" as "navel gazers" writing "civic journalism for the soul. Never," he said, "have so many shared so much of so little." In a review in the *New Republic* of what he termed the "crisis memoir," he complained that in the past people kept their personal secrets to themselves. "Now the problem is the opposite: getting people to put a cork in it." And he added: "We're approaching saturation agony overload." Wolcott could certainly turn a snappy and biting phrase, but also, you might wonder, why, down deep, he protested so much.[1]

Wolcott's list of books by "navel gazers," those who should put a cork in their revelations, included *Angela's Ashes* (Frank McCourt), *The Liars' Club* (Mary Karr), *Drinking: A Love Story* (Caroline Knapp), and *Autobiography of a Face*

—

(Lucy Grealy), all of which had been published over the previous half dozen years. These were really terrific books, I thought, and together they had sparked the rather sudden popularity of memoir; all of them were powerful, informative, and sometimes shockingly but necessarily revealing.

Angela's Ashes recounted McCourt's impoverished and generally miserable childhood and troubled family life growing up in Limerick, Ireland. It was awarded a Pulitzer Prize. *Drinking: A Love Story* was about Knapp's years of alcoholism and how it took over her life. Knapp passed away in 2002 at age forty-two of lung cancer, and her book *Appetites: Why Women Want,* about her experience with anorexia, was published a year after her death. In *Autobiography of a Face,* Grealy wrote about her childhood experience fighting the rare and often fatal cancer Ewing's sarcoma, which she overcame with radiation, chemotherapy, and surgery to remove half of her jaw, as well as the reconstructive surgeries and the tormenting teasing she experienced as a result. It was published internationally and added to many high school and college curricula. Grealy died in 2002. *The Liars' Club,* on the *New York Times* best-seller list for more than a year, may seem on the surface like a typical coming-of-age memoir in the hardscrabble South—until you begin to read it. It's got all the family rivalries and resentments, along with the cruelties of poverty and alcoholism. But in the hands of Karr (an essayist and a poet; *The Liars' Club* was her first memoir) the characters and conflicts are developed with vivid sensitivity. And no matter how grim the narrative, there are many tension-relieving laugh-out-loud moments.

Wolcott also attacked Daphne Merkin, Annie Dillard, John McPhee, and Cynthia Ozick, with a special and over-the-top emphasis on Kathryn Harrison's memoir, *The Kiss.* Wolcott had already published a lengthy, disapproving review in the *New Republic* of Harrison's book, about an incestuous relationship between the author and her father, a Presbyterian minister. Harrison had previously published two well-received novels based on this same affair with her father, but when she published a version of her story as a memoir, a true story, it stirred controversy and debate—to say the least. In the *New Republic,* Wolcott devoted little time to the writing itself; he focused more on the story content and Harrison's judgment in both the affair and deciding to publish the book. He labeled her a consenting adult, as opposed to an abused victim, suggesting that she published this book only for the money and recognition after her fictionalized versions of the story didn't have the desired result, and accused her of harming her children and invading her family's privacy by publishing the book.[2]

Wolcott was not alone in his dismissal of memoir, especially of *The Kiss*. He had a prestigious compatriot. Jonathan Yardley of the *Washington Post*, perhaps one of the most influential book critics at that time, was so incensed by Harrison's revelations that he wrote three reviews of the book, nearly back to back, calling it "shameful, slimy, repellent, meretricious, cynical, and revolting." I'm not sure he accomplished what he was trying to do: discourage readers. The book is still in print today. And I would take three reviews in the *Washington Post*, no matter how malicious.[3]

Yardley was not only concerned with what should or should not be written about in a memoir or personal journalism or an essay; he seemed also to want to legislate how old a writer should be before one was authorized or qualified to write a memoir. In a review of *Epilogue: A Memoir*, in which the thirty-four-year-old Will Boast is reunited with his family after a decade of self-isolation, Yardley concludes: "We really do not need yet another memoir by a person too young to have undergone any genuinely interesting and instructive experiences — or, having had such experiences, too young to know what to make of them — and too self-involved to have any genuine empathy for those whose paths he crosses, but here we have just such a book."[4]

I guess he forgot about Lucy Grealy, Dave Eggers, and Barack Obama, who all wrote compelling and lasting memoirs before turning thirty-five.

Several months before Wolcott's *Vanity Fair* piece, the columnist Ellen Goodman also published a critique of the memoir genre in the *Washington Post*, inspired by the revelation, earlier that year, that Wanda Koolmatrie, known as the "urban Aboriginal girl," author of the memoir *My Own Sweet Time*, was actually a forty-seven-year-old white man named Leon Carmen. When his identity was revealed, Carmen blamed editors and publishers for his ruse, claiming he had been unable to break into publishing as a white male. Goodman hypothesized that Carmen's success came not from changing identity, but from switching genres. Publishers might well be more interested now in memoir, she wrote, partly because it was easier than fiction to promote, as it was "easier to put an author on tour than a main character." More than that, she wrote, memoir was growing in popularity because the form, more easily than fiction, seemed to satisfy readers' "search for authenticity."[5]

Goodman did not know then that she was predicting the future course of many memoirs, most especially of a book by James Frey in 2003 that topped the *New York Times* nonfiction best-seller list for fifteen weeks and became the leading book on Amazon. It went on to be published in twenty-two languages worldwide. In this book, *A Million Little Pieces,* Frey confessed his many sins — he was an alcoholic, a drug addict, and a criminal — and the terrible things that happened to him before he found himself and changed his life in a rehabilitation center in the Midwest. "Over the course of 500 pages," Laura Barton wrote in the *Guardian,* "he wrestles a swarthy rage he names 'the Fury,' battens down his cravings, sprays spit and snot and blood and urine, recounts his misdemeanors, finds friendship, and falls in love. In one memorable scene he undergoes back-to-back root-canal surgery, but as he is in withdrawal he is forced to weather the entire procedure without anesthetic, pressing his pain into two tennis balls until his fingernails crack. It is a brutal, foul-mouthed, utterly compelling book."[6]

But in spite of this "compelling" story and the way he wrote it, publishers seemed uninterested when his agent first submitted it — as a novel. There were many rejections. But when *A Million Little Pieces* was resubmitted as a memoir, he hit pay dirt, almost immediately. Not only did he find a publisher, he found Oprah Winfrey. Or Winfrey found him as a selection for her very popular book club. His destructive past and then his heroic efforts to save and rehabilitate himself were perfect for the kind of content Winfrey loved to feature. Frey appeared on her television show billed as "the man who kept Oprah up all night." The book, Winfrey told her viewers, is "like nothing you've ever read before . . . we all loved the book so much."[7]

It was the *Oprah* appearance that piqued the curiosity of *The Smoking Gun,* a website that specializes in investigative reportage. The website published an in-depth exposé of the book, based on a six-week investigation, that outed Frey as a liar and a phony. Among many exaggerations and fabrications, Frey had not gone to jail for more than half a day, the root canals without pain medication never happened, and the way he described a friend's suicide was untrue.[8]

The hoopla over Frey's lies, exaggerations, and manipulations went on for a long time. It was big news almost everywhere. Humiliated, Winfrey attacked Frey on her show and lambasted his editor at Doubleday, Nan Talese, who had been invited to appear and explain or justify how and why the book had been accepted and then promoted as real life. After Winfrey interrogated her, often unjustly, Talese surely regretted her appearance and maybe even regretted having ever met James Frey.[9] A special on *Larry King Live* highlighted the dispute soon after. Frey's mother was a featured guest, attesting to her son's character and honesty — until even her honorable son admitted his duplicity.[10]

Frey was not the only writer who conjured up a life story; plenty of memoirs were totally fabricated by authors who did not exist as they presented themselves and embarrassed and angered those who had praised and supported their books. Not long after *A Million Little Pieces* was published, Michiko Kakutani in the *New York Times* praised *Love and Consequences* by Margaret B. Jones as "humane and deeply affecting."[11]

Jones's story was riveting. She grew up as a foster child who was half white and half Native American, and became a member of the Bloods outlaw motorcycle gang, living a life of crime and drug abuse. But soon after Kakutani's review, Jones's real identity and background were revealed by her sister. She was, in real life, Margaret Selzer, who grew up in a posh suburb in the San Fernando Valley with well-to-do white parents and attended a private Episcopal day school. So even after "Wanda Koolmatrie" and James Frey, it was still possible to fool publishers, who did not then, and do not now, fact-check the books they publish, relying on writers to do their own legwork. Often to their own peril.[12]

But even with the pushback, criticism, and scandal, and the protests of Wolcott, Yardley, and many others, memoir or personal stories have become the most popular form of creative nonfiction today and, for some writers, a way of magnifying their own "brand," sharing what they have learned about the art of the memoir with others who may think they have true personal stories to tell, and perhaps earning a few dollars in the process. Or more than a few dollars.

Meghan Daum (*The Problem with Everything*) began her weekend seminars in 2018 with the goal of helping developing writers polish their work. Fees for her classes, usually taught from her Manhattan apartment, some of which included chef-cooked meals, ranged from $1,200 to $1,800. Joyce Maynard has

---

hosted eight-day seminars in a Mayan village in Guatemala at the price of $3,000, while Dani Shapiro offers two-day retreats in Salisbury, Connecticut, for $3,500. Some of these teaching events have snappy and alluring titles, like Susan Shapiro's "Instant Gratification Takes Too Long" and Cheryl Strayed's "Brave Magic."

Not that there's anything wrong with using what you know, imparting all the wisdom a writer has gathered after many years at the keyboard, often faced with rejection and a struggle to pay bills. Workshops like these have become rather common, as hopeful writers and many who have never tried to write before want to learn how to share their personal stories or their family stories, not necessarily for publication or fame and fortune, but more as a legacy to pass on to future generations.

Lately, there's been a lot of research about how stories affect human behavior and enhance communication and understanding. Writing your life story – or hiring professionals to do it for you – can help you put into context experiences from the past, even if they were negative and hurtful. It can, in some cases, improve your health and help you achieve professionally. One study suggests that family stories are especially affecting for young people, helping them "make sense of who they are in the world." Bottom line, telling stories about our lives, experiences, pursuits, and beliefs is a fundamental human impulse, and not likely to go away anytime soon, as research by Dan P. McAdams, a professor of psychology at Northwestern University, suggests.

McAdams, the author of *The Redemptive Self* (2005), has conducted studies and experiments that make three significant points about the power of story: First, that people remember facts longer and more completely when those facts are embedded in or part of a story. Second, that people are persuaded more quickly and effectively when information and ideas are presented in story form. Third, that people, when asked to relate their life stories, will usually do so by isolating and recreating selected events, like "the day I failed chemistry in high school" or "the year of my cancer scare" or "my parents' struggle over assets during their divorce" – situations that lead to traumatic experiences and life lessons. McAdams points out that his subjects when interviewed about their life stories usually describe several crucial scenes in minute detail, complete with a list of characters and suspenseful and surprising turning points. He concludes

—

that people use these stories to decide whom to marry, whether to take a certain job, and an array of important life decisions based on memory and their vivid re-creation of a scene.[13]

James Wolcott may never participate in a memoir workshop like those offered by Daum, Maynard, or Strayed. Or for that matter teach a creative nonfiction or any creative writing class. He once told a reporter that he learned everything he needed to know about writing when working for the *Village Voice* selling and writing want ads. But he eventually did have a change of mind or heart about the genre he had torn apart throughout the 1990s. In 2011, he published his own memoir, *Lucking Out: My Life Getting Down and Semi-Dirty in Seventies New York.*

Wolcott's roasting of the memoir and creative nonfiction genre, read by at least some of *Vanity Fair*'s million-plus readers, created a great deal of buzz, and the commentary and attention it let loose turned out to be one of the best things to happen to creative nonfiction, the genre and my journal. And maybe, I don't know, to me.

I wasn't so sure that being named the "godfather" behind the genre was a good thing for me, especially considering my status or lack of status in my department—until I figured out how to "spin" it. Or how to own it and use it. A colleague, Bruce Dobler, helped me figure it out.

I had stayed close to home for a few days after that article came out, hoping that my English department colleagues did not read *Vanity Fair*. Which was a good bet; *Vanity Fair* was much too commercial and "slick" for their tastes. But as I ventured out to the supermarket, or drove my son to school, or worked out at my gym, people were suddenly congratulating me. Even those who had been at most nodding acquaintances were looking and treating me differently and saying stuff like, "Saw you in *Vanity Fair*!" Or, "You are a celebrity!" Although most of the time they couldn't remember exactly why I was in *Vanity Fair*, something to do with something, a few noted, called "noncreative fiction."

I was kind of perplexed; I didn't exactly get it. Wolcott had thoroughly annihilated me and a bunch of good writers I admired. It was great that I was featured in *Vanity Fair*—with a cartoon, by the way, quite a flattering caricature — but not so great that there was absolutely nothing in the article of any positive value, at least to me.

———

PART 2

I went to campus a few days later to teach a class, and as I waited at the elevator to get to my fifth-floor office, the doors slid open and there standing before me was my writing program colleague Bruce Dobler, a short, broad-shouldered fellow with an ever-present toothy smile. When he noticed me, he raised his eyebrows and then suddenly did something that helped me put the *Vanity Fair* roasting in perspective. He looked at me, paused thoughtfully, and then dropped to his knees, grabbed my hand, and said, with breathless reverence, "I kiss your hand, Godfather." And then, as I watched, confused and astounded, he did just that—with a loud, wet *smmmmmmmack!*

With that simple gesture, Bruce reminded me of the Oscar Wilde quip: "There is only one thing in the world worse than being talked about, and that is not being talked about."

Becoming the Godfather behind a genre was not at all what I had anticipated when I walked into the CL for the first time thirty years before. How could I, of course, since creative nonfiction did not exist, and I had only the vaguest idea that I could become a writer someday? But now as the Godfather according to *Vanity Fair* I noticed that people seemed to be listening to me more closely and acknowledging my newfound status. Lots of invitations to speak, and always being billed as the Godfather.

At first, it made me feel uncomfortable, like a pretender or a phony. And it diverted attention from the work I was doing as a writer. Invariably, at parties or dinners, I'd be introduced as the Godfather, rather than the author of whatever book I had most recently published. Or as a writer or a professor. This still happens today, so many years later, and it still makes me uncomfortable. But I did what many creative nonfiction writers do when presented with a new opportunity: I went with it and used it, immersing myself in the role, playing along, and sometimes milking my fifteen minutes of fame. I had been somewhat of a figure of authority before, but after *Vanity Fair*, I had suddenly become the absolute go-to guy ready and willing to discuss and debate—and fight for the genre.

Writing programs and students bought into the Godfather thing. Like the time I was scheduled to speak at a conference in Lancaster, Pennsylvania. The MC provided a very nice introduction, but when I walked on stage, microphone

—

140

in hand, the theme to the Godfather movie began to play, as a full-sized image of Marlon Brando looking old and evil in a tuxedo was projected on a screen behind me. A few months after I spoke at the University of New Hampshire, I received a link to a movie the students had made in which a student portrayed me as a Brando-esque character, threatening the literary world that they better soon start accepting creative nonfiction – or else. Near the end, the Gutkind-Brando character chillingly proclaims, "I'm gonna make them an offer they can't refuse." I often received gifts after appearing on campuses, invariably the same gift: a boxed set of all the Godfather movies on DVD. I own four of them.

I often wondered why Wolcott had written that column. He had never interviewed me or anyone else he roasted for that piece. The magazine just appeared on the newsstand one day and the shit hit the fan. I eventually got an answer to my question – and it turned out to be a disappointment.

I had written to Wolcott at *Vanity Fair* right after his article appeared and sent him a copy of my response – my regular column in the *Creative Nonfiction* journal. He didn't answer, and I hadn't expected him to. Time passed. I figured someday I would run into him at a conference. I had no agenda in mind; I just wanted to ask him how he had heard of me and my journal, and why he had decided to roast us.

I never did run into him, and I waited for a long time to reach out to him again, this time when *Creative Nonfiction* was about to publish its seventy-fifth issue and celebrate its twenty-fifth anniversary. I asked for an interview, and after going back and forth a half dozen times over six months or so, he finally agreed. We had drinks at a New York bistro on Fifty-Seventh Street. He was not in any way what I had imagined, which was basically a tight-assed intellectual; he was pretty much down to earth and quite friendly. I can't remember what Wolcott was drinking – I had a glass of red wine – but he ordered a plate of French fries and nibbled away at them while we were talking. French fries were not how I pictured James Wolcott. I figured him as a caviar guy.

Over the years, I had read articles about Wolcott and reviews of his books. He had a lot of not very nice things to say about the people he wrote about or knew, as Marion Maneker described in *New York* magazine in 2001: "Wolcott uses his pulpit – *Vanity Fair* as well as lengthy pieces in *The New Republic* and *The London Review of Books* – to deliver mordant, personal attacks. His columns

---

141

aren't just critical reviews or clever commentary, they're laced with humiliating zingers."[14]

He often went after prominent media personalities. He labeled Rush Limbaugh "the cuddly master-blaster of conservative diatribe." Charlie Rose frequently "gets tangled in a 'verbal ball of yarn.'" Maneker and others have pointed out that, for some reason, he goes after fellow writers with a vengeance.[15]

Gloria Steinem, Wolcott has written, has "the nun-glow of a strict forehead"; Martin Amis was "the scowl of a new generation" who made writing look "insolently easy"; David Denby is "the boy who cried wolf. Easily excitable and always concerned." Jay McInerney and Bret Easton Ellis write a "ticker tape of dropped names." Wolcott compared one of Joyce Carol Oates's jumbo-size novels to the monster in the movie *The Blob*. (He called it "a word-goop with a ravenous case of the eaties.") And he made minced meat of Richard Ford's taste for hunting: "Well, now we know who killed Bambi's mother! It was Richard Ford on one of his death strolls." The death stroll comment came from an interview Wolcott had with Ford. Asked if he liked walking in the woods, Ford replied: "I don't walk. I hunt. Something dies when I stroll around outside."[16]

When I read these put-downs, I didn't feel as bad about being categorized as the Godfather and a human octopus—at least temporarily. I imagined or hoped then—giving myself much more credit than I deserved—that I and creative fiction were part of that cadre of writers that Wolcott had taken on to roast.

At the bistro, I was expecting something meaningful to discuss. Memoir? Navel gazing? How creative nonfiction had changed the literary landscape? But when I finally got to the point, telling him about how he had changed my life by anointing me the Godfather and in the process called attention to the genre and the journal, and introduced us to his million-plus readers, he was, it turned out, completely in the dark. The best he could remember about writing that article was that someone had sent him a copy of the journal and one of the anthologies I had edited. At the time he was facing an upcoming deadline for his column. And so he had given us a kick in the ass to make his deadline. There was nothing more to it than that.

I felt kind of funny and deflated at the end of our conversation. I had thought that there would be more substance to it, that we would go deep, maybe go back and forth about nonfiction, fact and fantasy, and everything in between, but none of that had happened. After all those years, wondering about Wolcott and why he had decided to pick on us and me, it had all come down to an accidental discovery of my work and a deadline. Which was, in many ways, another kick in the ass.

PART 3

CHAPTER 14

AFTER ALL, GENTLEMEN, WE ARE INTERESTED IN LITERATURE HERE—NOT WRITING

I began turning myself into a teacher of writing in 1970 at the Community College of Allegheny County in Pittsburgh. These were part-time informal (non-credit) courses mostly for adults who believed they had stories to tell about their lives. A few of them did—they would be writing creative nonfiction today—and I helped them develop their ideas as best as I could. I knew nothing about teaching, and I had never addressed a group of people in any way, formal or informal; I had always kept to myself, watching and listening like the outsider I thought I was. It had never occurred to me that I had anything important or interesting to say or contribute in high school or in the military. Even when I was working at the agency, I remained in the background, which was why I had not told anyone about my Johnny Carson letter; I think I was fearful of making a mistake or revealing my many inadequacies. But all those books I had been reading, all that new journalism I was soaking up, combined with the notion that I could become a writer, somehow, someday, provided the substance I had been missing and the desire and ability to motivate others. There was also Monty whose friendship and support inspired the confidence I needed to, let us say, come out, take chances, reveal myself.

I had discussed my teaching at the community college with Monty, who paved the way for me in the English department at Pitt to teach courses in expository

—

writing. It was kind of amazing, actually, if you think about what an outsider I was in that milieu. I was the only person in the entire department teaching without an advanced degree. But by then, my motorcycle book, *Bike Fever,* would soon be published, which gave me some credibility. And a bit later, my *Sports Illustrated* articles. I would soon, a year later, enter the tenure track as an assistant professor. So even though I was a schlep, degreeless, I had published more than anyone else who was teaching writing courses at the time. And even though I was the guy who did not fit in at the academy, I was the perfect fit for my students, who were restless and rebellious in the early 1970s and hell-bent on making some changes.

One change I made right away is how to define or write in an expository manner. If good expository writing meant introducing a main idea, developing it with facts and supporting details, I saw no reason why this couldn't be done in a new journalistic way. Writing scenes, recording dialogue or experiencing what you are writing was the best way to eliminate the boring formulaic part of expository writing. You'd still have a main idea with facts and details; it would just be more relevant to what was happening in the writing world at that time. Students would be challenged and engaged. They needed to know, although verboten in the English department at that time, what new journalism was all about.

I tried to make my classes all cinema—capturing the spirit of the genre and my own newly perceived motorcycle persona. I wore big black motorcycle boots with cleats on the heels and the toes so that my footsteps reverberated on the tiled floor in the CL as I approached the classroom. Then? Burst through the door, dump my helmet and backpack on the conference table and immediately light up a cigarette. The students always waited for the cigarette—the signal that it was time to get serious and pay attention. I paced back and forth and around the room. Sometimes shouting and waving my arms to make a point, sometimes throwing chalk or jumping on the desk, all the while lighting cigarette after cigarette. A one-hour class was a four-cigarette class. My students counted them as I quashed each butt on the floor as I paced and preached about this new way of writing, this literature of reality—writing in scenes, recording dialogue, looking for intimate details—stuff that readers would not necessarily know or expect — all part of this marvelous, irrevocable movement — this "new journalism." I am guessing that many of my students were not particularly thrilled with me or my persona. But they were, mostly, excited and intrigued with my new journalism message.

Right from the beginning, I pushed these students out of the classroom to do immersions. Shoemaker shops, five and ten cent stores (there were such things back then), churches and synagogues, especially if it was not a denomination they had practiced; fire or police stations; it didn't really matter where; what mattered was that they would find a story to write about what they experienced and learned. Once, I even pushed them out of the city.

One weekend, I led a group of my students to Cook Forest, three hours north of Pittsburgh on the edge of the Allegheny National Forest, to do an immersion. The idea was to show them that stories were everywhere, people with things to say; lives that may have seemed so ordinary but were rich with secrets and eccentricities that could teach readers a lot. One student discovered a "bear lady," a woman who hunted bear every year, ate the meat and preserved the coats, hanging them in a shed behind her house. Another met a researcher from an insect museum doing fieldwork and spent the day with him. And another got lost in the woods. They all wrote stories about their experiences with dialogue, description, and more, all the stuff that I had been preaching; each story had to pass the new journalism test.

When I think back to that Cook Forest new journalism adventure now, I can't help but smile. Could a university professor get away with such a stunt today? I didn't inform my department chair or request permission or fill out any forms; that stuff never occurred to me. And even if I had filled out a dozen forms and went up the university chain of command, the idea of this adventure would be considered preposterous for too many reasons to count. But we're talking fifty years ago in an anything goes (nearly) atmosphere. And it worked. Especially for a small cadre of undergraduate students who were on the staff of the student newspaper — *The Pitt News*. They wanted more new journalism, not under the guise of expository writing or descriptive writing or whatever other courses I was teaching. They wanted new journalism to be, let us say, "official," and decided to take action.

———

———

We are in a conference room on the fifth floor of the CL for the monthly English department faculty meeting. Lots of the normal business on the agenda — potential faculty hires, programming updates, upcoming conferences, the usual stuff. But at this particular meeting we have a special guest, Bill Larsen, one of my students, who was the editor of the *Pitt News*. (I've changed some names here in this story.)

It was unusual for an undergraduate student to address our faculty, probably any faculty at a large university. Mostly the students who attend these meetings are at a graduate or even post-graduate level. But this young man had a mission, and he wanted to be heard. Previously he had gone to see the department chair requesting that the department offer a "new journalism" course — either in place of the regular expository writing or essay writing offerings or in addition to it. I was not at the time the only person teaching expository writing; it was a core course and they were all taught somewhat differently, although none focused on the new journalism, except for mine.

The chair, John Whitehead, explained that he lacked the authority to approve, let alone encourage, a course so out of the mainstream of contemporary literature. Maybe it would belong in a journalism department — that would be in its domain — however, Pitt did not have a journalism department. But in the spirit of free speech and openness reflected in the early 1970s, Whitehead allowed Larsen to make a presentation to the faculty at its next meeting.

I will never forget the scene.

Larsen was bespectacled, with straight brown hair hanging in bangs down his forehead. And he was pretty nervous, as he stood at a hand-carved wooden podium reading from the sheaf of notes he had prepared, about the history and relevance of new journalism and its many practitioners, to a totally silent collection of mostly aging, scraggly dressed professors. He spoke for five or ten minutes.

There may have been a few questions — I don't remember — but after Larsen's presentation, a balding, flat-nosed guy, Norman Moses, stood up, carrying one of those massive, flat-bottomed leather briefcases that fold out like an accordion, so you can carry around half of your library, as well as lunch and dinner. Clearly,

———

he had come prepared for our special guest—and he was ready for battle. He plopped the case on the table beside the podium and, facing Larsen, who had retreated to one of the back rows, began pulling out books—Faulkner, Thurber, Fitzgerald, Thomas (not Tom) Wolfe, Welty, and on and on—holding each one up in the air and providing us all with a succinct description of its literary value and inherent brilliance and then slamming each down on the table beside his briefcase, *kaboom, kaboom,* until the massive briefcase was empty. And then, peering across the room and addressing Larsen, he said something to the effect of: *Until you and the other* Pitt News *staffers read all of these books and learn to appreciate and understand them, this department should never support such lightweight and insignificant work as what you think you are calling writing that is "new" in journalism or nonfiction.* That was the gist of the finale of his illustrious presentation.

Listening to Moses pontificate was too much for the other members of the department, who all burst out in debate over the books he had selected as classics—which didn't have anything to do with the subject at hand, but that was typical, I had learned since joining the faculty. And anyway, Moses's incredible rudeness had also annoyed them. There was really no reason to treat an undergraduate, who had the courage to present an idea to the entire department, in such a dismissive manner—especially the editor of the student newspaper, who could wreak revenge on the English department should he choose to. You had to give the kid some credit and respect, even though maybe his idea was worthless.

Finally, the chair, Whitehead, attempted to tone down the rhetoric and move to another subject, reasoning, "After all, gentlemen, we are interested in literature here—not writing."

We few writers paused for a moment to allow that to sink in. This, of course, was the crux of the matter—the ambivalence displayed by literature professors toward those who wrote or might one day write the work they would teach or study. A conflict that would play out through the 1970s and 1980s. (There were, by the way, some women in the room who clearly felt uncomfortable, but held their fire, although they weren't "gentlemen.")

I was so damn angry at Moses for putting Bill Larsen on the spot, embarrassing him by being so superior and self-righteous. And I also felt more than a little discomfort—and shame—because I had not read many of the books he had been waving around in that conference room, hadn't even heard of some of them. And it took me a couple of years to realize that although Moses was being a supercilious ass, he was right. If we new journalists or, later, creative nonfictionists, wanted to be considered respectable and acceptable, we should be familiar with the great works of nonfiction narrative that came before us. But why, I wondered then—and still do now to a certain degree—couldn't he and his colleagues help us, instead of blowing us off and making us feel so inferior?

This didn't discourage me or convince me to back down; it fueled my efforts to continue what turned out to be a decades-long contentious literary rivalry. In fact, I stood up and stomped a cleated boot down hard on the CL floor to get more attention and asked Moses what stuff he had ever written that real people—non-academics—could appreciate and understand. Did he ever come down from his academic cloud of papers and conferences that no one in the real world ever paid attention to or cared about to notice what his students were concerned with in their daily lives? To consider how his teaching would prepare them for the future? Did he know why the new journalism was so important to share with our students? Did he understand its place in literary history?

I don't know if he did or didn't, or cared, for he failed to answer. I am certain that a lot of what I said did not make sense. Discussion and debate, resistance to change, was expected in these departmental meetings, but downright anger—a genuine tantrum—was rare. No one in the room said a word until I sat back down. The meeting continued as if nothing had happened.

But in the next few days and weeks, the *Pitt Newsers* pressed the issue. They weren't about to give up. And eventually a course was introduced, called the "new nonfiction." This name was a compromise, avoiding the taint of the "J" in the curriculum. That changed a few semesters later, when new nonfiction became what it was supposed to be—new journalism. But this literary battle over nonfiction continued on many levels for many years after.

I look back now at that incident as life-changing—my first "literary fist-fight" over creative nonfiction. Of course, creative nonfiction did not exist then—or at least it did not exist in the way we know it today. There were two literary genres—poetry and fiction—and if you wanted to stretch it to include drama, three. Nonfiction didn't belong. Nonfiction was not a genre; it was a hodgepodge — essay, journalism, travel writing, nature writing, biography and autobiography, all of which were closely protected and siloed by their practitioners. They all had put up barriers to protect against interlopers that might taint the purity of their artistry (and compete with them), although "artistry" is not what the traditional journalists would have called it then.

At the time I didn't think there was a lot of difference between those factions. There were different flavors of nonfiction just as there were different flavors of fiction and poetry. As far as I was concerned, these ways of writing nonfiction were close enough together to be put in the same pot and certainly just as important to study and teach as anything else. They were all under the same general umbrella. Although not a lot of people agreed with me for a long time.

CHAPTER 15

BRICKS, UNDERWEAR, FAKE VOMIT—AND A GUINNESS WORLD RECORD

I have been teaching for a long time, mostly at two large universities, and I have no idea how many students have run through — or maybe struggled and squirmed through — my classes. But with a few exceptions, the *Pitt News* students I came to know and work with are the most memorable. I have watched them grow in different directions, as they have watched me, and sometimes even joined me as we grew together.

When they graduated and began to shape a new life, these *Pitt Newsers* all went in different directions, but the idea of breaking boundaries and barriers always stayed with them. Scott MacLeod began working for the United Press International (UPI) in Pittsburgh after graduating and was soon transferred to the state capital in Harrisburg where he became bureau chief. He had once told me during the first day of class — when he was a freshman — that he wanted to be a foreign correspondent. I had laughed as did others. It was a great goal, but maybe just a pipe dream. After all, this was Pittsburgh and not New York. And only the best and the brightest and the most tightly connected — Harvard, Yale, Princeton, and so on — got those dramatic jobs.

MacLeod, despite my pessimism, was soon transferred to the UPI London bureau and then to Beirut to cover the Gulf War of 1982 between Lebanon and Israel. He remained in the Middle East for the next half dozen years, reporting

---

154

in the thick of the battles. He went to work for *Time* magazine and was transferred to South Africa for seven years to cover Nelson Mandela's release from prison and subsequent election as president. Later and for the next twenty-five years, he was the Middle East correspondent for *Time*, interviewing and writing stories about all of the adversaries, including Yasser Arafat and Osama bin Laden. He was one of the first journalists on the scene following Princess Diana's fatal car crash. Diana had been having a very public affair with the playboy billionaire Dodi Fayed, who was also killed in the crash.

The trust he had gained among the non-western combatants in the area he had covered over the years led to his access to the Fayed family, and he and Thomas Sanction, Paris bureau chief at *Time*, co-wrote a book, *Death of a Princess: The True Story Behind Diana's Tragic End,* providing an inside view of the events leading up to the crash and the many suspected conspiracies — in contrast to the stories and speculation of the western media. *Death of a Princess* became a *New York Times* best seller.

It was hard to keep up with Jess Brallier, who had been *Pitt News* arts editor. Or understand what he was doing. Brallier earned a master's degree in communications at Boston University and then was head of marketing for Little, Brown, book publishers, where some of his innovative ideas helped turn two creative nonfiction books into longtime best sellers. Learning that those who purchased *Blue Highways: A Journey into America* by William Least Heat Moon were not only buying it to read, but also buying it again, he assumed that, since the holidays were approaching, they were buying copies as gifts. How better, he thought, to build upon that consumer behavior than to offer already gift-wrapped copies of the books in retail? So, following Brallier's lead, Little, Brown's sales director contacted buyers at the major bookstore chains and offered to ship them gift-wrapped copies of the book for retail sales. Little, Brown received orders for ten thousand of the books by the end of that day. Those gift-wrapped copies pushed *Blue Highways* onto the *New York Times* best-seller list, where it stayed for forty-two weeks.

The anticipated sales for Tracy Kidder's *Soul of a New Machine,* also a Little, Brown book, were minimal, Brallier remembers. The book focused on a company on the outskirts of Boston, Data General, and its creation of one of the first

---

mini-computers, long before the Internet. Data General was located along the technology corridor lining Route 128, what public officials were then calling "America's Technology Highway," not unlike Silicon Valley today. People who worked in this area should know about the book and would find it most interesting and relevant to the work they were doing, Brallier reasoned. But how to reach them? Brallier made a list of fifty people he thought were a must-read for the book, mostly near Route 128. He went home to his small apartment and his typewriter, and punched out personal letters to every name on the list, hand-addressed mailing envelopes, and sent them free copies of the book.

But he wasn't finished. He loaded a pile of books in his car and drove up and down Route 128, dropping off copies at reception desks of these companies, and when he could get access, tables in company cafeterias. The cafeterias, he thought, were perfect; that's where people took breaks, relaxed for a bit, and talked to one another. So how to get more books into cafeterias? Which made him think about . . . milk! Who goes into a company cafeteria if they don't work for the company? Milkmen. Milkmen (or women) are a rarity today, but this was in 1981. So Brallier called up Hood, a New England milk company, and offered them an opportunity to give a gift to their clients. "I sent them 150 books," he told me, "and they put them on their trucks, and the drivers went around to the different cafeterias of the digital companies and placed a book on a few tables. Someone, I figured, would pick it up and read it and talk about it or pass it on."

Brallier doesn't know and will probably never know whether it was the letters he sent or the cafeteria milk deliveries or a combination of both that did the trick. The book soon sailed to the best-seller list.

Brallier had a knack or a genius for figuring out how to make good books appeal to readers — and to bookstore buyers. Working with another publisher, Addison-Wesley, he helped develop an informal learning line of children's books with an imprint called Planet Dexter. The series was a big success, in great part because Brallier insisted on introducing texture to the books' covers to increase their appeal to kids. Most notable was a book about the human body with fake vomit on its cover, attached (or removed) with double-sided tape. He persuaded Barnes & Noble in New York to put the book with this unusual new cover in a Fifth Avenue store window to see what might happen. Four days later they were asking for an additional six thousand copies, and it became a six-month *Times* best seller. The title of the book? *Grossology.*

Later, he turned his attention to digital publishing, and helped develop the educational website FunBrain.com. He published a book by Jeff Kinney, *Diary of a Wimpy Kid,* on FunBrain. Within four months of launching the site there were eighty thousand kids a day reading it. The book soon found a traditional (print) book publisher, and there are now seventeen books in the series, plus a spinoff book series. By November 2022 the books had been on the *New York Times* children's best-seller list for 714 weeks (the longest running series, one week ahead of *Harry Potter*).

Brallier continued to innovate, working with Kinney to develop Poptropica, an online role-playing game set in a virtual world, where kids would travel to virtual islands and complete game quests, including going to museums to solve a counterfeit art mystery (and learning about artists along the way—just like creative nonfiction), climbing Mount Everest, figuring out how things work in space, and so on. In only fourteen months, Poptropica became the most popular kids' site in the world, with more than eight million visiting a month.

Ken Gormley came to the *Pitt News* a few years after Brallier. There was no one on the staff more turned on by the new journalism than Ken, who was super-inspired by one of the early new journalists, George Plimpton.

Plimpton took the whole idea of the new journalism much further than most of his colleagues. Instead of just hanging out, he made himself part of the story. He immersed himself with an NFL football team, the Detroit Lions, training and coexisting day to day with the players. He was in his mid-thirties, a former college athlete, tall, slender, and fit, so he was able to endure the arduous work-out sessions in the gym and on the field. He actually became part of the action, a featured character in his story, and he even got into the real battle by appearing for a series of plays in an exhibition game—with disastrous results. His appearance on the field and the book he wrote about the experience, *Paper Lion,* created a lot of buzz in the right places, mostly in the media, because Plimpton was not just a journalist; as the founding editor of the *Paris Review,* he was very much a part of the literary world, a card-carrying member of the same New York intelligentsia that Wolfe had parodied in *Radical Chic.* His book was cool and amusing and connected with a wider audience, not just because it was about football, but also because the narrator was a likable character, living a dream undoubtedly shared by millions of other Americans. *Paper Lion* was required reading in some of my classes.

For one of his participatory pieces, he had played instruments with the New York Philharmonic, directed by Leonard Bernstein. Plimpton was also an actor who later appeared regularly in the long-running TV series *ER*. He was politically active as well. Robert F. Kennedy had been a friend from boyhood, and in 1968, Plimpton was one of the two men in San Francisco who grabbed Kennedy's assassin, Sirhan Sirhan, and held him down. *Paper Lion* was made into a movie, with Alan Alda, the star of *M*A*S*H*, playing the author. Perfect casting.

Plimpton inspired Gormley, who took the idea of immersion more seriously and literally than any of his classmates. Late one Saturday, he and a friend began paging through the *Guinness Book of World Records* to figure out what record they could try to break so they could write a new journalism story about it. There was an annual brick-carrying contest in New South Wales, Australia, they discovered; the reigning world champ had walked forty miles with an eight-pound twelve-ounce brick, nearly twice the weight of a regular brick. The rules said it had to be carried in one ungloved hand in a downward position, without dropping it.

This was it. Gormley trained all early summer, and in July, walking in eighty-degree heat and listening to "Thick as a Brick" by Jethro Tull, he broke the record—ending his odyssey in front of the CL, forty-three and a half miles away from his start with an eight-pound fifteen-ounce brick. Gormley stayed in the record book for several years before his record was broken.

He wasn't finished, though. Between taking classes at Pitt, Gormley wrestled a nine-hundred-pound black bear, Victor the Wrasslin Bear, hopped a freight train from Pittsburgh to New York (he was detained by the railroad police, who sent him home on a Greyhound Bus, and he never made it to the Big Apple). He went up in a hot air balloon, jumped out of a plane, slept in a haunted house, rode on a coal barge on the Monongahela River down to West Virginia, and wrote stories for the *Pitt News* about each of these experiences. One story, when he assisted in a cremation at a local cemetery, won the first *Rolling Stone* college journalism award for feature writing. He spent the summer writing for *Rolling Stone* magazine, covering concerts, sitting on stage at Madison Square Garden, while staying at a YMCA in Manhattan. He wrote a story about that, too.

After graduation, Ken Gormley went to law school at Harvard. But his Guinness world record and his no-limits new journalism ideas never left his mind. He has written two creative nonfiction books, *Archibald Cox: The Conscience of a Nation* and *The Death of American Virtue: Clinton vs. Starr,* both of which won many awards. *The Death of American Virtue* made the *New York Times* best-seller list.

His current immersion? He is now the president of Duquesne University.

You didn't meet a lot of writers in Pittsburgh back then. We were a sports town and a steel town. Blue collar was a badge of honor, representative of belonging. White collar not so much, even for those who had worked their way up. There were writers, to be sure, lots of wonderful writers who have won prizes and awards, have become respected and famous throughout the world—from Pittsburgh. August Wilson, Annie Dillard, John Edgar Wideman, Gertrude Stein, Rachel Carson, Jack Gilbert, Gerald Stern, David McCullough, and many others—playwrights, poets, novelists, historians, had two things in common. They were either born or rooted for a certain amount of time in Pittsburgh. That was one thing in common. The other? They all left town. And became famous writing about Pittsburgh while living somewhere else.

I tried to connect my students with real writers, as often as I could. Just to show them that there was not a lot of difference between those who wrote and made an honest living that way and those who wanted to write and even those who had no interest in writing. We were all, in one way or the other, just doing our jobs. I was learning that myself in those early days. We all, every morning, no matter who we were, to employ the old adage, put our pants on in the same way. Or, as one of my students from that *Pitt News* crew, a guy with a funny but distinctive nickname Bill ("Dinty") Moore, was to find out, we all needed underwear. ("Dinty" was a nickname his mother bestowed on him, originating from a comic strip character from the 1920s and 1930s. Moore has no idea why his mother thought naming her son after a comic strip character was a good idea, but, he told me, she took the secret to her grave.)

———

I had drafted Bill—or Dinty—to escort Nelson Algren around town the afternoon he was to speak at an evening event at the CL. Algren was a novelist mostly. His third novel, *The Man with the Golden Arm,* won the first National Book Award in 1949. And his fourth novel, *A Walk on the Wild Side,* added to his credibility as one of America's great writers. During that time, I was trying to show my English department colleagues that nonfiction or, then, the new journalism could be as artful as fiction and poetry. So when funds were available I tried to pick an author who could go both ways.

Algren, then in his late sixties, had written a lot of nonfiction, essays and articles—nonfiction was often how novelists and poets paid the bills. Algren was an eccentric but down-to-earth character—kind of the way we Pittsburghers like to think of ourselves. He lived in a cheap walk-up flat in Wicker Park in Chicago, the Polish neighborhood that was the setting for his most famous book, *The Man with the Golden Arm.* Around that time, he was embroiled in a long-distance and very public relationship with the philosopher Simone de Beauvoir.

I couldn't predict what Algren would want to do the afternoon before his evening talk, but Moore was a pretty easy-going guy with an irrepressible sense of humor. He was almost always joking. You could hardly have a conversation with him without him saying something funny—or trying to be funny. And he usually did a super job of that; he was most often clever and self-effacing.

Moore was excited; maybe he would learn something about writing and literature from Algren, some secret to his genius. But he was surprised to learn the great novelist's agenda for that afternoon: buying underwear. Moore escorted Algren from the Webster Hall Hotel across the campus down to the commercial district on Forbes Avenue to a Woolworth's store and hovered around him as Algren sorted through the racks and tables with a varied selection of underwear. He eventually purchased three pairs of boxer shorts.

Then, Moore remembers, Algren wanted a drink, but not back at the posh Webster Hall Hotel where he was staying. As soon as they exited Woolworth's, they walked past Frankie Gustine's Bar and Restaurant and suddenly Algren stopped and pointed to the front of the place and said, "Let's go in there."

Frankie Gustine had been a major league baseball player, a catcher for the Pittsburgh Pirates, and his place was overloaded with Pirates memorabilia, although Algren didn't seem to have any interest in baseball when Moore brought the subject up.

Algren ordered a martini, and then the bartender asked Moore what he wanted, and Moore, a college student, really only had one drink in his alcohol repertoire. "Beer," he said.

"No," Algren said. It seemed to be the first time since they had met at the hotel that Algren had shown any enthusiasm. "Give him a martini."

Moore had never had a martini. Maybe he didn't even know what a martini was, but if Algren wanted him to drink a martini, then that's what he would do.

Algren was on his second martini when he asked Moore what he thought of the drink. "This is great," Moore lied. He really thought it tasted like "piss." Algren seemed delighted, and if the great Nelson Algren was pleased, then Moore felt he had done his escorting job quite sufficiently.

They returned to the hotel soon thereafter. Algren seemed to be a bit unsteady after two martinis, so Moore walked him to his room. But Algren couldn't seem to unlock the door. This was long before the era of plastic keys — these were real — and Moore took the key and unlocked the door for him.

And before they could say goodbye or "thank you" or "nice to meet you," or anything else that might have been appropriate, Algren dropped himself on the bed and immediately fell sleep.

"I put the key down, closed the door, and hoped he would show up at the Student Union at seven o'clock that night," Moore said.

And Algren did indeed show up on time, and for an hour and fifteen minutes he lambasted creative writing programs, creative writing conferences, creative writers in general with special emphasis on the ineffective spineless English departments that were out of touch with the real world.

When he graduated from Pitt, Moore began his career as a reporter for a wire service, but it didn't really interest him. In the following few years he became a filmmaker, an actor, and a modern dancer before focusing his efforts on the writing life. He received an MFA in fiction writing from Louisiana State University, and his first of many books, published in 1995, *The Emperor's Virtual Clothes: The Naked Truth About Internet Culture,* was one of the first books to put a human face on the digital world. The titles of some of his nonfiction books — he was writing and is known today as Dinty W. Moore — since then

---

capture his rare and humorous takes on life and literature, including *Between Panic and Desire* and, perhaps most memorably, *To Hell with It: Of Sin and Sex, Chicken Wings, and Dante's Entirely Ridiculous, Needlessly Guilt-Inducing Inferno.* He is the founder and editor of *Brevity,* the very popular online magazine for that ever growing subgenre Moore has dubbed "flash nonfiction."

I can't say that his afternoon with Nelson Algren was a significant or defining moment in Moore's life, although he did learn that what was important to famous writers was just as important to everyone else, including things that might not seem to go together, like underwear and martinis.

You never know as a teacher how what you say or do or ask of your students will affect them one way or the other. These days I hear a lot from my former students about what they remember about our time together—letters and e-mails that come out of the blue about certain moments in class that may have not resonated with them at the time that made a difference in their lives sometime, often much later. I am always amazed at what they remember, or even that they remember me at all. But there are those very special students who are never far from my thoughts who made as much of an impact on me as a teacher and often quite later as a colleague, as I did them, like Dinty W. Moore. For those who teach—no matter how many books or essays we publish—our students are our legacy, as I was for Monty.

CHAPTER 16

WRITERS INVADING THE ACADEMY

There was always, it seemed, some sort of fight to navigate in those early years in the department, not just over new journalism and later creative nonfiction, but over many other issues related to the much bigger issue – creative writing.

We debated about the very existence of the new journalism and whether it should be part of a creative writing program curriculum. Or did it even deserve to be in or belong in the English department? And when that was reluctantly conceded, and a number of undergraduate courses in nonfiction were offered over the next decade or so, we debated over whether nonfiction was worthy enough to offer an advanced degree in nonfiction writing – we eventually did – and then we debated over whether that degree should be an MFA, a master of "fine" arts, as was offered in poetry and fiction, rather than just an M.A., a less worthy degree, fitting the second-class status of the work we were doing.

We debated over whether nonfiction degree students had to take critical theory courses as prerequisites, as students seeking advanced degrees in literature, rhetoric, or composition did. We debated over the whole idea of studying narrative and the marriage between facts and narrative, which was, to many scholars, an essentially useless construct and was in its own way a lie. We debated over whether to grant tenure to the writers we were hiring in our department to teach in other genres, and whether their creative work, novels, short stories and poems, could and should qualify as worthy academic credentials on par with the papers, journal articles, and scholarly books expected from prospective faculty.

Although I was constantly annoyed – pissed off – I realize now, my colleagues were not bad people; they were civil enough, displaying a subtle air of tolerance for my lack of credentials and even a little bit of respect for my work and for my willingness to fight for what I believed in. But they were on the defensive.

Before writers infiltrated the academy, English departments in colleges and universities were conservative places that kept faculty and their favorite graduate students siloed, safe from outside interference. Even though these departments were burdened with the responsibilities of teaching freshman English (responsibilities mostly dumped on graduate teaching assistants), and even though they watched with frustration and resentment as budgets for the sciences and other departments were often generously increased while the humanities remained relatively the same, and barrels of money were poured into athletics, life and work in English departments was secure, especially if you were tenured. You could do your research and teach your specialty, go to a conference or two every year (sometimes, alas, on your own dollar), commune with like-minded colleagues, and live a good, safe, siloed life.

But then came the writers and the atmosphere changed. Writers were not really a legitimate part of the academy – writers didn't fit. We didn't even look right, with our ponytails and sandals and me with my motorcycle helmet, leathers and boots, and we thought the endless meetings were dumb and conflicted with our writing time. We were taking up space and resources that might have been allocated to another Milton scholar or some other prestigious expert in the romantics. We were occupying their turf; they didn't like it; it was threatening. And they did what they could in their traditionally genteel scholarly way to resist, sometimes passively and sometimes quite actively, *the invading writers*.

This tension – or should I say "power struggle" – was ongoing in the academy throughout the mid-1970s and 1980s, not just at Pitt but all over. In an article in the AWP newsletter, a retrospective published in 2012, Phil Raisor described the atmosphere at that time at Old Dominion University, where he was then teaching. "Head-knocking power struggles were going on between writers

—

and scholars, programs and university resources. Some senior faculty, curious at first and then apprehensive about the energy of the new wave, retreated to defensive postures. All would be well, they argued, if the university would provide new positions for the writing program. Otherwise, growth would require more pillaging of literature and linguistics." The scholars, to say the least, were threatened.[1]

In an article from that time in the *AWP Chronicle,* Mary Carter, a novelist and the director of the University of Arizona's creative writing program, tried to make peace between the two factions. "The traditional separation between Literature and Creative Writing faculties," she wrote, "the writers' air of defensiveness, the sense of hard-won turf closely and vigilantly guarded; the scholars' air of uneasy indulgence, the tendency to regard the Department rather the way conservative hard-liners regarded the Panama Canal (we built it, we paid for it, we won it) — persists, like the separation of Church and State, to varying degrees in most of our universities. It is rooted in history, in the social evolution of establishments and institutions, in the persistent sense of Them and Us. Rather than trying to 'win,' it would be more useful for us to encourage an ecumenical approach."

By the time Carter's article was published in 1986, creative writing programs were pretty much a fait accompli in English departments across the United States. That didn't mean the animosity had in any way ebbed; the scholars could still win some battles. Like not awarding tenure to a poet or fiction writer who lacked the precious piece of paper that they — the lit folks — had struggled to earn: the Ph.D. Even if these writers had published in the very best magazines and journals; even if their books were well-reviewed. To earn your tenure as a writer, you still needed to prove that you were a scholar by publishing critical articles in journals and presenting papers at academic conferences.[2]

Carter in her article was also striving for an ecumenical approach between the professor-writers themselves. There were, as time went on and creative writing programs began to grow, those who wanted "creative writing" to go off on its own — separate departments — disconnected from English.

I was at first all for it — Let's just get away from these whiners and complainers and jealous road-blockers — until I began asking myself who would run the creative writing department. This was a full-time job, not a lot of time left over for writing. Which was why so many writers fought their way into the academy in the first place. Teaching provided security, a regular schedule, financial support and time to do what they most wanted to do, which was to write. So, it would have to be a failed writer, someone who had given up the ghost, thrown in the literary towel, to lead a pack of writers and manage their various and often crazed eccentricities. Who was going to admit to that—even to themselves? Or put themselves in this untenable position? Or raise the money—resources—to achieve independence? Despite the revolutionary fervor in the air at that time, not a lot of creative writing programs broke off from English departments, which, even considering the ongoing *tsuris,* had become their own bastion of safety.

Which was a reality that we would all come to appreciate. If it wasn't for English departments and the creative writing programs they very reluctantly supported, living the writing life would have been much more difficult, and for some, not really possible in the long run. For me, if not for my safe haven in the English department, I would undoubtedly not be writing this book—or maybe writing at all, and the story of creative nonfiction would be much different, if there was a story at all.

It may well be that English departments resisted change for various reasons at the beginning, but they also opened the doors and provided a place—a destination—for all of us creative nonfictionists to come together, dialogue and share our work, and earn a certain legitimacy that had been denied us from the beginning. I was much too engrossed in fighting the good fight and establishing my own turf to realize any of this. It was too early to look back and consider the bigger picture. There was no doubt that respect for the literary value of nonfiction would grow—it was growing—but creative nonfiction was different from what Mailer and Capote and Talese and Ross were doing or saying about what they were doing; it was a flavor, an attitude, a more expansive way of thinking and writing, and even debating, a process of evolution which, I have now realized, only the academy would allow.

I continued to teach nonfiction writing at Pitt, and with Monty's support I got a full-time tenure-track position. But the student demand for nonfiction writing courses led first to a readjustment or, let us say, a transfer. A colleague,

Margery Gulbransen, had taught children's literature, and when her program was phased out, she was transferred over to nonfiction. Or maybe dumped there. Gulbransen was a real team player and another voice and vote in the department. This switch of fields – the transfer – would not be condoned so easily today, but it was assumed then, and for many years thereafter at Pitt and in writing programs everywhere, that nonfiction was simple and formulaic, and with a little bit of preparation, or maybe no preparation at all, anyone who was well-educated, with an advanced degree, who read newspapers and magazines, could pretty much do it – especially for undergrads. This "almost anyone could do it" notion for teaching nonfiction was pervasive in writing programs throughout the 1980s and early 1990s.

Pitt added another nonfiction faculty tenure-stream member in 1979, Bruce Dobler, so I had another partner – a fellow fist-fighter – along with Gulbransen. Dobler was mostly a fiction writer, having published three novels in the years leading up to his hiring at Pitt. But he was a great teacher and super encouraging for students. So even though there were three of us nonfictionists, we really didn't have, at the time, a complement of writer-professors who were actually practicing what we were trying to teach.

At that time, there was always the question of where to find qualified and experienced nonfiction faculty members. Journalists were obviously out, although we did receive a fair number of applicants who had paid their dues in the newspaper world, mostly veteran journalists who imagined how they could live out their remaining years in the halls of ivy, sharing their wisdom and smoking their pipes. It was difficult to find faculty with experience, and with an advanced degree – which was a non-negotiable departmental requirement – no matter how many real professionals applied. I was the exception, but it was pretty clear the department wouldn't be breaking the rules a second time and hiring an outcast. Although, one new hire in the writing program, a poet with a Ph.D., turned out to be as much of an outcast as I was – because of her belief in the literary value of nonfiction.

We were in a conference room on the fifth floor of the CL, discussing with a group of graduate students in writing and composition – I think they were all teaching assistants – potential summer support, or lack thereof. Let's face it,

English departments being English departments, there's never a lot of money to go around — and in the summer, there's a lot less. That was especially true in the 1970s and early 1980s, when the third term was not such an essential income-generator for universities as it is now. And if anybody got paid any decent amount for summer or third-term work, it was (and still is) the full-time faculty. Grad students are invaluable teaching assistants, or they help out in the department office, tutor challenged students, especially from other countries, and perform a number of support jobs during the academic year. But the summer is tough, and these people, mostly ranging in age from their mid-twenties to early thirties, were feeling pressured and panicked. "We are in a crisis mode. We are desperate," said one woman working on her Ph.D. in composition, as she made her tearful plea for funding during this meeting. And a young man with shoulder-length hair and a stringy beard commented — jokingly, but clearly unhappily — "I better call my dad."

This was one of those meetings we were dragged into from time to time — obligatory, but in actuality unnecessary because there was really nothing to say. There was no money to promise these students; we all knew it, even the grad students themselves knew it. The real purpose of the meeting was so the grad students could voice their frustrations and the faculty members who felt obliged to attend would listen and sympathize, although I admit that I was not particularly on the same sympathetic wavelength as some of my colleagues.

The book I was working on at the time, profiling the world of organ transplantation through immersion, trying to live in the shoes of all of the actors involved in the transplant experience, surgeons, nurses, and most especially patients who were fighting for their lives and their families, was about real desperation; the people I was writing about were actually seeking support to *live* through the summer. In fact, the chances of half of them living from then, the late spring, to the early summer were considerably dimmer than the slim-to-none likelihood of these grad students being awarded a summer stipend. So maybe I was not in a particularly receptive frame of mind to empathize with these students.

I sat there during the meeting with my mouth shut, wondering why they didn't just get jobs — like at the local McDonald's or the Pitt Tavern around the corner from the CL, where they could pour fifteen-cent drafts all night for minimum wage plus tips and drink for free after hours with the regulars. Or get in a car and drive across country, doing odd jobs. Or stick out a thumb on some back road in Amish country and see where it led. Do something to prepare for life in the world at large — which, for a writer, might be the perfect start to a path toward publication and into the academy later on. I admit I was being cavalier; it was easy for me, Mr. Tenure, to take a hard line. After all, I had it made.

The conversation continued until a young poet on our faculty, Diane Ackerman, addressed the young people sitting in that room with a simple suggestion. *Why not write nonfiction — creative nonfiction? You can be poetic, informative — and you can make a living that way. It's a perfect avenue for young people, poets especially. This is what I intend to do. I won't give up poetry; I can do both.*

I am obviously paraphrasing, but that was the gist of her message. And the students in that room, quite honestly, to my deepest recollection, looked at her like she was speaking in tongues. They would have laughed if they were not so surprised and so traumatized by their fear of leaving the confines of the university and finding other avenues of support. Nonfiction? Was this poet crazy? Had she lost her pride and her literary presence? For journalism? So formulaic, just like plumbing? Writing nonfiction was not an option or an idea to consider at that time — not for these grad students. The meeting ended soon without any resolution, as everyone had known it would from the very beginning.

I had thought that, because Ackerman had worked and studied with Carl Sagan and her poems dealt mostly with the scientific and natural world, I would soon begin to read her essays about science or nature, and of course I would read her two best-selling books, *A Natural History of the Senses* and, four years later, *A Natural History of Love.* But what surprised me was that she first chose to do immersions, just like a new journalist, experiences that both touched the natural world and dealt with — beautifully and poetically — the challenges and intricacies of real life in unexpected milieus.

In *Twilight of the Tenderfoot,* her first nonfiction book, she captures the life of a modern-day cowboy in New Mexico during one summer and the challenges of ranching. She had intended to write about the aesthetics of horses, but the story, as creative nonfictionists doing immersion work often discover, took her in another direction. For her next nonfiction she was still riding — this time in the sky. In *On Extended Wings,* she learns how to fly and, in the process, earns her private pilot license. Later, in *A Slender Thread,* she immersed herself for five years in a mental health crisis center. But in all her books, no matter the milieu, her work reflects, as she once explained to Linda Richards in *January Magazine,* "a poet's heart and a poet's sensibility." She often writes parts of poems she's been struggling with into her prose. "I end up insinuating into the prose sometimes what I think of as unrequited poems," she told Richards. "They're ones I've been working on for a long time and for whatever reasons I couldn't make them sort out but they're extremely relevant to what I'm writing in the prose, so they just slide in. . . . If I had my druthers—which is an interesting word—every prose book I wrote would be like inhaling jungle. It would all be at a level of poetic intensity that I would find satisfying word by word. Sentence by sentence. Page by page."[3]

She once showed me the books she was reading about science, wildlife, and philosophy—lots of environmental material, also—to prepare to write a profile for the *New Yorker.* She prepared in a similar way to write poetry. Her library and her reading list were impressive, but the scrawling annotations in the margins of each of these books, page after page, astounded me.

Our English department was not a good fit for Ackerman, who departed the following year, moved to a different university, and became a model for other poets and fiction writers, encouraging them not to be afraid to cross genres into nonfiction and experiment. To look at it as an adventure and another part of their literary arsenal. I often wonder if any of those grad students sitting in the CL conference room that day remember that conversation and after further consideration followed her advice.

CHAPTER 17

DRAMA AND TRAUMA

The writing program at Pitt got big and bigger and it was really terrific to be able to hang out with other writers finally — not being so alone. We had a community. Until egos got in the way of camaraderie.

First, we hired Chuck Kinder, who had published two well-received novels, *The Snake Hunter* in 1973 and *The Silver Ghost* in 1979. Now he had a big book he was working on, he said, when he came to town. And by big, he wasn't joking. He had, depending on when you might talk with him, a thousand or two or even three thousand pages of this book in progress. He obviously didn't suffer from writer's block. He had no trouble writing every day — sometimes all day. He had trouble not writing — more and more. He couldn't stop.

Revision to Kinder meant adding pages. He did not know, nobody really knew, if he was working on a book, or a number of books, or if there was, in this massive manuscript, a book to salvage at all. And he made no secret of his dilemma. But he did it in such a congenial and self-effacing way that you couldn't help but think that behind his obsessive turmoil, there was a masterpiece brewing. "I wrote ten pages today!" he would tell you excitedly, in his charming West Virginia drawl. Or he would laugh and shake his head and confess, "My magnum opus may never end!"

It was fun to be with Chuck, to hear his stories — and quite frankly hang out

—

and party with him. His presence in the writing program, his connections and contacts, helped solidify the program inside our department, and provide opportunities to students and faculty to interact with other writers. He had earned his MFA in fiction on a Stegner fellowship at Stanford, which is where he met Richard Ford, Tobias Wolff, Scott Turow, Larry McMurtry, and Ray Carver and loyally kept them as friends for life. You could hardly name a writer that Chuck did not know and have something to say about — something good and complimentary. And from time to time during his long tenure at Pitt, he brought many of these friends to campus to give readings or just hang out. You would go into the Squirrel Cage, a neighborhood bar where Chuck did his early evening drinking, and he might be sitting (and bragging about how many pages he had written that day) with any of his friends, especially the novelist Theodore Weesner, who was teaching at Carnegie Mellon University. And there were the weekend writers' raft trips he organized annually down the Gauley River in West Virginia, near his birthplace, and again you would never know who might be sitting in a wetsuit beside you. It could be Ed McClanahan or Toby or Richard or Jayne Anne Phillips — or a young editor who had founded the Vintage book fiction series, Gary Fisketjon, who would eventually publish Chuck's book.

Chuck, scruffily bearded and big all around, was a self-described outlaw from deep in the backwoods — a different kind of outcast than I was. He gradually began moving his classes to his home — and hosting weekend parties. Not just with students and colleagues, but with the characters he met while barhopping. You never knew who you might meet at a Kinder gathering; you'd only know that they'd be a rough-and-tumble good old boy that Chuck had somehow befriended. I don't think any of the writers in the department could have so easily escaped ridicule and scorn from colleagues for such antics, but Chuck handled it perfectly. He just did what he wanted to do, without making any fuss. And the students loved it. One of his students, the arts editor of the *Pitt News*, would eventually make him mythical.

In a book published in 1995, a raucous rebel writer, addled by alcohol and suffering from severe writer's block, faces his demons at a writer's conference in Pittsburgh. His name is Grady Tripp, and the book, written by Michael Chabon, was called *Wonder Boys*. (Chabon was also a *Pitt News* alum and one of my students.) A few years later, the book was made into a movie of the same name, starring Michael Douglas, about whom Kinder said, in joking objection, "He's not as cute as me."

The following year, Pitt added another fiction writer to our program, Lewis (Buddy) Nordan, who had just published his first book, *Welcome to the Arrow Catcher Fair,* at age forty-five. Nordan, a native of Mississippi who wrote exclusively about the South, fit in well in the department. That same year, a third fiction writer, Eve Shelnutt, who was also a poet and a Southerner, came on board. But she was far from a "good ole boy." For when Shelnutt came to town, she brought her own grad students—five young men, students she had been working with at the University of Western Michigan at Kalamazoo, who were immediately labeled "Eve's boys."

When Shelnutt arrived in Pittsburgh with her five boys, our program, quite amazingly to all of us, became the largest creative writing program in the country, and admission had become quite competitive, if you were a fiction writer. But the competition for students who had been admitted to the program quickly grew intense. Suddenly Kinder and Shelnutt were literally battling for student attention and adoration. In a way, it was like they were two politicians campaigning for office.

Shelnutt was a very different kind of writer from any of the other folks on the writing faculty, especially Kinder. Rather than writing the big book and shooting for big-time publication in the *New Yorker* or *Esquire* or *Rolling Stone,* or reviews in the *New York Times,* as did Kinder and his cronies, she published her work in little or literary magazines. And really wanted no publicity whatsoever. Seemingly, she was way above any of the commercialism that affected the literary world. She focused on her writing and devoted a great deal of time and attention to her students.

And she ran her classes differently—in opposition to what might be called the "workshop way." So instead of sharing the written work of her students first in printed form, as in most any writers' workshop, in Shelnutt's classes, the author had to stand up and read the story to fellow classmates aloud, so students could judge the work without distraction and, at the same time, hone their listening skills.

Fiction writing—and poetry, she insisted—were rooted in the oral tradition of storytelling, so that's where criticism must begin. She talked incessantly about literary idealism and purity of style and form and intention, and she was articulate, exceedingly well read, and most important, passionate. A conversation with Eve Shelnutt was more like psychotherapy. She cracked through student ambivalence or insecurity and provided direction and purity of vision. As time passed, the tension between Eve's boys only wanting to study with their mentor and the Kinder followers caused as much dissension in the department, perhaps more, as the rifts between the scholars and the writers—and the fight for or against creative nonfiction.

I was a little surprised. I had not expected that once writers, even those who danced to their own individualistic drummers, became part of the academy, "turf" would suddenly become a personal issue and a battleground. I just thought that the more real writers we could recruit into the English department, the more influence and persuasive power we would have to offer more courses, provide more opportunities for our students and, sooner or later, find a place for acceptance and equality for nonfiction as an art form, just like poetry and fiction. But I was being a bit too idealistic and hopeful. Sometimes the vanity of the writer (or teacher) becomes more important than the stories they tell and the work they do. But personal drama I guess is also part of being a writer, even when it is self-destructive to your work and mission and your friends and colleagues.

Unlike the infighting among the literature and composition folks, which was mostly over resources—travel money for conferences or a course off for research—the rift in the writing program was way out in the open, having more to do with the perceived charismatic personalities of professors involved. The department had never before experienced such nearly cult-like displays of loyalty. Not only did the students have their cliques; they seemed to travel in packs, attending meetings three or four at a time where they sat together, inseparable. First had come the invasion of writers, and then, to make it worse, their brash and unconventional behavior. The literature professors stood back and watched with surprise and amazement as it all played out, not really knowing what to make of it. And maybe they were also a bit jealous. They resisted the way all academics resist change, by discussing and debating and using their majority, the power of their numbers, to keep all the writers in check. Or, at the very least, slow down what was, in the end, inevitable.

—

Over the years, creative writing would become the most visible and dominant program in many English departments because of the passion displayed by students, not just for their teachers but for their commitment to the subject matter. Writing students, unlike those studying literature, were not just studying the masters such as Milton or Shakespeare or Faulkner or Melville, they were trying to emulate them. And they were vocal, energized and focused, often dragging the typical Mr. Chips academic into the twentieth and then the twenty-first century. I am not saying creative writing programs saved English departments, but creative writing was the adrenaline to allow them to grow. In the very same way creative nonfiction would soon become the adrenaline of the creative writing programs, but not quite right away. It was much easier for English departments to learn to work with poets and novelists—kind of a natural fit—but nonfiction was another animal entirely.

I was not such a charismatic personality as Kinder or Shelnutt. I remained during all of this time pretty much the loner I had always been. I did not have classes and parties in my house. I did not date or marry any of my students or anyone in the department. My circle of friends, limited as it was, rarely included connections to the academy. I worked really hard to maintain a safe distance, mostly to keep my loner image alive and free up time to do the research necessary to write immersion books. Which did not mean I did not have my loyal student followers. But in the bigger picture it wasn't me these students were following; it was, rather, my message and my relentless (and what seemed sometimes as ridiculous) campaigning for the genre, whatever you wanted to call it.

But what was also happening, even with our meager nonfiction troops—an outcast, a kiddie lit specialist, and a novelist turned nonfictionist—was that we were attracting a bit of attention and an increase in enrollment, in nonfiction. Perhaps in part because of the popularity of our super fiction corps.

In 1982, we snagged our first MFA student in creative nonfiction, Jeanne Marie Laskas, although she might have had second and third thoughts about coming to Pitt, both in the wake of the Kinder-Shelnutt standoff and in her general feeling of isolation as, she soon learned, another outcast nonfictionist. For it wasn't just the literature faculty that questioned the legitimacy of the genre; even the students in poetry and fiction, as Diane Ackerman had discovered, were at the most ambivalent about connecting to, bonding with, those of us — students or faculty — in creative nonfiction.

The atmosphere in the department and the writing program at that time, Laskas remembers, "was not normal. A bunch of eccentric characters dueling for legitimacy and attention." The squabbles between Eve's boys and the Kinder crew was like small-town politics. It was, she said, "drama — and trauma."

Laskas was the first teaching assistant to be accepted and funded in the newly established nonfiction MFA track of the writing program — the first and the only MFA program of creative nonfiction in the country. There were a half dozen fledgling fiction writers and another half dozen fledgling poets who had received teaching assistantships in the program that year. And then there was Laskas for creative nonfiction. There were dozens of young writers working on MFA degrees in both genres who had not received assistantships and were paying their own way by various means — and only three in all, including Laskas, in nonfiction.

But it wasn't being a loner, Laskas told me when I interviewed her years later, or in a minority that bothered her, as much as it was her status — or lack of status. Her feeling of isolation. Though she was now part of a creative writing program, she was not really thought of as a "creative writer." Maybe actually no one came out and expressed those feelings, face to face, but she knew — she could feel — the lack of interest and respect accorded to what she was trying to do: learn about writing artful nonfiction. And, of course, write it.

Not that she knew then what to expect in a creative writing program when she arrived at Pitt. She had no idea, as an undergraduate literature major at St. Joseph's University in Philadelphia, that graduate degrees in creative writing actually existed. Few students were aware, across the country, of this rare but growing option for study. There were undergrad courses at St. Joseph's in creative writing — fiction and poetry — and in journalism. "You lucky people," she would say to friends and acquaintances, "you get to write stories!"

But she had never taken any of those courses and had had no idea that you could actually go on and get advanced degrees in writing until her senior year when, like all of her classmates all across the United States, she had to decide what to do next in life. Although she had appreciated what she had learned studying literature at St. Joseph's, she had been an intern, the summer of her junior year, at *Philadelphia Magazine,* and she had enjoyed proofreading and editing and writing that summer more than anything else over her four years of college. So she began to investigate where she could go, how she could pursue what she was calling "magazine writing." And there were only two options then—the University of New Hampshire and the University of Pittsburgh. She chose the latter because there was a guy there, Lee Gutkind, who seemed to have experience teaching nonfiction. And, of course, she had received a free ride. But she had not expected feeling so apart from everyone else. It was traumatic.

Leslie Rubinkowski, even though she came into the nonfiction program a little later than Laskas, shared a similar experience as a nonfictionist—being "shot down and rejected," she remembers, "just on the basis of the work we were trying to do. It felt as if we were being cheated—and attacked—even though we had been accepted into the program and paid our tuition. Being told again and again about what I was attempting to do was just so riddled with flaws. It felt as if the reason we were there—to study nonfiction and to write it—didn't matter. That what we were doing—or trying to do—was, essentially useless."

Rubinkowski came from a different background and orientation, as a working full-time reporter at the *Pittsburgh Press,* and in a way, because of that, familiar with criticism of using story and narrative from both editors and colleagues. Despite her journalism degree, she had never read John McPhee or Tom Wolfe's anthology, and neither had any of the staff at her paper. Or at least they never discussed the narrative work or valued it enough to bring it up. All this narrative, she remembers one editor stating in a training session, "is simply throat clearing, depriving the reader of information they need to know."

Enrolling at Pitt, she had assumed, there'd be a different vibe—and there was, to a certain extent, primarily in the meeting of the minds of her fellow students, and in the readings she was assigned in our writing classes. Finding John McPhee was "a major discovery," especially at thirty years old, with a journalism degree and a half-dozen years of reportorial experience, mostly writing features. "Even though McPhee had been writing, marrying facts and narrative, since the 1960s. And Lillian Ross—and Norman Mailer and Annie Dillard. I always just found it strange and still find it strange looking back that people I was working with at the newspaper were resistant to something that really was there all along."

—

Rubinkowski and Laskas remained with the program and received their degrees. And with that and what they had learned, they were on their way to successful careers as writers and teachers. Rubinkowski turned her MFA thesis into a book, *Impersonating Elvis* (she had spent many months attending Elvis conventions and interviewing fake Elvises), that was published by Faber & Faber soon after she graduated. She continued to write and publish essays and articles and teach as a part-time lecturer in the English department. Today she is the director of the Goucher College creative nonfiction low-residency MFA program.

Laskas left the department immediately after graduation, served a stint as associate editor of *Pittsburgh Magazine,* and then went into business as a creative nonfiction writer. And I really mean "business." Unlike other freelancers, Laskas rented an office in a downtown building and established regular nine-to-five hours and carved out a career. Over a few years of being in business, she became a columnist for the *Washington Post* and a crack profile writer for *Esquire* and *GQ,* a modern-day Lillian Ross — with revealing and often surprisingly dramatic revelations and observations about a range of figures from the most famous (like Joe Biden, LeBron James, Tom Cruise, Barack Obama) to the infamous, like Joe Paterno. And a host of people we would never know anything about, like the housewife who invented the Slinky toy. She is the author of the book that inspired the movie *Concussion,* which eventually led to the NFL's radical reforms. Three decades after leaving the academy, she returned to the English department and soon became the director of Pitt's creative writing program.

CHAPTER 18

MUD AND COCONUTS

The resistance to nonfiction, not just at Pitt, but throughout the academy, went on throughout the 1980s. It had first been a turf issue when the writers invaded English departments and the resistance came from scholars in literature and composition. Later the resistance was coming from inside the writing programs, from other writers, as Laskas and Rubinkowski had to confront. The well-worn "nonfiction as a non-sequitur" objection came up constantly and seemed to be a good joke that gave everyone an opportunity to shake their heads and chuckle or shrug with more than a little arrogance. The attitude was: Nonfiction compared to poetry or fiction? Well, there was no comparison.

Unless of course you were writing essays, or the right kind of essay, the kind that was very literate and philosophical and did not rely on narrative and did not involve the lives of other people and did not pay much attention to accuracy or reality or literal truth. Perhaps I am exaggerating or being defensive, but there was a certain entrenched elitism among many writers in the academy when it came to nonfiction, writers who resisted change and wanted the literary world to remain small and exclusive and not immerse themselves in the Mississippi mud. At least that was how William Least Heat Moon put it in a panel discussion at the AWP annual meeting in 1983.

That was the year a nonfictionist, Annie Dillard, had been selected as the keynote speaker—the first in nonfiction—for the conference. Dillard had won the Pulitzer Prize for general nonfiction in 1974 with *Pilgrim at Tinker Creek*, which was very much a work of creative nonfiction, although not categorized as such when it was published. The book was poetic, informative, and very personal, a spiritual exploration—a surprising choice from the predictably conservative Pulitzer committee, which had pretty much selected books by journalists or historians in the past. She was perfect for this group of writers at AWP who were also academics, not journalists, for her literary work reflected their interests—the essence of writing and literature combined with her focus on the natural world.

Dillard did not live up to the hype, however. Her remarks during the talk were thought to be rather rambling and contradictory, especially concerning the idea of the meaning of truth and integrity in nonfiction, which became a running theme that year. But if any of the substance of her talk is remembered today by those who attended, it is for what she said about the very memorable and now often shared anecdote that opens *Pilgrim* about a cat she once owned, "an old fighting tom, who would jump through the open window by my bed in the middle of the night and land on my chest."

This, she revealed, was actually an image that had been shared by one of her graduate students, which Dillard had borrowed and "reconstructed—with permission." Her surprising revelation set the tone for the panel that followed on the last day of the conference, which brought together the essayist William Gass and William Least Heat Moon along with Dillard in a packed auditorium.[1]

Least Heat Moon's book, *Blue Highways: A Journey into America*, the story of his travels in a 1975 Ford Econoline van with bald tires and a faulty water pump, had been published in 1982 and became a best seller—perhaps with my student Jess Brallier's help. The book was not only about his travels and experiences; Least Heat Moon was on the run, looking for answers after he had been fired from his job—as an English professor.

He was the first speaker and, capturing the spirit of creative nonfiction, he immediately woke up the audience and his fellow panelists. It was pretty dramatic, especially for the mostly sleep-inducing panels at AWP. Least Heat Moon stood up, slowly took off one of his boots, and placed it with a flourish in the middle of the table right between Dillard and Gass. This boot, he declared, was a symbol of the essence of the roots of nonfiction and a message to all nonfic-tionists to get out of their own way, to restrain their efforts to pontificate about words and ideas, meaning essayists and, of course, academics. First (and I am paraphrasing here), put on your boots, go down and immerse yourself in the Mississippi mud, connect to the people who live there and write down their words and ideas rather than your own.

Peter Schneeman, in an AWP annual report following the conference, summed up Least Heat Moon's colorful opening statement as a "*Blue Highways* kind of epigram, about a man who would climb a tree to tell a lie when he could stand on ground to tell the truth," an epigram that became the leitmotif of the discussion from then on.[2]

Least Heat Moon was immediately staking out a position in opposition to the essayist William Gass, the next speaker, who countered in his own meta-phoric way by declaring right at the beginning, as an essayist, "I like to lie." And, he added, "I like [to climb] tall trees from which to throw down coconuts."

The essay, he said, has been largely a movement of mind over texts. "It is essentially words about words. Even when the title says that this particular essay is 'On Carrots,' it will turn out to be as much about what other people have written about carrots as about the little root itself."

The debate went on in this manner throughout the hour, mostly about the importance of fact and reality, the use and place of imagination in nonfiction, and where or how the imagination and fact intersect. Near the end of the con-versation Dillard summed up the positions that both she and Gass embraced, which was, I thought, a rather arrogant pronouncement, dismissing Heat Moon's boots on the ground Mississippi mud metaphor: They were both, she and Gass, in favor of not only climbing the tree, Dillard said, but of making the tree. "Fact and reality is only part of the writing of nonfiction," they agreed. "We are the inventors of texts." Truth, she said, turning to Least Heat Moon, "isn't good enough." And then she added, somewhat illogically, "Truth has nothing to do with it."

Although Dillard's final statement left most in the audience scratching their heads, it turned out to be a precursor of all the major conflicts and debates not only over the next few years, but through the evolution of the genre up to the present day. What is truth, what is fact, how are they defined and differentiated?

—

And how much do they actually matter when you are writing creative nonfiction? It was clear to me that until these conflicting ideas — boots on the ground versus coconuts tossed from trees — could somehow be accommodated by both factions, the acceptance of the genre in the academy would remain in limbo.

Nonfiction was the focus again at the 1985 annual meeting, keynoted by Edward Abbey, the author of *Desert Solitaire* (1968), about his seasons at Utah's Arches National Park. Abbey, like Dillard in 1983, devoted a great deal of his talk to truth and fact in nonfiction. Echoing Least Heat Moon, he distinguished fiction from nonfiction: "Nonfiction is about actual events and fiction is about imaginary events." He named a number of writers he most appreciated — Joan Didion, Edward Hoagland, Paul Theroux, Dillard, and Barry Lopez, who had introduced him that day. What these writers had in common, he said, no matter the variations in style, subjects, and ideologies, was a dedication to the truth. "Real writers have a responsibility to the truth," but then he added, "the truth that gets you in trouble."

I thought then, as I considered Abbey's remarks, that it was an endorsement of what the new journalists had been saying and doing in the previous decade: for writers to be daring in both style and content, to push the limits of the ideas and observations and the events they were writing about. But I think I got it wrong, for later in his remarks, he criticized writers — journalists primarily — who write for magazines and TV networks who are too compromised by the needs of marketing and advertising to write what they really think or mean. "Trouble to them was something to avoid."

Abbey knew something about causing trouble. In his books and public appearances, he lamented the loss of natural landscapes, speaking against the building of roads, dams, mining, and other infrastructure he thought was destroying the integrity of the landscape of the Southwest. Writing in *Salon*, Philip Connors describes how Abbey even burned or cut down billboards himself during his grad school years, and sabotaged bulldozers later, actions he categorized as "field research." He was investigated by the FBI for advocating burning of draft cards.[3]

Although Abbey was not completely wrong in his assessment that writers, mostly journalists, are at the mercy of the market and advertisers, he was also reflecting the bias in the academy that writers of nonfiction, creative or not, were tainted by commercialism. This was the same kind of bias that I was confronted with at Pitt. The common belief in the academy, that we writers, writing on assignment, writing for money, writing for a market, are arbitrarily rejecting the purity of the creative experience. And since few editors or publishers would assign a writer to write a poem or a short story, the taint of commercialism fell securely on the backs of the nonfictionists. Not that poets or fiction writers should not be compensated for their work — Abbey certainly was — but there was a distinction here between those who wrote for the joy of it, for the opportunity to infuse in their work a higher and more sacred purpose, and those who wrote, at least to a certain extent, to pay the bills.

In a follow-up report of the AWP proceedings that year, Rodger Kamenetz, then the director of the Louisiana State University creative writing program, took Abbey's critique one step further. Students in creative writing programs, he said, should be urged to ignore realism, professionalism, and most especially the marketplace. Writing for the market was too much of a creative compromise. "Pragmatic compromises produce great politicians, but not great writers."[4]

Today that mindset has largely changed. Editors and publishers are demanding and expecting professionalism and respect for and understanding of the marketplace. Most editors want to see proposals for nonfiction books, an outline of what the writers want to write before they agree to it, and agree to pay for it. The rise of social media has contributed to these changes, with many positive effects for nonfiction writers. A strong presence on Instagram and Twitter can be a deciding factor in obtaining a book deal.

But the sentiment and belief that any interference or support relating to the business of writing and literature — the crassness of professionalism — somehow tainted the purity of the literary experience lingered for quite a long time. And in many ways, it inhibited many writers in the academy who wanted and deserved a larger and more diverse audience. Publishing in an obscure journal often meant much more to colleagues when tenure time rolled around than publishing in a major magazine. Those most affected were nonfiction writers whose obvious outlets were commercial. Nonfictionists who were publishing were invariably writing for the people and not for the in-group choir. To make it in the academy, they were in a spot that might be described as "between a rock and a hard place"; in many ways, they were trapped.

But by avoiding a general readership, writers wedded to the academy were trapping themselves. Those trees that essayists were climbing, from which they were hurling their coconuts, were that safe haven so many academics were enjoying and protecting. Up in those trees they could speculate, ruminate, philosophize, and criticize, but not a lot of people were listening, except for other essayists. Their words about words were quite often about each other, who were not only mostly men, but a certain kind of men.

Joseph Epstein, the editor of *The Norton Book of Personal Essays* and the author of a dozen collections of personal essays, described the essay as a "middle-aged genre. One's early thirties," he said, "is too young to dabble in it."[5] Phillip Lopate had once explained, describing the essence of the essay, that common to the genre was what he called "a taste for littleness."[6]

This elitism was the problem and the challenge Robert Atwan was confronting right about the time the AWP-ers were pontificating and debating. Atwan, an editor, writer, and critic, had this idea of shining light on the essay form, hoping to revive and reintroduce the essay to a general reading audience by publishing an annual collection of the best essays that appeared the previous year. Publishers were wary, especially those who wanted to discover new voices and sell books that contained big ideas. The taste for littleness, especially from middle-agers, was not commercially appealing. The "E word?" many agents and editors would joke, when writers would propose collections of essays, "God forbid!" If you want to sell your collection of nonfiction, call it something—anything—else.

It took a while for Atwan to sell his idea. He had offers from small publishers, but he held out for a bigger one, until in 1986 Houghton Mifflin bought in. I make the commercial or "trade press" distinction here because Atwan knew that if he published his proposed annual with a literary or university press, the work would fall into the same ambiguous and quite ignorable, commercially limited category of all essay collections. Even in the academy, he said, the status of the essay form had been "compromised"—relegated primarily to the composition departments.

—

Atwan did not necessarily have a category of reader, an intended audience, in mind when he proposed his anthology, although he had pretty much written off those interested in journalism. "Your hard-boiled journalist at the time considered the essay as a form of 'thumb-sucking' or 'navel-gazing,'" he told the literary journal *Assay* in 2016. "At least those were the terms some magazine editors used when talking to me about the sort of writing they were not looking to publish."[7]

The E word was also a hurdle, even at Houghton Mifflin. Wasn't there a better word for "essay"? Atwan was committed. "It had to be Essays," he wrote in an article for *Essay Daily*. Even though, during the process of negotiation, he suggested appeasing (and unappealing) alternatives: *The Best American Articles, The Best American Nonfiction, The Best American Pieces, The Best American Thumb-Sucking!* Ultimately, they agreed: *Essays* it would be."[8]

Atwan was realistic about the potential of the book, at least at the beginning. "Because of the anxiety I sensed about the book's chances of success, I also asked for a two-year publishing commitment, so the series wouldn't be abandoned as a result of disappointing first-year sales. They agreed to that also." Two years was quite enough to prove that Atwan's annual collection of essays had an audience. A new collection has been published every year since 1986. Atwan and his prominent guest editors continued to engage in the decades-long conversation about the essence of the essay, but the most significant impact of this series was that, practically speaking, it broadened the appeal of the genre. The essay would no longer be trapped and contained in the academy.[9]

Elizabeth Hardwick, a poet, essayist, and co-founder of the *New York Review of Books,* was the first guest editor, followed by Gay Talese in 1987 and Annie Dillard in 1988—very different voices. Talese as a guest editor, especially early on, was a brilliant selection, bringing the new journalists—the mud guys—into the essay fold, blurring distinctions and divisions. Over the years many other prominent writers with contrasting ideas worked with Atwan as guest editors, including David Brooks, David Foster Wallace, Mary Oliver, Cynthia Ozick, and Joseph Epstein. For the first dozen years or so Joyce Carol Oates assisted Atwan in culling the thousands of essays sent to him by editors of various publications—from the slick mags like *Vanity Fair* and *Esquire* to little magazines with few subscribers.

PART 3

The Best American Essays did not change everything about the form and function of the essay, but it did help to reduce the insularity of the essay in the academy, the mistrust of narrative, and the perceived taint of commercialism. It shed light on the great potential of the E word as a vital part of the expanding nonfiction literary spectrum. By the early 1990s, the evolution of the creative nonfiction genre began—finally—to take hold.

PART 4

CHAPTER 19

HOW CREATIVE NONFICTION
BECAME *CREATIVE NONFICTION*

I can't tell you exactly when I started to feel it — not a day or week or month to pinpoint — but sometime around late 1989 or early 1990, there seemed to be the beginning of a creative nonfiction buzz. I wouldn't say that people in and out of the academy were jumping on the creative nonfiction bandwagon, but I began to sense an acknowledgement, whether reluctantly or excitedly, that this thing, this way of writing with a rather outrageous or inappropriate name or label, did, in fact, sort of, exist.

Previously when I was asked what I wrote or taught, and I said, "creative nonfiction," the responses were either glassy-eyed stares, people wondering if I was joking, or, at best, noncommittal. "Cool!" they might say. Or "Interesting," as they moved on to another subject. But I began to notice a bit more curiosity and some conversational give and take. "What's that all about?" Or, better yet, "I've heard of it." Or even better, when talking with colleagues at other universities, "Yeah, we're thinking about introducing a course on that — whatever it is."

I did not think we were at a tipping point, to use Malcolm Gladwell's overused phrase, but something was happening. Creative nonfiction was less of a joke to shrug off with a nod or a wave of a hand; it was becoming, ever so slowly, a real thing.

A couple of things were going on that might explain this buzz. The collective

—

force of all of those books I have talked about here by Mailer and Didion and Capote, and way too many others to profile — like the magnificent *On Boxing* by Joyce Carol Oates and *Pine Barrens* by John McPhee, as well as Atwan's anthology — had gradually given nonfiction a certain literary status it had never in recent times enjoyed. Maybe bookstores were still shelving McPhee in the nature section and *On Boxing* with sports, but critics and professors alike could not help but acknowledge that the stature of nonfiction had been elevated. It was beginning to feel like nonfiction was not just considered journalism or even new journalism anymore. Or rambling essays by the literary intellectuals, talking to one another about themselves. There was something more going on here — something that might not necessarily be new but that maybe finally deserved to be acknowledged. And, something else was happening, something big — sort of. Creative nonfiction became almost official.

Sometime between 1989 and 1990, the National Endowment for the Arts, in an effort to increase applications from nonfiction writers, had changed its previous nonfiction category for its creative writing fellowships from "belles lettres" to "creative nonfiction." I suspect that belles lettres (meaning beautiful letters in French) had been the designated nonfiction category because the NEA's advisory committee on literature had been made up mostly of academics rather than working writers, but belles lettres was kind of inappropriate because it could also refer to poetry or fiction or drama. And it was hard to imagine that *In Cold Blood*, or "Frank Sinatra Has a Cold," could be characterized as beautiful letters. I gather from conversations with those who participated in the NEA's deliberations that creative nonfiction was not the overwhelming choice to replace belles lettres, but the talk had centered around the fact there was some rebel back in Pittsburgh who was making a lot of noise about creative nonfiction. And since they could agree on no other name, creative nonfiction was a reluctant compromise. But it didn't really matter. The genre, or what was to become a genre, now had a name — or at the very least an official, vetted category.

Of course, few general readers paid attention to the goings-on at the NEA. It would still take a while for the news — the name and what it meant — to be generally recognizable, even in the academy. And, certainly, to the rest of the world.

—

I once asked one of my MFA students at Pitt, Michael Rosenwald, how and when he had decided to study creative nonfiction. Two years before enrolling at Pitt, he told me, he had thought he would be a journalist—a sportswriter. As an undergraduate at Southern Illinois University, he had taken a few courses with the novelist Ken Haruf, and he had tried his hand at fiction. But he had been uncomfortable and just plain old unable to make things up, even though he appreciated the craft he had learned in Haruf's classes. One day, he went to Haruf and explained his dilemma. He liked doing research. He liked talking to people—interviewing. And he also liked the craft that Haruf was teaching. How, he asked, or where, could he put them all together?

Haruf was sympathetic and helpful and introduced him to the work of many writers of narrative nonfiction and magazines like *Esquire* and even the *New Yorker,* which Rosenwald had rarely, except for sports stories, ever read. Haruf suggested that he take a course from a visiting professor, Lisa Knopp, from whom he first learned about my journal and heard the term "creative nonfiction." This was in 1995, nearly a half dozen years after the NEA had designated creative nonfiction as a category. So, recognition, even among those who should have known about creative nonfiction, took a while.

But gradually the word was getting out. Yes, in the academy, but I mean really out—in the world. With real people. Folks I would call literary outsiders. I was getting many invitations to tell people what creative nonfiction was all about, what it meant and how to do it. Not just at universities, but even more so from book clubs, or independent writing groups, mostly adults who had as many college degrees as they wanted, lawyers, physicians, engineers—writers or folks who wanted to be writers who were lost or just plain old confused about genre and what to do with the writing they were producing. Where it might fit.

These were like the people I had met when I was a nontraditional student at Pitt in the late 1960s. Many were writing true stories about their lives or the lives of others. But they were perplexed. Some of these folks had no idea what genre they were writing but were inadvertently pushing the limits of nonfiction or journalism, letting loose and using literary techniques like dialogue, character description, and writing in the first person just because it felt right. Mostly they were from what the New York literati would characterize as the hinterlands—

—

Oklahoma, Alabama, Kansas. But they had a lot in common with my students and even my colleagues. They wanted to write and most definitely they wanted to get published.

Of course, it would be wrong to say that this stuff, whatever you wanted to call it, was not being published. But let's get real. How many of these writers I was meeting on the road from Oklahoma or Alabama or anywhere, or instructing at universities or book clubs, would be breaking into the *New Yorker* anytime soon—or ever? For one thing, every one of those publications named here was based in . . . where else? New York. And the writers were kind of on the same literary and journalistic treadmill. Tom Wolfe, Gay Talese, Jimmy Breslin, Norman Mailer, Truman Capote, Joan Didion, Joyce Carol Oates, and others like them were appearing in *Esquire, Harper's, Rolling Stone,* all New York based, repeatedly. John McPhee, Susan Orlean, John Hersey, John Updike—I could go on and on—were writing exclusively for the *New Yorker.* And why not? It was the best magazine in the world. Of course, there were exceptions; other writers from other parts of the country were appearing in these "slicks," but the reality was that it was a very closed circle and there were not a lot of opening slots. The odds of you—or me—breaking into it were, to put it gently, rare to none. There were a few other magazines trying to break barriers, like *Ramparts,* or *Mother Jones.* But precious little space for the outsider.

Which is how my idea for a literary journal that would publish creative nonfiction, exclusively, had started to take shape. First, literary journals were easier to produce than magazines—no pictures, advertising, or color. And much more important: I had become increasingly aware of literary journals when I came to work in the English department. Maybe I had known about them before I became a professor, but I paid little attention. I began to understand the impact they could make, though.

Like many young men at the time, I had been quite taken with Hemingway, and I tried to read all of his work and lots of biographies about him. Hemingway spent time working for newspapers. That's where he began to develop the spare, crisp style for which he is known, as well as his ability to capture and recreate people and places with vivid and unforgettable detail. But the development of his "literary" career, in sync with his reportorial accomplishments and maturation as a writer, was all about a bunch of magazines most people (including me) had never heard of. Most of them were defunct long before I was born – but a long line of these literary "little" magazines supported and showcased Hemingway and others as they matured.

While he was still in his early twenties, Hemingway's work appeared in the *Little Review* (as did the work of Gertrude Stein and Ezra Pound); the *Transatlantic Review,* edited by Ford Madox Ford; and another little magazine called *This Quarter.* Most of these little magazines were based in Paris, where many American literary ex-pats were hanging out at the time. Most were startups that existed for a few years, supported by an impassioned writer or editor, made an impact, and then disappeared when the founders ran out of money or spirit (and sometimes both).

Literary or little magazines supported Hemingway at a key developmental moment in his career. Without their support and encouragement, and without the exposure they provided to critics and other editors, maybe Hemingway would not have ascended to such fame, might not have won a Nobel Prize for literature, might not be regarded as one of the most famous American artists ever to live. Perhaps I am exaggerating – but look: the *Little Review* was first to publish the Hemingway vignette "In Our Time," which not long after was reprinted with minor edits in Hemingway's second book, *In Our Time.* ("Big Two-Hearted River" was also in this collection.) Then the *Transatlantic Review* published Hemingway's brilliant short story "Cross-Country Snow," and *This Quarter* published "The Undefeated," a story about bullfighting that eventually was adapted into a screenplay. These stories had been turned down by *Harper's* and the *Saturday Review,* respectively.

And it was not just Hemingway. *Transition,* launched in 1923 (and now out of print), featured early segments of *Finnegans Wake,* by James Joyce, and essays, poems, and stories by Gertrude Stein, Hart Crane, Samuel Beckett, Dylan Thomas, and Rainer Maria Rilke. Some of these writers were just finding their voices. And maybe they would have not found a voice or an audience if it wasn't for the littles that had supported them when they really did need support and encouragement. What would have happened to these writers and their careers, if not for the literary publications that first believed in them? Probably they would have achieved fame and fortune eventually, but the littles were undeniably a bridge to the "bigs."[1]

I knew my department colleagues were quite appreciative of these "little" or "literary" journals, perhaps because they were indeed little and exclusive to a certain kind of writer and reader to whom they could relate. If you looked in the department's library or on the shelves in the offices of literature profs, you'd see some of these publications — the *Georgia Review, Partisan Review,* and others popular at the time. They did not display *Esquire,* the *New Yorker, Harper's,* or the *Atlantic Monthly* in their offices. Maybe these magazines were in their living rooms, bedrooms, and bathrooms at home — but not in the academic workplace. And even though there was this creative nonfiction buzz, they still resisted the idea that new journalism or creative nonfiction was something students might want to study and write in a "literary" or literature department.

So I began to make a plan. What if there was an actual literary magazine that published creative nonfiction exclusively? Not something bold and brassy but something — how should I say it? — unpretentious? On nice paper — not glossy — and page after page of type. No photos, no ads, just words — lots of words. It would have to seem to be scholarly; the less style and personality, at least visually, the better.

Somehow all of this — my colleagues' awareness of the critical importance of literary magazines, the interest in the genre out in the "hinterlands," came together for me. I don't exactly remember a day — a light-bulb moment — when idea and inspiration turned to action and mission or purpose. It just nestled in the back of my mind for a while. The plan took shape slowly; I was only vaguely aware of it until, suddenly, one day: Commitment! This was what I was going to do — launch a journal, *Creative Nonfiction* — and that was that.

First, I tested the idea around the department, fishing for funding. That effort went nowhere. So, I went out and marshaled resources on my own, mostly from students or former students who volunteered to set type, lay out pages, and help proofread. Printing from Paul Mathews, whose family owned a printing business, legal counsel from Cris Hoel, a former editor of the *Pitt News,* now an attorney. For design of the journal — a really cool paper tear on the cover — I went to the most prestigious design organization in Pittsburgh, sort of barged in and asked for help and received it from one of the younger designers on staff, Mona MacDonald.

But now the big challenge: I had to prove my point and publish pieces that were literary and nonfiction, that reflected exactly what I was looking for. Work that I sensed was out there by writers inspired by narrative and story who were frustrated by a lack of market or academic interest. Work by people who had led and were leading consequential lives. Where would I find creative nonfiction good enough for a literary journal — stuff that reflected what I thought creative nonfiction was all about?

My nonfiction colleagues in the writing program, Bruce Dobler and Patsy Sims, who joined the faculty in 1991, helped me. I'm not quite sure they thought this was a totally good idea, but they knew how difficult it had been, how long and hard I had battled to wedge the idea of creative nonfiction into the writing program. If it had not been for the expanding roll of nonfiction students, in fact, there would not have been a place for them.

Bruce and Patsy had provided some names of writers they thought might be interested in contributing. I took that list of names, along with some I had gathered on my own — a list of about 170 folks who I suspected had some interest in nonfiction — and wrote letters (real letters!) explaining what I wanted to do and asking for advice, comments, and, most of all, submissions. I got some nice return letters, telling me what a great idea an all-creative nonfiction journal was. And people sent submissions, too. I think I got about forty in all.

I won't say that most of the manuscripts sent my way — for not only that first issue, but the first few after word spread that there was a new journal seeking creative nonfiction — represented bad writing, whatever that is. I mean, lots of bad writing comes across the transom of any literary publication. Bad writing was not even a fair classification; it was writing that didn't fit — for us. What people sent as creative nonfiction — what they thought the term meant — was difficult to fathom. We got some poetry, for example, because the poems were true, the writers said. I was okay with that, in principle, but it wasn't what I had in mind for the journal. More often, we received submissions of poetry interspersed with nonfiction prose. The poetry was the "creative" part, the writers said when questioned. Today mixing poetry with prose is no big deal, but that's not what I was looking for either. Too radical — then. And it would give the wrong impression to those nonfictionists on the journalism side of the spectrum that the creative part meant anything you could throw into a story or an essay without regard to any nonfiction standards whatsoever.

———

195

We got lots of fiction; the writers explained that the stories were based on fact, and more or less true, so why not just call them creative nonfiction? Today filmmakers and TV producers call that stuff BOTS (based on a true story). We got screenplays. Prose poems. We got personal letters, many of them — parents to their children expressing disappointment or encouragement, angry patients to their doctors, citizens to public officials. People had wild ideas — or no idea at all — what creative nonfiction was. *Well,* they must have figured, *let's just throw it against the wall, or in this case, submit it to Creative Nonfiction, and see what sticks.* These way-out-of-whack submissions kept coming in quite regularly for the first few years. They were entertaining to read, but it really showed that we had a lot of work to do to define our identity.

Sifting through these submissions and trying to figure out what to publish, I began to recognize at least one clear mission of the new journal: since no one could agree on the essence or meaning of creative nonfiction, we would publish work that demonstrated the core and fiber of the genre. We would select essays or articles or prose pieces — whatever you wanted to call them — that would help writers define and understand the parameters of the genre through example. We would — as any good writer is supposed to do — show, not tell. I wanted narrative — stories — that were compelling and passionate and, at the same time, informative. Stories that had a point, a theme, what I began calling a "main point of focus." I wanted readers to not just read for the joy of it all, for the entertainment value, but to benefit from the reading experience. To learn something. And of course, I wanted what we published to be true — or as true as possible.

My idea of the essence of creative nonfiction would be soon debated; that debate is still today going on in many quarters. And well it should be; creative nonfiction has become an open-door genre. What I thought creative nonfiction was in 1991 is not what others thought then and especially now. I was surprised and quite circumspect about the lyric essay, for example, when Deborah Tall and her student John D'Agata introduced it in her literary magazine the *Seneca Review* in 1997. "The lyric essay," Tall wrote, "partakes of the poem in its density and shapeliness, its distillation of ideas and musicality of language. It partakes of the essay in its weight, in its overt desire to engage with facts, melding its allegiance to the actual with its passion for imaginative form."[2] The lyric essay

———

is now being regularly taught in MFA classrooms and published in many little magazines, including *Creative Nonfiction*. Lots of work by such writers as Zadie Smith, Claudia Rankine, and Maggie Nelson can be described as lyric essays. I often felt, especially in later years, that I couldn't keep up with the rapid evolution of the genre once it got started. I look back now at some of the stuff I wrote, diatribes about holding the fact line, with a bit of surprise and discomfort, and some of the pieces I rejected for the journal then might be accepted today. As the genre evolved, perhaps I did, too.

There were some gems in the first round of submissions, work that beautifully represented what I thought creative fiction was then. Work that jumped out at me — and it was really exciting to discover them. Like Peter Chilson's "Bush Taxi Commandos," about his journey across West Africa, traveling the way the natives traveled from one place to another, stuffed into cars and piling into pickup trucks, bodies squeezed together, almost in layers. His essay was part of a larger writing project he was working on, dealing with the violence of the African road, "a living entity here, powerful and frightening. The road carries the necessities of life, and it takes life away with intense violence." Chilson clearly knew his stuff from a boots-on-the-ground situation, like Least Heat Moon. And this was different from getting an assignment from a magazine or a book contract; Chilson was living the life and then writing about it on his own time and money. A different orientation. Not that Chilson wouldn't have preferred a magazine commission from the *New Yorker* or *National Geographic,* but he immersed himself into his subject anyway simply because he wanted to do it. And he wasn't a writer or just a writer. He was one of these outsiders I have been talking about. He had done some reporting for a few small newspapers, but mostly he was kind of an adventurer, having served for two years in the Peace Corps and as an English teacher in West Africa.

"Bush Taxi Commandos" was, I knew right away, the perfect piece for the first issue. It was very action-oriented and took readers to places they had never been. And it wasn't typical travel writing that you could find in newspapers and magazines of the day. Maybe Bruce Chatwin would take a bush taxi, but probably not a writer or reader for *Travel and Leisure*. And the way Chilson wrote about it was exactly what I had been hoping for — nonfiction with dialogue, description, personal point of view — bringing the reader to the face of the action quite immediately. He was showing what creative nonfiction was all about, at least as I wanted to demonstrate to my readers. It was a memorable piece.

Twenty years later, when I traveled across Tanzania on a bike with my son, I saw those bush taxis, just as Chilson had described them. "Bush Taxi Commandos" would eventually be, years later, the first chapter in Chilson's first book, *Riding the Demon: On the Road in West Africa*. I read the review in the *New York Times*: "Chilson's book, as vivid in places as a nightmare, has all the revelatory power of the early explorers' narratives, with their shreds of myth and rumor snatched from the borders of terra incognita."[3]

Carolyn Kremers's essay, "How Tununak Came to Me," also in that first of many slush piles, was really appealing, fast-paced, personal and dramatic, and again reflected exactly what our genre was all about, recounting her two years teaching in the Alaskan outback village of Tununak. Tununak, we learn, "sits right on the edge of the Bering Sea, totally unprotected, no trees for 125 miles. . . . The wind blows at fifty miles an hour all winter. . . . Tununak is the foggiest, windiest village in the Delta. . . . Wind chill can bring the temperature down to 90 degrees below zero." And while this was definitely an adventure story like "Bush Taxi," a young woman alone, confronting loneliness and hardship, it had a back story, a love story that provided a warm three-dimensional element to the essay. "How Tununak Came to Me" became the first chapter of Kremers's book, *Place of the Pretend People: Gifts from a Yup'ik Eskimo Village*.[4]

There were other new voices that would appear in the first issue, but also pieces that reflected other aspects of the rich possibilities of the genre. "If and When" was a very personal piece by Mimi Schwartz about confronting and living with breast cancer, a piece that might be familiar today, but was new and different — and personally revealing — unusual at the time. And even more personal in a way was Jill Carpenter's "Consanguinity." Carpenter was a biologist — from Alabama, no less — as far away from the literary world in some respects as were Alaska and West Africa. Carpenter's piece was pretty daring for that time, focusing on blood and AIDS and cancer and "the blood of miscarriage, the blood of birth, the confused spattering of menopause."[5]

I did not know Chilson or Carpenter or any of these folks. Their work just popped up in the slush pile over a period of weeks. It was pretty exciting to go to my mailbox every day, see stacks of brown envelopes with postmarks from all over, and tear them open. And Chilson, Carpenter and Kremers were not academics; they were people living extraordinary lives, opening doors that we professors might never experience or know about. This was exactly what I had wanted to do, bringing writers from the outside — inside. So that writers from the inside would value and understand what there was on the outside.

That first issue also included what my colleagues would have called "pedagogy," a word that I had to look up after attending my first few faculty meetings in the 1970s. And I am not sure I thought of pedagogy when I put the first issue together. The essays included were examples of what I thought creative nonfiction was or could be, but I also wanted to begin to try to define the genre and to deal with the controversies and objections surrounding it. In that regard, Natalia Rachel Singer, then an assistant professor at St. Lawrence University, sent a manuscript based on a talk she had given when she was applying for the St. Lawrence position. It's a great essay, very informative and personal at the same time, but it was the title that caught my attention. It was like a proclamation, a definition of doctrine: "Nonfiction in First Person, Without Apology." It knocked my socks off, it was so apropos! I know Wolfe and Talese, Didion and Mailer and God knows how many other hotshots were demonstrating this to the world with their work, nothing new, but Singer was making this statement to some very judgmental folks in the academy and out in the world as well. This was something I too could have said — and did say, frequently, to anyone who would listen — but it was much better coming from someone who was not such an avowed true believer.[6]

But if any one particular piece was to make a difference, it came from Michael Pearson — who was then a lone wolf in a writing program, teaching creative nonfiction, more or less, at Old Dominion University. Michael did not submit a manuscript; rather, he wrote a letter offering to conduct a Q&A with John McPhee. Pearson had interviewed McPhee once before for an academic article he had written, so they were acquainted. Over the past ten years or so, in three books published from 2013 to 2020, McPhee has written extensively about his work, how he researches and writes and doggedly rewrites. And he provides lots of behind-the-scenes access, stuff left out from the original pieces published first in the *New Yorker* and then collected in more than forty books. But at the time he was resistant to writing about his process, although many others had studied McPhee carefully, most significantly his Princeton colleague William Howarth, whose forty-page introduction to the first *John McPhee Reader* in 1982 was incredibly detailed and thoughtful and remains today the best writing about McPhee ever written.

I have mentioned McPhee frequently in this book, and for many good reasons. Back then, in the heat of all the disagreements between writers in the academy and journalists, the one common denominator, the one writer who put together style and substance, the creative and the nonfiction, acceptable to both, was John McPhee. His acceptability was not just because he was a great writer, but because he was also a naturalist, very appealing to academics; for a long time, creative nonfiction was considered to be nature writing or sometimes travel writing. The writers who were most admired, like Thoreau, and the writers featured at AWP, Dillard, Least Heat Moon, Abbey, fell into those categories. As did, some would say, McPhee.

McPhee was not only a working writer, by the way, but also part of the academy, teaching one course a year since 1975 at Princeton, his alma mater and hometown, where he had earned a B.A. in 1953. Later, when I first met McPhee, I learned that he did not write when he was teaching; he devoted all of his time and attention to the sophomore writers he accepted in his class each year. Which was quite impressive considering his incredible productivity of books and articles.

So this would be a gigantic coup for the journal if Michael could get an interview with McPhee — and he did. It was quite a feat, not least because when he arrived at McPhee's office, tape recorder in hand for his "Twenty Questions," McPhee told him to put his tape recorder away. "You'll get a better story without a tape recorder. Besides, the question-and-answer format is the most primitive form of writing, you realize. Writing is selection. It's better to start choosing right here and right now."[7]

We published Pearson's piece in the first issue: "Profile of *New Yorker* Writer John McPhee" was right on the cover. What could be more fitting and perfect to give birth to this journal than beginning with McPhee on the cover?

CHAPTER 20

THE FIRST ISSUE

A Dining Room Disaster

It sounds as if we had all of our ducks in order, so to speak, and with McPhee anchoring the cover, we did. But also, as it turned out, we didn't.

We, by the way, was my then wife, Patricia Park, one loyal student, Kathleen Veslany, and my son, Sam, who was two years old and occupied his time in a high chair, as Kathleen, Patricia, and I sat around our dining room table, by throwing food in every direction in protest for not getting the attention he deserved.

("We" is a term I will be using as I describe the evolution of *Creative Nonfiction* through the years and the staff who supported my ideas and appreciated – loved – the genre.)

The dining room table in our apartment in the Squirrel Hill section of Pittsburgh was headquarters for our literary startup, to use today's terminology. This was where we spread out the manuscripts that had been submitted, selected those that we planned to publish in the first issue – there were nine essays in all – and established the order in which they appeared in the journal.

I spent a lot of time contemplating what the first essay would be. The first essay in the first publication devoted exclusively to the genre would be the most important one we ever published, and maybe even the barometer of how many issues we would eventually publish. I always stress to my students the importance of leading their essays with excitement, intrigue, and substance all in one package. Because first impressions make a big difference. Readers are busy; they have little time to read. And they are impatient. You can't count on their attention for too long, unless you hook them early. So too, I reasoned, with our little experimental magazine. I wanted the first essay to be not only well written, obviously, but an example of how nonfiction – information – could be seamlessly integrated with narrative, all the while reflecting the potential of the genre and the journal. This was a big decision. I finally selected "Meander" by Mary Paumier Jones.

"Meander" describes how a writer can wander among various subjects and ideas while keeping the substance of her ideas together from start to finish, kind of like a meandering river. The piece was also short, just a couple of pages. Readers could zoom through it, and then, hopefully, seamlessly, without pause, dig into the heavier stuff with Chilson in Africa and Kremers in Alaska and onward with Carpenter and her blood.

The issue went to press and was delivered back to my house in a couple of weeks. Cartons of Issue #1 were scattered through the house. The day before we went public, sending the journal out to our very select readership, I was very nervous and more than a little surprised to realize how important this journal had become to me. I had already, more or less, cemented my place in the department as a tenured associate professor. Soon I would be a full professor – in addition to being a working published writer. So what did it really matter now? But it did matter a hell of a lot. This had to work.

The genre was clearly growing, in small ways, in other writing programs across the country. But it was quite a fragmentary movement, a here and there sort of thing. Not a lot of people were convinced, in and out of the academy, that it was a movement and not a passing fad. Was it something to look back at ten years hence and laugh about? *Remember creative nonfiction – what a joke!* But I had staked my reputation, or to be more precise, made my reputation, such as it was then, fighting for recognition inside the academy for creative nonfiction and insisting that it was the wave of the future, that there were hundreds – thousands! – of unknown writers out there in the hinterlands, just waiting to be acknowledged, discovered, published. And maybe, in one way or another, they would become part of the academy, as students, teachers, supporters. Mary

Paumier Jones was kind of an outsider herself, and the perfect example of what I had been talking about, in that she was a librarian in real life. "Meander" would be one of her first published essays.

But, anyway, here we were, Patricia and I, Kathleen and Sam, around this table ready to "go public" with the finished product. It was hard to take our eyes from it, as we slipped each issue into envelopes, admiring our work and virtually pinching ourselves that we had done this from start to finish—or almost finish, pretty much alone. It did look like a legitimate literary journal, although a rather skimpy one. It was perfectly bound, ninety-two pages plus the cover, where the names of all the contributors were listed, just like most other literary journals. Nine essays and a couple of ads. Nothing ostentatious. On the upper righthand corner: "Volume 1 Issue 1." (I was being optimistic.) Just like most of the journals I had examined. The paper tear flowed over to the back cover where there was a bar code and our mission statement: "Here is a publication—the only one in the world—for writers, editors and readers of the emerging genre of creative nonfiction, exclusively." At that moment, at the dining room table, it felt to me—to us—like a final dress rehearsal in the theater, after a long series of rehearsals, anticipating our inevitable upcoming opening night. Or journal opening pages, in this case.

That night, after we mailed the issues, I could not sleep. I tossed and turned and worried, and finally I went downstairs to the dining room to admire the first issue again. I opened the magazine, flipped past the TOC, and began reading, for maybe the twentieth time, "Meander." Suddenly I realized as I read—how could it be?—that something was terribly wrong: Two paragraphs—a significant chunk of text—were missing from the middle of the essay. A gaping hole of vital connective tissue inexplicably gone from Jones's original piece. How could this have happened? I had no idea, except, obviously, for my lack of competence, my editorial or proofreading failure. What happened to all of my talk about standards? And more to the point, what could be done about it? I was sure Mary Paumier Jones would be livid, and the journal's and my credibility would be shot.

But there was no turning back. Couldn't go banging on the door of the post office demanding my 173 white envelopes back. And besides, we had printed 500 copies and had already shipped most of them to Tempe, Arizona, for our really big "opening night" — our debut, our coming-out party, at AWP the following month. Where all that debate had taken place over the past ten years over how or when to be creative, over the boots in the mud and the coconuts in the air and how nonfiction writers, tainted by the marketplace, would never quite fit in.

I had attended AWP off and on over the previous decade and had participated in a few panels, including the one featuring the "imaginative essay." That was the same year Abbey had delivered the keynote. The panel this year was called "Creative Nonfiction in the Academy." I had put this panel together and I regarded it as a make-or-break event for us, for the journal and maybe the genre's future in the academy. This would be the first time, as far as I was aware, that writers and teachers of the genre — not nonfiction, but creative nonfiction — would gather together from universities across the country in the same space. (I hoped that Mary Paumier Jones was not one of them.) So there was a lot riding on AWP for me and the genre that year — like I said, a big leap. So much at stake.

I had recruited some good panelists: both Michael Pearson and Natalia Rachel Singer had agreed to speak, and I had also invited Jane Bernstein, who had just joined the faculty at Carnegie Mellon University. Bernstein was in Tempe at the time, researching a memoir based on the murder of her sister when she was a student at Arizona State University in the 1970s. Singer and Pearson were from the beginning of their careers academics; Bernstein had earned an undergraduate degree in journalism, but had realized early on that she was unsuited to be a reporter. She had written a novel first, and then published a memoir, *Loving Rachel,* about her developmentally challenged daughter, and with that book had gradually gravitated to creative nonfiction. This was the path that so many other writers were following, dissatisfaction with journalism, frustration with trying to become a novelist and eventually finding opportunity and success somewhere in between with creative nonfiction.

We all met before the panel to make certain we were on the same page, joking all the while that we might be talking to ourselves — either because attendees didn't know what creative nonfiction was or because they thought they knew what it was but were amused or appalled by the thought of it.

The morning of the panel, I steered clear of the designated room and kept myself occupied with other matters. Even though I was the moderator and the initiator of the event, I intended to be if not late, then right on time. Not early, for God's sake, because I feared that standing there with my fellow panel members, watching an empty room not fill up, would make me crazy. I walked around town and drank an extra coffee, with my heart literally pounding with anxiety. Patricia and Sam were at the table at the book fair, displaying and selling the journal. Or trying to sell the journal. Or, more accurately, trying to entice passersby to stop and look. At that point, a few people had come around, but although there was a lot of interest – which was encouraging – we had made few sales.

Anyway, I waited until the last minute and then hurried to the conference room. I had checked the room out beforehand. It was pretty big. I had counted the chairs: one hundred and twenty-six. Why had they given us such a large room, I thought? If no one showed up – or only a few – it would make us seem even more pitiful and laughable. I knew I was being overly dramatic. That there'd be at least a few people sitting in those seats and that we were all professionals and our show, no matter what, would go on. When you are a writer doing an event, you may hope for the best but expect the worst. All of us have had events, most often in bookstores, when only one or two people show up, not necessarily to see you, but to help themselves to the complimentary cookies and coffee.

But when I finally decided to go to the room and make my entrance . . . I couldn't get in; I had to push and shove to get through the door, explaining to those fighting for seats that I was the panel moderator. The place was packed. People were flopped on the floor everywhere. Many of the attendees knew exactly what we creative nonfictionists were all about, as it turned out, and others were intrigued by the idea, thinking that they had all along been writing and reading this stuff and wanting to learn more about it. It was an eclectic, curious, and enthusiastic crowd.

The buzz had indeed been growing. I took it as confirmation of my theory that creative nonfiction was how many writers had always wanted to write – if only they had a place to publish it or a classroom where they could learn more about it or a community with which to discuss or debate it.

Near the end of my introduction to the panel, I made a pitch for the journal.

I tried to be sincere and passionate. "Now there is a potential home for the work you have been writing or have been wanting to write but have had no idea where to send it or who might publish it. Or even pay any attention to it. It is the new journal *Creative Nonfiction*. Come and see it at the table at the book fair—buy and subscribe and give to the cause. Your commitment now is crucial. Patricia and Sam are at the table, ready to show and sell," I said. I hadn't forgotten what I'd learned at the agency and on the road selling shoes: "No matter what the situation and circumstance, always ask for the sale."

After the panel, the conversation continued, with people jamming the podium and lingering in the hallway in front of the room as we cleared out. People were all over the place, incredibly excited, and it was hard to break away—and I did not really want to break away, if truth be told. I was enjoying this feeling of making a connection. It was like coming out of a dark alley, having wandered aimlessly, seeking an exit. I can't tell you what emotion I felt more at that time, elation or relief or even a bit of trepidation. Would this make any difference? What would happen next?

When I got back to the book fair table, most of the copies of the journal that we had shipped to the hotel had been sold. The event, the panel, the launch—it had all been a big hit. Like I said, my emotions were mixed. I knew that something really good had happened, and I wished that all of my doubting colleagues in Pittsburgh had been around to witness it. But it didn't matter in the end. The genre and the journal were on their way to establishing something significant to writers and readers everywhere.

A final note, re: this first issue: As soon as I returned to Pittsburgh, I made copies of "Meander," the entire essay, the missing two paragraphs included, and mailed them off to our subscribers with a note of apology. No one responded or complained, so I guess they appreciated my extra effort. Or maybe those who had purchased a copy at AWP just didn't notice. A testament to Mary Paumier Jones, whose essay held together, even though her editor had bungled it big-time.

A couple of other things happened during that AWP conference that were very encouraging and sort of surprising. I learned that I wasn't as much of an outlier as I had always assumed, that others were working on closely related projects in tandem with my own efforts.

I met Michael Steinberg, a guy I did not know and had never heard of. He was a big gangly sort of fellow with oversized ears and nose, tall and awkward; seemed more like a freshman entering the university than the Michigan State English department faculty member he was. And he was a gusher; I mean, he couldn't stop talking about the dream he had had for quite a long time of doing exactly what I had actually done: start a literary journal not just publishing exclusively creative nonfiction but digging deep into the pedagogy of the genre and mining its potential. He was trying to convince his English department colleagues to support him and fund it. I was surprised. I had been so obsessed with what I was trying to do that it had never occurred to me that someone else might have the same idea. And frankly, considering that he was going to rely on his university for funding, I figured that he had no chance to succeed. If I had waited for my dean or department chair to put up the bucks for my journal, well, I think I would still be waiting today.

But Steinberg's enthusiasm and persistence were obviously hard to resist, and five years later, in 1999, he achieved what he wanted with the first issue of a journal that continues to publish biannually today. When I met him in 1994, he had already found a name for his journal. When he told me what it was, I was impressed and a little jealous. It was so perfect. Why hadn't I come up with that? Steinberg really tagged what creative nonfiction was and could be with the phrase I have been using since the beginning of this book: *Fourth Genre*. Steinberg remained at the helm of his dream child until he retired in 2009 to pursue other writing projects. He died in 2019.

I did not meet Joe Mackall or Dan Lehman that year at AWP, but I soon found out that they too shared this idea of starting a creative nonfiction literary journal. In many respects they were typical of the kind of writers and teachers who were beginning to transition into the field. Both had been working journalists, Mackall at first with the *Washington Post* and then later as editor of *Cleveland Magazine*. And Lehman had reported for three newspapers, in Washington, D.C., Charlottesville, Virginia, and New York. Both had not necessarily wearied of journalism, but their work enhanced their interests in studying nonfiction as a literary form that led to advanced degrees. Lehman eventually earned a Ph.D. in nonfiction at Ohio State. They met at Ashland University, a small university in central Ohio, where they were both faculty members, and their interest in creative nonfiction immediately clicked. They realized that they were kindred souls. And they had the same wild idea.

"One day Joe came into my office," Lehman recalls, "and said: 'Why don't we start a journal?' I had been thinking about a nonfiction journal for a few years as well, but my idea was more of a scholarly journal *about* the study of nonfiction, not a literary nonfiction journal itself. But Joe's enthusiasm for the project carried the day. David James Duncan lent us his name and wrote an inaugural essay. . . . We assembled an editorial board just by daring each other to contact our writing and reporting heroes and set out our shingle. The whole damn thing came together on chutzpah. I did all the layout and production in the early years and we did it on a shoestring and sold it out of the trunk of Joe's car at conferences."

So now there was another literary journal of creative nonfiction: *River Teeth: A Journal of Nonfiction Narrative* went live right after *Fourth Genre* in 1999. *Creative Nonfiction* was five years ahead; we were already live. But momentum was building—and again, I was surprised.

Also during that AWP in 1994, I was interviewed by the writer Philip Gerard at the Starbucks around the corner from the Mission Palms, the hotel hosting the conference. Gerard was teaching at the University of North Carolina in Wilmington, and he told me he had a contract with a very fine midsized publisher to write a book about creative nonfiction. I admit that I was annoyed at first. Why hadn't I, "Mr. Beating the Bushes," been asked to write a book about creative nonfiction? But Gerard was thorough and professional, and I quickly realized that he was the perfect person to do such a book. I was way too close to the subject—no distance or objectivity for me. I was a "you gotta believe" guy—my way or no way. *Creative Nonfiction: Researching and Crafting Stories of Real Life* was published in 1996.

Over the years, Gerard wrote or edited a half dozen books about the genre, the most popular of which, an anthology, was particularly targeted to writers in the academy: *Writing Creative Nonfiction: Instruction and Insights from the Teachers of the Associated Writing Programs.* This was edited with the poet Carolyn Forché, whose work and reputation added to the credibility of the collection.

Gerard's background very much mirrored those of Mackall and Lehman—journalist turned scholar, with an attempt at fiction writing early in his career.

But even as he worked his first job as a general assignment reporter for a small-town newspaper, he was a creative nonfictionist at heart, jumping out of a helicopter with Marines making a mock amphibious assault on a beach, cinching bulls for the Cowtown Rodeo, performing two shows as a clown with the Clyde Beatty–Cole Brothers Circus and writing stories about his antics. Eventually, after writing what he describes as a "bad novel," he entered the University of Arizona's creative writing program to write a good novel. Edward Abbey during that time was hired to teach nonfiction, and although Gerard did not take any of his courses, he frequently interacted with Abbey and came away with what he describes as "my first glimmering that nonfiction could be just as literary as fiction." Unfortunately, Gerard died suddenly, in November of 2022; he was sixty-seven years old.

At the end of that weekend at Tempe in 1994, I was still not convinced that creative nonfiction had finally arrived as a real thing that folks in and out of the academy would take seriously, but how could I deny these signs of progress and acceptance? A book about creative nonfiction by a mainstream publisher, other literary journals in the works, a packed house for my panel and a sellout of issues of my journal?

I had flown into Tempe with Sam and Patricia not knowing what I would discover and fearing that I would discover nothing—indifference at best. And instead I had discovered allies, true believers like me, who I had not known existed. I had presumed, up until that point, that the future of creative nonfiction was a nearly one-man crusade. Heading home, I realized that I had been naive and way too self-centered. Truth was, I had allies. Or, if not exactly allies, then like-minded colleagues. And there was a difference between our approaches. Steinberg, Gerard, Mackall, and Lehman were assuming that creative nonfiction was a fait accompli, while I, on the other hand, remained in the trenches, on the defensive, ready and willing to confront—or attack—anyone who resisted the notion of creative nonfiction or took potshots at it.

But a lot of that—the chip on my shoulder—had to do with keeping my little journal afloat. It seemed to me then that *Creative Nonfiction* was . . . creative nonfiction. That the journal had to be the flagship of the genre, and that without it, the movement toward legitimacy would gradually fall apart. I am not sure, thinking back thirty years, after experiencing the creative nonfiction groundswell in

Tempe, that I was thinking straight; maybe creative nonfiction would have made it without my journal, although perhaps it might have taken a bit longer. Regardless, in 1994, I was sure that the fight to keep my journal and the genre going was far from over—and I was right about that.

Still, I couldn't deny the fact that there was this buzz. I wasn't imagining it. It would grow louder and louder and eventually turn into a roar.

CHAPTER 21

DO POETS WRITE PROSE?

How to proceed with a second issue? I really had no plan. I had figured that I would just wait for AWP—maybe we'd bomb—and get the first issue out to as many as possible and then make some sort of determination about moving ahead. But we got a lot of submissions right away—a good sign—and with those submissions a few surprises.

If all went well, I figured, I would receive work from some of the contacts I had made on the road, plus a scattering of academics from creative writing programs. But I honestly thought—assumed, really—that we would be inundated with work from the journalistic world. All you would hear when talking to reporters was that they were sick and tired of writing in inches, which is what newspapers compelled them to do, and of being formulaic, all while attempting to maintain the guise of objectivity. But there weren't many journalists represented in the stacks of manuscripts we were receiving. Likely they simply had no idea that *Creative Nonfiction* was around, but also, it might not be so easy to jump from news to narrative.

Mackall, Lehman, and Gerard had made the transition, but not without an intercession in the academy for contemplation and study. Jane Bernstein had published a novel before turning to nonfiction. This was the best path forward for those who became leaders, pioneers, of the genre. Boots on the ground and coconuts combined. I had taken a slightly different path; I had never sought an advanced degree. But my fortunate immersion in Pitt's English department, Monty Culver's mentorship, and the influence of my colleagues had led to my own self-study, nonfiction reading work—Huxley, Orwell, Twain, and beyond—I might not otherwise have encountered.

I also thought we would receive submissions from advertising copywriters, who had expressed similar frustrations. Mostly these were men trying to write the great American novel at night after the wife and kids had gone to sleep and they were finally alone. Hadn't Joseph Heller written *Catch-22* in his office during lunch hours while he worked as a copywriter in an advertising agency? Well, maybe. The frustrations expressed by my agency colleagues—which I'd heard again as I traveled the country talking to writing and book groups—were among the many reasons I had decided to get out of that profession before it was too late.

But we were not getting stuff from the advertising community any more than from the journalists. Either they didn't know we existed—or, perhaps more likely, we weren't *Esquire, Playboy,* or the *Atlantic,* and thus were simply not worth wasting the paper their manuscripts were printed on. So many would-be writers then wanted to start at the top, efforts that would invariably be fruitless and discouraging. I had hoped that *Creative Nonfiction* would offer a way of bridging the gap, of allowing them to cut loose and receive approbation. Getting them published and helping them feel encouraged, knowing that there was a road ahead if they kept working at it, kept trying. Instead of just thinking about trying. Nothing worse than a would-be writer who dreams of publishing in the "slicks" or writing a great book who doesn't write.

But as I spread the submissions out on the living room floor—too many now for our dining room table—and put them in order from those I would have to reject for various reasons to those I intended to read carefully that I thought maybe would work, I suddenly realized that the best of these submissions came from a totally unexpected group: Poets! "What the hell is this?" I thought.

I hadn't even considered poets when I began soliciting submissions for the first issue. But here they were—en masse—a road sign, so to speak, and a literary gold mine. Not that I thought poets couldn't write nonfiction; Henry David

Thoreau, May Sarton, Gary Snyder, Terry Tempest Williams — way too many to name — were poets who wrote nonfiction and fiction. I just assumed, quite naïvely, that poets were kind of a closed group, a literary elite who would not want to taint their work and vision by associating it with a publication devoted to nonfiction. Or worse, journalism. What was I thinking after spending time with Diane Ackerman and listening to what she had to say to our grad students?

I hadn't been all wrong in not considering poets, I discovered later, talking with the poets who were submitting to us. Most poets were attached in one way or the other to English departments at colleges and universities; after all, very few could make a living as a full-time poet. They needed to teach in order to survive and write more poetry. And given the attitude about journalism in English departments, it was best to simply not be identified with the profession, especially when it was called new journalism. But through the mid- and late 1980s and into the 1990s, it became increasingly acceptable to write nonfiction. Ironically, the word that journalists so vociferously objected to — *creative* — made nonfiction much more palatable and approachable to poets and fiction writers.

In any case, these submissions were talking to me, and, as it turned out, providing a road map that I could learn from and follow and take advantage of. So, the "what to do next after Tempe" decision turned out to be a slam-dunk. We published essays by Charles Simic, Margaret Gibson, Judith Kitchen, Adrienne Rich — all of them poets of great prestige — and called the second issue "Poets Writing Prose."

The fact that these poets were sending their nonfiction over the counter, through the slush pile, such as it was, to us, was quite eye-opening. And assuring. Would Simic, who had won the Pulitzer Prize for poetry in 1990, have sent his very "creative" essay (a series of memory fragments about friends, family, music, art, and wartime), aptly titled, for our issue, "The Necessity of Poetry," to the *New York Times* or the *Washington Post*? Probably not. What would be the point? They wouldn't have accepted it anyway. Not because they wouldn't have admired it, but where would it go in a newspaper? It wasn't news, a feature, or an opinion story; it was the kind of essay that pretty much didn't fit anywhere — until creative nonfiction became a recognizable genre. And in those early days, *Creative Nonfiction* was the best of few, if any, options. We later published another essay by Simic, "Dinner with Uncle Boris," in our twenty-fourth issue. Both of his essays were republished in Atwan's *Best American Essays*.

Perhaps I should have realized what might happen when a literary journal (where the work of most poets mostly appeared) began to accept and encourage out-of-the-box nonfiction prose. It was an opportunity for poets to achieve more and to appeal to a more diverse audience with their literary pursuits. Diane Ackerman once told me that she often doesn't know what genre she is going to work in when she sits down to write — poetry or creative nonfiction. She writes for a while and decides at one point or another what she needs to do to achieve her literary or intellectual objectives — what the subject and the focus demand, prose or poetry. I wasn't a poetry reader and had rarely spent time with poets, until I joined the Pitt faculty and met a few of them and discovered that they were not as breathless and overly dramatic in person as when they were up at a podium reading from their work. In fact, they were much more fun to be with than the journalists I tended to hang out with; poets, I quickly learned, could smoke and drink and swear the average journalist under the table.

In my "What's the Story" column, which introduced each issue of the journal, I said that contrary to popular belief, poetry is much closer to nonfiction than one might imagine. On the most basic level poems are, in essence, nonfiction — spiritual and literal truth — presented in free form or verse. In addition, the skills and objectives of the best poets are the skills and objectives most vital in the writing of "fact" pieces. Poets, I said, seem to be more able, because they tend to work in such small places, to manage structure. And to maintain a concentrated focus or theme. Journalists, I said, will often ramble; they will write good scenes, capture incisive and revealing dialogue, but sometimes the full import and meaning of their articles and essays can tend to not fall together.

But that was just me in 1995 trying to connect the different flavors of the literary world, lure them in, get them to buy in, to this new thing called creative nonfiction. And it was me, the ex-hippie motorcyclist and undereducated "rebel," trying to catch up with all I had missed by not studying literature when I was younger. I was pontificating, reaching for a connection — and I pissed a lot of journalists off.

Today poets are a significant part of the creative nonfiction world. So much nonfiction is written by poets that you really can't call them just poets anymore.

—

Are Mary Karr, Maya Angelou, Mary Oliver, Terry Tempest Williams, just poets? Or are they writers who write poetry and creative nonfiction or fiction? The fact that prominent poets took the leap into creative nonfiction at that time was a symbolic endorsement of the potential and legitimacy of creative nonfiction.

Going forward, as I had done with "Poets Writing Prose," I continued to listen and learn from the submissions we were receiving. I thought – hoped – that people would continue to send their work, and that I would eventually discover pieces, like those of Chilson and Mary Paumier Jones, that seemed to fit for one reason or another, and that sooner or later I would have a third issue. At the time I was saying that *Creative Nonfiction* would be published biannually, but really, I was riffing. At first, we did manage, more or less, to publish two issues a year, but that was only with luck. We were very makeshift, piecing the journal together instinctively and looking for or waiting for some sort of message or opportunity to guide us.

And so, just as the submissions by poets had provided a direction and a theme for the second issue, the slush pile determined our third issue. Lining up the submissions, I discovered that there were many more women writers submitting to us than men. Today, of course, this would be no surprise, since the presence of women writers, editors, agents, and readers pretty much dominates and drives the genre. But women writing nonfiction had been given a rough ride over the years, I knew, as Nellie Bly, Gail Sheehy, and so many others would attest. Not just because the profession was more or less closed to women unless they would sneak or fight their way in. But because, also, so many of them seemed, to the men guarding the publication doors, too emotional, too revealing, too whiny and complaining, too in your face with their personal challenges and problems.

So then there was the third issue of *Creative Nonfiction* – "Emerging Women Writers," followed a couple of years later by the twelfth issue, "Emerging Women Writers II." That first women-only issue achieved something that I had hoped for when I launched the journal. "Poets Writing Prose" had featured very prominent writers; to do so had been and would continue to be part of our mission. But also part of our mission was discovering and showcasing new and unpublished writers, and thus the word "emerging." While it was true that writers then determined the substance and definition of the genre, the new writers, those who were just testing themselves and the field, would determine its future.

We had really good writers in that issue, including Jane Bernstein from the AWP panel and Jeanne Marie Laskas, who, you will recall, had been Pitt's first nonfiction teaching assistant in 1982. When we published her story about a town (Colon, Michigan) that existed for only four days each year when more than a thousand magicians from all over the world came together to meet and trick each other ("Magic"), her career was already escalating, so the word "emerging" was, to say the least, a stretch. But not so with another writer we published in that issue; as would happen at *Creative Nonfiction* from time to time, we fulfilled that other part of our mission. Or to put it another way, we would hit pay dirt.

This story starts at the Harvard Book Store in Cambridge in 1994. A young writer, browsing the magazine section, spotted *Creative Nonfiction*'s "Poets Writing Prose," and began thumbing through it. (We had been fortunate to quickly find a national distributor for *Creative Nonfiction* and get it placed for sale in key prestigious locations like this, as well as Borders and Barnes & Noble.) I can just imagine her reaching down, picking up the journal, flipping through it, reading an essay or two, feeling the quality of the paper. (We had upgraded it for our second issue, in an act of purity; we didn't want the type shining through from one page to the next.) And then I imagine her lifting her eyes in recognition, nodding slowly and thoughtfully, like this is something really special – it is speaking to her, eureka! – and then heading home to pack up her manuscript and send it to us at *Creative Nonfiction*.

I wasn't there at that important moment in the Harvard Book Store, and maybe I am being way too dramatic in my imagined scene, but the writer told me this story many years later when I visited her in a town not too far from Cambridge.

She's had a controversial career, to say the least – international criticism about her writing and research in relation to the psychiatry community and, at the same time, ghostwriting for the stars, such as Rosie O'Donnell. But her work remains brilliant, controversial, and revered. And it started, in some respects, at the Harvard Book Store thirty years ago — with *Creative Nonfiction*.

I don't for one moment want to give the impression that we inspired her or that if it wasn't for *Creative Nonfiction* this writer would not have made an impact in the literary world. To the contrary, she made an impact with me — first, because she sent her book manuscript to me and I had the chance to read it before anybody, almost. There's a story I have heard — I am told that there's more than a grain of truth in the story — the late editor (and brilliant baseball writer) Roger Angell was once seen running up and down the corridors at the *New Yorker*, waving a manuscript he had snared from the slush pile and shouting, "Look at this!" It was a story by a young writer named Garrison Keillor, and it turned out to be the first of many dozens of publications by Keillor in the magazine. And this happened to me, too.

I received a big box in the mail from somewhere near Boston, and I put it on the corner of my desk, recognizing it as a book manuscript. This actually annoyed me to a certain extent; I had said I would read essays — I mean, I wanted to read essays, that was what *Creative Nonfiction* was all about, and I guess it was also what I was all about right then, and I had encouraged people to send them, even if they weren't sure what they had written was creative nonfiction, which was, at that time, often the case. But I was already getting weary plowing through all of this stuff — and reading my students' work at the same time. And now — a book?

But anyway, we are talking here about a night, a Friday night, I remember, although I don't know why the day is so clear in my mind. I remember I had been at it for a very long time, reading submission after submission, working my way through the slush pile, which, it seemed, was getting higher by the day, no matter how diligently I was reading. (Although this was often a task I had to work my way through, it was also the most exciting part, because you never really knew what to expect, what you might find when you ripped open the yellow manila envelope, pulled out the sheaf of 8½ × 11 white bond typing paper and scanned the first couple of pages of the manuscript. It was kind of a mini-mystery story every time.) But that night, my eyes fell on the box that had come in the mail earlier that day, and just for a change, a diversion from the

---

217

stack of manila waiting for me, I cut open the paper it was wrapped in, lifted the manuscript, maybe three hundred pages, out of the box, and, well, you know what happened next. My incredible Roger Angell moment. Eureka! Holy shit!

The manuscript was *Welcome to My Country*, the first book by the brilliant memoirist, and also a psychotherapist, Lauren Slater, who eventually sold the book to Random House for a substantial six-figure advance. Michiko Kakutani later raved in the *New York Times:* "Ms. Slater writes about her patients with enormous compassion and insight, making the emotional and physical realities of their illnesses palpable to the lay reader. At the same time, *Welcome to My Country* gently unfurls to become a revealing memoir and thoughtful meditation on the therapeutic process itself." Slater went on to write *Prozac Diary* and the best seller *Lying: A Metaphorical Memoir,* among other great work.

Anyway, I went crazy, read all six of the long essays in the book that night, mostly about her work as a psychotherapist treating schizophrenic and border-line personality patients. It was a powerful, real-life narrative made especially vivid because the author, the doctor, also suffered so severely from her own borderline personality diagnosis that she had been institutionalized for many years as an adolescent. I stayed up half the night reading the manuscript, slept fitfully into the early morning, then phoned the author up on Saturday, offering to publish the book—telling her of course how brilliant it was, repeating it again over the phone.

Judging by the way she responded, she must have thought that I was going a little overboard with the praise. But I thought my enthusiasm would be at least partially offset by the fact that I wanted to publish the book but could only afford to offer her a $1,000 advance. And even that was a real stretch, since I knew even less about book publishing than I did about magazine publishing. But I had been talking with a small press from nearby Duquesne University about starting a creative nonfiction book series, and I figured maybe *Welcome to My Country* could be the first book. It was an exciting possibility—until a few weeks later when Slater phoned to tell me, quite apologetically, that on the advice of friends she had also sent a copy of the book to a New York agent, who, of course, recognized the work for its power and brilliance.

The agent was amused—sort of—for she knew the moment she read the manuscript that she had discovered gold, a real treasure, and she wasn't going

—

to allow this young, unknowing writer to give it away for $1,000 to a no-name press. The agent presented *Welcome to My Country* to publishers in an auction situation—which is how Random House eventually got it, weeks later, by out-bidding dozens of other houses.

But Slater was grateful for my encouragement and enthusiasm and offered first serial rights for the publication of any of the essays in the collection. I chose a piece called "Three Spheres," a narrative that begins with her boss assigning her a patient with borderline personality diagnosis, and a call from the treatment team meeting at a hospital in the suburbs of Boston where the patient has been voluntarily committed. The reader finds out in the narrative that Dr. Slater has been anxious to avoid visiting this hospital throughout her career as a therapist, and she tries to refuse taking on the patient.

In the end, she capitulates and accepts the assignment. What else can she do? And then, as the narrative progresses, the reader discovers the biting and fright-ening truth: that Slater herself spent time as a patient in the hospital as an adolescent. Midway through the story, she and the treatment team take a bath-room break, and she wanders out in the hallway, ending up at a bathroom in one of the patient wards. A nurse notices, and Slater fears being revealed, stripped of the professional demeanor she has fought so hard to attain.

When we published "Three Spheres" in "Emerging Women Writers," issue three of *Creative Nonfiction*, we also wrote a news release and sent it out. Here I was using my agency skills as a public relations expert; most literary magazines then and now don't really publicize their issues to target markets other than their own readers. We sent the press release to the *Boston Globe* and other media in the area. It sparked some interest and a subsequent feature story in the *Globe* about Lauren, the patient turned therapist, and suddenly, the telephone in our tiny office was ringing off the hook with calls from readers who wanted to order the journal, buy a subscription, and learn more about it and the genre, generally. Many people said to me over the telephone the week the Slater story appeared in the *Globe*, "Gee whiz, I have been writing this stuff all of my life and I never once knew what it was called." So the genre and the journal were still on an uphill climb for recognition, but getting there.

———

———

Those first few issues had been a great struggle, not just to get each issue out and in the mail, avoiding, of course, my Mary Paumier Jones mistakes, but to showcase the genre and offer examples of the different ways it could be approached by a potential slew of writers just waiting to be heard. And more than that, to confirm in my own mind, to reassure myself, that all the effort, the single-minded craziness and the defensiveness of my creative nonfiction obsession had been worthwhile. So the next issue, "Creative Nonfiction Classics," was a step back, kind of a way to tie up loose ends and to make the point that the work that had been done by the masters, then thought to be reporters and new journalists, and the work being written by new and emerging voices in the genre like Lauren Slater, were in essence, give or take a certain imaginative literary wiggle room, one and the same thing.

For this issue, I reached out to Gay Talese — cold turkey. This was quite spontaneous. I had found his telephone number in the directory for Ocean City, New Jersey, where he had a summer home, dialed the number, introduced myself, and asked him if we could reprint "Frank Sinatra Has a Cold." I am pretty certain that at the time he was totally unfamiliar with the journal — or even the idea of creative nonfiction as a genre, but he was friendly and interested — and generous, by providing permission to publish the essay.

This interaction was the beginning of a long and fruitful friendship; if Monty Culver had been my first mentor, then Talese was certainly the second. He and I immediately discovered that we had some mutual interests, beyond writing: we both had summer homes in South Jersey. I was, over the years, to spend many evenings talking life and literature on his winding front porch across from the ocean, sometimes with his wife, the editor Nan Talese, his children, and often with guests he had invited. Or just one-on-one.

Every few weeks he would call and invite me to meet at a restaurant at the edge of the bridge connecting Margate to Ocean City for dinner with his mother. Because of its location — and maybe because of its food — this restaurant eventually went out of business. We were often the only diners in the place. And sometimes the conversations were kind of awkward; his mother, a tiny, somewhat shriveled woman in her nineties, didn't have a lot to say, and when she did speak it was mostly in Italian. But being with Talese in such an intimate way, the guy who helped start it all, was exhilarating. I felt fortunate and privileged — me, the guy who thought he would never fit in, finally connecting with a man he never imagined he would ever have the good fortune to meet. And with his mother, of all things.

Talese has been under fire recently for an off-the-cuff remark, at a conference at Boston University in 2016, when he was asked to name women writers who had inspired him. He first named Mary McCarthy, but then, thinking awhile, he replied, after a long pause, "None." Later at the conference and in the subsequent Twitter backlash, he tried to explain himself, rather unsuccessfully. For Talese, then eighty-four, and for all of the writers and editors who admired him, it was an uncomfortable and unfortunate incident.

But Talese was one of the first new journalistic "rock stars" who helped legitimize the idea of creative nonfiction — and the label. "Frank Sinatra Has a Cold" was one of two classics featured in that fourth issue of *Creative Nonfiction*.

The other "rock star" we included in that issue was John McPhee. I had also reached out to him, pretty much on a whim and a memory. Way back in 1972, the same year Wolfe wrote his *New York* magazine piece, I had read a short article called "The Conching Rooms," in the "Talk of the Town" section of the *New Yorker*, and like all articles there at the time it was unsigned. You never really knew who you were reading — Joseph Mitchell, Lillian Ross, John Updike, or God knows who else. It was frustrating in a way, but a cool guessing game, trying to figure out, through style and voice, who the anonymous writers were.

Years later, I heard an interview with McPhee on NPR, discussing his writing process and the challenge that every writer goes through — knowing when the piece you are writing is done. Or at least that you have taken it as far as you could. In this interview, McPhee discussed a piece he did for "Talk" about the Hershey chocolate factory and the highly refined taste buds of the principal character in the essay, Bill Wagner, who alone determined that the chocolate being made was of "Hershey" quality. Wagner was actually a highly sophisticated taster; he roamed the factory and was called in — for a taste — when a batch of chocolate was nearly ready to be prepared for sale. Wagner had been employed at Hershey's for his entire adult life, nearly forty years, and he knew from experience and his own sense of what was worthy, and right after a taste, he would pronounce, "That's Hershey's." And then the process of bringing Hershey's to consumers could proceed. (The "Talk" piece he was referring to was "The Conching Rooms.")

This, McPhee had said in the NPR interview, reminded him of his own writing process and how he finally decided to release his work to his editors. "I complain about all of the difficult and painful aspects of writing, but at the same time, I have always felt lucky that for better or worse, right or wrong, I seem to have a sense within myself [like Wagner] of when it is 'Hershey's' or right for me."

When I called McPhee to ask if we could include this piece, he remembered the interview Michael Pearson had conducted for the first issue of the journal. And he quickly agreed. Which led to another opportunity not much later.

McPhee and I had had a number of back-and-forth conversations mostly related to acquiring the rights to "The Conching Rooms," controlled by the *New Yorker*. As we chatted, McPhee told me that he had been putting together other pieces of his writing that, like "The Conching Rooms," had never been published in book form—or published at all outside of the *New Yorker*. This included articles from his earliest days at *Time* and a number of unsigned pieces written for the "Talk of the Town." It also included random unpublished notes, about 250,000 words in all, which he had refined into about 75,000. His aim, he explained, was not merely to reproduce and reprint, "but to present a montage of patches and fragments of past work that he had picked out and cut and trimmed (and edited and touched-up and sewn together as if it were an 'album quilt'"). Developed in Baltimore in the 1840s, album quilts were custom-made for individuals, and often commemorated technological innovations but also dealt with personal histories. McPhee explained that *An Album Quilt,* although considerably altered and rearranged, was still a draft. So once again, I took a shot and asked him if I could read it.

Some months went by until we actually settled back into our respective offices and McPhee was able to locate a copy of *An Album Quilt* and send it off. For the next week, I set aside an hour a day, tucked *Quilt* under my arm, and walked up the street to my favorite coffee shop to read. The experience was fulfilling—on a number of levels. In reading *An Album Quilt,* I discovered some old, unsigned favorites I hadn't seen for many years, such as the "Talk of the

Town" piece about the poor, absentminded professor (McPhee) who locks his keys in his car in downtown Manhattan near the Fulton Fish Market. There were profiles of Mort Sahl, Joan Baez, Jackie Gleason, the latter two beginning with classic descriptions (identities withheld), which capture the essence of the subjects with bell-ringing clarity, along with Marion Davies, Richard Rodgers, Cary Grant. Aside from the notion that this was pure, terrific, original McPhee, the real joy in reading *An Album Quilt* was the fact that each turn of the page offered another unpredictable, delightful surprise. As I read through *An Album Quilt* (twice) at my coffee shop, I earmarked a half-dozen of these pieces as "special" because they illuminated a heretofore veiled, personal side of McPhee. I approached McPhee about publishing these pieces. And again, to my surprise, he agreed.

McPhee had also included a copy of a letter to his publisher Roger Straus, a co-founder and chairman of Farrar, Straus and Giroux, dated October 15, 1995, explaining that his intention at the time was to publish the book in "a couple of years." But those couple of years turned out to be nearly a quarter of a century. *An Album Quilt*, or a different and pared-down version, was finally published in 2017 as *Draft No. 4*, followed by more from *An Album Quilt* in *The Patch*, published in 2018.

McPhee, by the way, had been teaching at Princeton a course he had inherited from Larry L. King in the late 1970s that King had called "The Literature of Fact." In the mid-1990s, not long after we published "The Conching Rooms," he renamed his "Literature of Fact" course for the then newly established literary journal called *Creative Nonfiction*.

CHAPTER 22

THE FIRST CREATIVE NONFICTION CONFERENCE—AND GEORGE PLIMPTON'S REVENGE

After that issue (four issues!), it was time to celebrate, to have a creative nonfiction party—or, to sound more literary, to have a conference. Not just a one-day affair. That would not be enough for all the creative nonfictionists who might attend to connect and bond with one another, and meet and interact with some of the big names in the field, who would not only provide advice but, more importantly, inspire them. We'd need three or four days, at least. I wanted these folks, whoever they would be and wherever they were coming from, to leave the conference with an aura of hope and excitement about the work they were trying to do or to understand and its potential.

But then, the first two essential questions: Where to have a conference and how would we pay for it? We would charge a fee, but we couldn't charge enough to offset expenses. Most attendees would not be doctors or lawyers or other professionals, whose conferences took place in resorts in Boca Raton or Maui; these were, for the most part, people who, even when they did get published, especially in a little magazine, were paid twenty-five cents a word or fifty dollars for an essay, if they were paid at all.

I did not want to have this conference in Pittsburgh, the obvious venue, considering our creative nonfiction program and the fact that the journal was published there. But the animosity and resistance to creative nonfiction remained ongoing, so much that I wasn't even confident anymore that I wanted to continue working at Pitt. Besides, I had staged conferences at Pitt before, all through the late 1970s and the 1980s, featuring all genres. I had learned a lot about planning and pulling off events from my Helium Centennial experience and those at Pitt were quite successful, as far as student attendance went. But faculty had boycotted these events. My department chair told me that my colleagues felt slighted because I hadn't consulted with them about whom I might invite. "After all," she added, "they know their stuff." Meaning — at least I took it that way — that maybe I didn't.

Perhaps she was right. I just thought that if they could only see how creative nonfiction fit in with other genres then maybe I could just, in a subtle way, convert or convince them. I was showing, not telling, like any creative nonfictionist might do. But it hadn't worked out too well.

My assistant at the time, the grad student I had roped in to help me coordinate the conference for a small honorarium, warned me about the animosity my cavalier actions had created in the department. He was a nice young man who later became a respected poet, and by the way he blushed and stared at the floor, I realized that he was under the gun, intimidated by those professors who could, should they want to, damage his career. He said he would finish the job he had signed on for, but he too did not plan to attend many of the events in person. He did not want to seem too aligned with or supportive of me. He was sorry. So was I. Maybe more consultation would have bridged divisions. I was taking it personally. I was taking everything personally then. It was hard for me to think clearly and rationally about all of this. I kept asking myself, "Is the villain here nonfiction — or me?"

The answer to both of those initial questions — venue and money for a conference — had come in a weird sort of way with a phone call from a guy named Larry Bielawski from Goucher College a few hours after I appeared on the ABC network show *Good Morning America* to promote my just-published book about child mental illness. I had received lots of phone calls right after the broadcast, mostly congratulatory from friends or from parents who were confronted with the challenges of finding diagnosis and treatment for their children. But Bielawski wanted to talk about creative nonfiction — or an idea I had posed on C-Span a while back about how a creative nonfiction low-residency

—

MFA program would be the perfect fit for those most interested in writing what they knew—folks who had already, perhaps, earned a degree, or many degrees, who did not want to devote two or three years sitting in classes with a bunch of students half their age learning the basics of the genre. My low-residency idea was not a brainstorm. There were a few colleges and universities offering low-residency options for poetry and fiction and at least one at the time, Bennington in Vermont, including nonfiction. But creative nonfiction? There were no options.

The meaning of "residency" in a low-res program varied. But the idea was more or less the same. Students would come to campus for a certain period of days—maybe even a week or longer—maybe once or twice a year and immerse themselves in the writing experience from morning to night—workshops, panels with guests, and most of all, lots of one-on-one time with a mentor assigned for a term and with whom they would remain in contact for the next three or four months. They would write whatever it was they were writing, and the mentor would evaluate and make suggestions for revisions, mostly by mail or telephone. This was long before Zoom became an option. Or even Skype.

This was what Bielawski was proposing for Goucher, and the idea had turned me on. Almost anybody's ideas or even just their interest in the genre turned me on. I was knocking on doors as often as I could, trying to make headway for the journal and the genre. But in this case, I hadn't needed to knock. Bielawski had opened the door and I walked right in.

Bielawski was not a writer or an English professor but an IT guy, a rare breed back then, especially at a small private college, who was charged with the task of computerizing the entire campus pretty much single-handedly. But as such he wielded a great deal of influence and resources at his disposal that he could use to help kickstart an MFA program. His real goal, it turned out, was to learn enough about the genre to write his own life story—a memoir. We negotiated for a while and made a deal. We would start with a conference—that party I referred to— and then I would help him build an MFA low-res program. And the conference would potentially seed the program by recruiting from the attendees.

So we launched the first conference, four days of workshops, panels, readings, informal talks, in 1996. We attracted a hundred people from all across the United States. One hundred people may not seem like a lot but considering where we were as a genre in 1996, I was ecstatic. Those hundred turned out to be incredibly enthusiastic and excited – giddy almost – with the very idea of meeting other writers like themselves, in an atmosphere where they knew they belonged.

Our speakers – there were dozens of them over the years – would arrive on campus or walk into the lecture hall, and our students would stop and stare and sometimes even beam at or poke one another and whisper. This was kind of ridiculous, but we didn't think so back then. These names, these people, Tobias Wolff, Susan Orlean, Joyce Carol Oates, William Least Heat Moon, George Plimpton, Mary Karr, John McPhee, were legendary. Of course, the participants might have seen them before at larger events, like AWP, but having personal contact with them would be unlikely. Goucher, set off as it was on nearly three hundred acres of rolling grassy hills and walking paths, and with only one hundred attending in all, was pretty damn intimate. You could get up close and look for details that made them seem like real people. Joyce Carol Oates, it was duly noted, wore sneakers. When Mary Karr and Kathryn Harrison sat around a conference table to discuss memoir, they took off their shoes.

These little but intimate details counted. Oates during her presentation and the Q and A afterward had repeatedly referred to the genre by its proper name, at least as far as we were concerned, creative nonfiction. Most of the guest writers during those first few years were unfamiliar with the term – or so it seemed. In the panels and workshops and readings, they would more often than not refer to their work or the work of others as essay or memoir or new journalism. So Oates scored a lot of points.

The dining room in the hotel adjacent to campus, where we all stayed, a cheesy three-star Holiday Inn, was situated beside the swimming pool; whatever you ordered to eat seemed seasoned with chlorine. But you could sit wherever you wanted, including right beside the guest writers. One night, Leslie Rubinkowski sat across from George Plimpton, who was wearing an ascot and a blue blazer. The following night she sat beside Barry Lopez, who asked the waiter what kind of salmon was on the menu – where it came from. The waiter replied, "I think we get it at the supermarket." That story went viral on campus.

Putting the conference together, and negotiating with the guest writers, who were agreeing to very low speaking fees, took not only time but in some cases

—

227

very complicated maneuvering, especially with Gay Talese. When I had invited him, he was immediately up for it—ready to go. But there was a caveat. He did not want to drive the four hours from his summer home in Ocean City to Towson, Maryland, on the northern edge of Baltimore or drive to Philadelphia to fly or take a train. He agreed to attend if someone would chauffeur him there and back. I couldn't do it; I was, after all, the conference director and couldn't leave the venue for an entire day, as much as I would have liked to. This was the second year of the conference, and control freak as I was and am, I wanted to make sure everything would go right—for CNF and for Goucher.

So I reached out to my most adventurous student, Michael Rosenwald, the guy who had come to Pitt from Southern Illinois University. I knew I would not have to convince him; Talese was his idol; he would have jumped into his car and cruised nonstop from Pittsburgh to Mexico City for the opportunity to be with Talese alone in a car, one on one. Even though their road trip began somewhat precariously. Rosenwald was then, and always has been, generally unconcerned about his attire. When he appeared on Talese's porch on the designated day, he was dressed in an untucked and wrinkled old shirt and baggy Levis. Talese, dressed magnificently as usual, eyed Rosenwald up and down, and asked, "Do you normally dress like this?"

When Rosenwald replied "Yes," or "usually," or something like that, Talese persisted. "You mean when you go to work, this is how you look?"

"Yes," Rosenwald replied.

"Well," Talese said, "you dress like a fucking apple farmer."

Rosenwald remembers that after the comments about his apple farmer clothes, Talese, always the curious journalist, immediately began interviewing him, nonstop, for the entire trip—so much that they got lost a couple of times trying to navigate through Philadelphia, and the expected four-hour ride turned into nearly six hours.

Talese complained throughout the ride, but this was the beginning of a personal and professional relationship that would last for their lifetimes. Rosenwald was to become a features writer for the *Washington Post* and a contributor to those publications that Haruf had introduced him to—like the *New Yorker*, and *Esquire*. He was often a guest at Talese's home, across from Central Park, where Talese revealed his extensive—let us say "obsessive"—files, which contained every note he had ever taken related to a published story, many of which were on shirt boards—beginning with the stuff he wrote for his high school newspaper.

When he works, Talese, forgoing notebooks and index cards, takes notes on small pieces of shirt board recycled from his laundered shirts. (Talese and I keep in touch regularly, sometimes via e-mail, but mostly he will send postcards, jammed with single-spaced typewritten messages. Or, for quick comments and observations, an envelope with a note inside in the shape of a reporter's note-book, but with carefully cut rounded corners—shaped from shirt cardboard.)

Rosenwald was to eventually comb through those shirt board notes and stories and forge them into a collection, published in 2010, *The Silent Season of a Hero. Creative Nonfiction* eventually published excerpts of this collection in our thirty-ninth issue, a satisfying outcome of an encounter in a car between a young man looking for a genre that suited him and an eccentric legendary figure, both for Rosenwald and for me, as the guy who put them together.[1]

There were always transportation glitches during the conferences. And amusing coincidences. And a few practical jokes. Especially when Dinty Moore was around.

The following year after Talese, I had sent Rebecca Skloot to fetch George Plimpton, our featured guest, who was traveling to the conference from Man-hattan by train. But when Skloot arrived at the Baltimore Amtrak station in plenty of time to meet Plimpton, she learned that his train was late—and it would, as it turned out, be very late. Skloot was in her first year at Pitt's MFA program. I had recruited her as my assistant for the Goucher conference.

Skloot doesn't remember now how long Plimpton's train was delayed—maybe three hours?—but as she sat in the station nervously watching the scheduling board as it updated arrival times, she pictured the scene back on campus—all those folks, many of whom had traveled a great distance to the conference, promised the opportunity to meet famous writers like Plimpton, now just stand-ing around in the lobby of the auditorium or outside on the patio smoking and pacing; maybe they were still excited, or had been excited until this long delay maybe diminished their enthusiasm and their patience.

But Dinty Moore, feeling responsible for keeping his students engaged and amused, had been telling people – or hinting – that he and George Plimpton were friends or at the very least familiar acquaintances. Of course, he was joking. But there was more than a grain of truth to his "exaggeration." He had indeed met George Plimpton – more than once, in fact. And they had conversed. Sort of.

The first time they met was twenty years earlier at Pitt when I asked Moore, after he'd done such a bang-up job with Nelson Algren, to chauffeur Plimpton from the airport to Webster Hall. Moore remembers very little of that experience because, as he told me, he was in his "heavier dope-smoking persona at the time," so he probably had had no more than an hour of sleep before dragging himself out of bed, driving to the airport in his beat-up old Datsun and feeling foggy and star-struck and babbling at Plimpton all the way to the hotel. And then more babbling a few hours later as he escorted him to the lecture hall in the Student Union.

They met again three weeks later, when Moore was at the Harrisburg, Pennsylvania, airport after reporting on some government hearings for the *Pitt News*. Sitting in the waiting area, checking over his notes and beginning to plan the story he was going to write that night, he looked up and spotted the man he had embarrassed himself with a few weeks before, George Plimpton. And he figured that now that he was sober and looked presentable enough in his reporter's uniform, jacket and tie, this was his chance to try to have a more coherent conversation and maybe even regain a bit of self-respect. Surely, he thought, Plimpton would recognize him, after forty-five minutes in that old Datsun. Plimpton was reading, his head deep into a book, slouched in a chair. Moore walked right up to him and said, "Mr. Plimpton?" Like it was a question.

Plimpton looked up, startled. In fact, Moore remembers, "He looked a little horrified," maybe because he had hoped he could maintain a low profile and rest after doing whatever it was he had been doing in town, or maybe because he had no idea who the young man addressing him was. And once again Moore realized that he had not done himself much good. As soon as Plimpton looked up, Moore felt star-struck again. He was certain he had babbled a bunch of stupid and inappropriate things, before he could back away apologetically and return to his seat.

Plimpton had been distanced, but certainly polite, the first and second times

—

they met. And that—was that. Until maybe a few weeks later, when Moore was in Manhattan, visiting a friend, a musician who wanted to look into buying some equipment at Manny's Music, an instrument retailer on what was then known as "Music Row," Forty-Eighth Street between Sixth and Seventh Avenues. Manny's Music was a great place to meet fellow musicians—rising and hopeful wannabes or superstars. Many of the world's most famous rock stars had purchased instruments at Manny's over the years. Bob Dylan, Johnny Cash, Buddy Holly, members of the Doors, the Beatles, the Who. You could never tell who might walk into Manny's Music on any day.

Moore looked around, turned on by the ambiance, but after a while, his friend still shopping and talking with salesclerks, he wandered out onto the street to soak in Manhattan. "And sure enough, right across the street were the offices of *The Paris Review*," Moore remembers, "and coming down the steps and out the door at that very moment, with a handful of manuscripts, was George Plimpton."

Their eyes met, and Plimpton had the most curious look on his face—"not one of joy for seeing me again, I can tell you that." Moore can't remember how long they looked at each other, maybe only a few seconds, but he will never forget how Plimpton suddenly turned away and hurried down the street, his back to Moore, as if he were being stalked.

Moore had shared these Plimpton stories with Skloot and the other faculty members from the moment the conference started in his own very self-effacing way, continuing to joke, asking, "Do you think he will remember me?"

Plimpton eventually arrived on campus. Skloot introduced him, and he was worth the wait; he was charming and articulate and generous with advice about writing narrative nonfiction and learning how to connect with the people we were writing about. At the reception after his talk, Plimpton signed books and mingled with the students and faculty. At one point, he spotted Moore and walked up to him. "Hey!" he said. "I remember you! How are you doing, Dinty?"

"I thought," said Moore, recalling that moment, "I honestly thought that I was going to faint. At least for a couple of seconds."

Until he realized that Plimpton had been briefed in advance. Moore had been set up by Skloot and other faculty members. Moore eventually wrote about his "relationship" with Plimpton. "I think," he told me, "that Plimpton enjoyed the joke as much or even more than my colleagues. He was a good sport."[2]

I wish I had kept a list of those many folks who attended the conference, and worked harder to keep track of them. Had the conference been helpful? Inspiring? What had they published since Goucher? But we were not too organized at that time and when the conference ended thirteen years later, the list of all of the attendees seemed to disappear. I did remain in close touch with one attendee who made her first contact with a publisher at the conference that featured Plimpton, which led to a contract for her first book and subsequently a whirlwind career trajectory of phenomenal success, prestige, awards, and fame: Rebecca Skloot.

Skloot's story is quite spectacular. It was, on the surface, looking at it today, a perfect publishing story, a dream come true. Here was a very inexperienced writer, a young girl from Oregon, coming to Pittsburgh to study and earn an MFA, and while doing so, wrote a book that would—seemingly overnight—not only become a best seller and a movie starring Oprah Winfrey, but make nearly as much of an impact on readers as Rachel Carson's *Silent Spring*. It was indeed a dream come true for Skloot, or so it seemed on the surface, but no one had worked harder or longer to turn dream into reality. There was nothing magic or overnight about it. All along Skloot knew that writing a book and publishing it would be a struggle and that maybe she would not succeed, but it never occurred to her—or to me at the time we were working together as professor and student—that the future of her book would eventually hinge on the acceptance of the genre she was studying and writing, creative nonfiction.

The book, *The Immortal Life of Henrietta Lacks*, recounts the story of how one woman's cell tissues—she was a cancer victim—harvested in 1951 without her consent, would be replicated billions of times, allowing scientists working with her cell cultures to develop cancer treatments, vaccines, including the polio vaccine, in-vitro fertilization, and cloning technology. Henrietta Lacks was from a family of poor black tobacco farmers from the rural town of Clover, Virginia. Before Skloot's book, most scientists and the people who benefited from her cells did not know her name.

Skloot first learned about Lacks in a high school biology class in the late

—

232

1980s when her teacher, Donald Defler, described during a lecture one of the most important tools in modern medicine, "HeLa cells." And as an aside, he added, "They came from a woman named Henrietta Lacks, and she was Black." Skloot was intrigued and after class began questioning Defler not just about the cells, but about the family, whether they knew anything about the vital importance of the cells and whether Lacks's race had anything to do with the properties of the cells. Skloot was especially curious about whether Lacks had children and whether they were around and able to support her while she was in hospital — and dying — and while, as it turned out, doctors were researching and discovering the "gold" of her cells.[3]

There was a personal reason, as well, as I was to learn later, as there often is in the creative nonfiction world when a writer is committed to devoting time — as much time as necessary — to a book project. During the time Skloot was taking Defler's class, her father was suffering from a mysterious illness. "He'd gone from being my very active and athletic dad to being a man who had problems thinking, and he spent all of his time lying in our living room because he couldn't walk," she recounted later. A virus, the family was soon to learn, had caused brain damage, and he enrolled in an experimental drug study — hoping for a more specific diagnosis and successful treatment. After class, three days a week, she would drive her father to the hospital and sit with the other caretakers and wait and watch as the research "subjects" went in and out of the laboratories and exam rooms with little understanding of what was happening or how long their loved ones might survive. She had asked Defler those questions because she suddenly that morning made a connection between Henrietta's children and her own plight with her dad.

Off and on, through the remaining years of high school and later when she studied creative writing at Colorado State University, Skloot couldn't let go of that symbolic connection. She researched and learned a great deal about cell biology, but there was very little to learn about the Lacks family. From the few articles she was able to turn up, the family seemed to know just a bit about Henrietta's amazing legacy. When she arrived at Pitt, Skloot was one of the few students who already knew what her thesis — her book project — was going to be.

If — and this turned out to be the big if — she could actually write the book the way she envisioned it. There was more to the story than the science she had been researching for so long; there was an equally important story to be told about the Lacks family, the way they had been marginalized and ignored by the scientific community that had benefited and profited from Henrietta's cells. But as hard as Skloot tried to connect with members of the Lacks family and gain their cooperation, she was hitting dead ends. Her letters were not answered, phone calls were ignored; for many months, she was unable to gain their trust.

Skloot's fight for access to the family, especially with Deborah, Henrietta's daughter, who had fought for many years for recognition for her mother's contributions, is vividly recounted in her book; it is, in fact, the heart and soul of the book—the creative nonfiction part—the aspect that not only made the science accessible to readers, but allowed her to delve into some of the issues surrounding the evolution of HeLa cells, including research, scientific policy, and politics—and the impact of racism.[4]

Skloot took many of my classes while she was at Pitt, and she worked as an assistant editor at *Creative Nonfiction,* as well as at the conference, so we interacted quite often. I clearly remember her moods, depending on the state of her efforts to win over Deborah, exuberant when she thought she had made progress and tearful when she had been frustrated and rejected. Fellow students sympathized and encouraged her, while others advised that she should walk away and find something else to write about, but she wouldn't and couldn't let go.

In the end, although she succeeded in gaining the family's trust, this turned out to be only the first part of her struggle. Her original book contract had been with a small publishing company that had been scooped up in a merger with a much larger company. The editor who accepted the book, based on Skloot's proposal, lost her job and Skloot inherited another editor, one with little affinity for the book and not much interest in the approach described in the proposal. They were both in awkward positions. Skloot was unmoored by the loss of support, while her new editor was stuck with a project he had not and would never have encouraged or even known about a few weeks before.

Skloot's new editor was on board with a book about HeLa cells, but had no interest at all in Skloot's backstory—her efforts to win over the family and the family's anger and resentment at being shut out and not receiving credit or compensation for their mother's monumental contribution to science. This was a science book, clear and simple, as far as he was concerned. He believed—

insisted—that Skloot's relationship with Deborah and her efforts to win her trust, and the racism and the resentment of the Lacks family, would be of no interest to readers. It was, at best, an unnecessary distraction, and he refused to cooperate and agree to allow Skloot to move forward.

Skloot was just as adamant; she and I had many conversations about her frustrations with her editor, a guy I had worked with and respected, and her attempt to persuade him to see the creative nonfiction light. Their dispute went on for many months, until Skloot decided to have it out, once and for all, with this editor. Either she would write the book the way she wanted, or he must release her from her contract. He had been unwilling to do that at first. Eventually they had a late-afternoon telephone conversation; they talked and debated for a long time, and in the end agreed that they would never agree about how the book should be written. But she thought then that she had made some progress and that he might release her from the contract, although it was late in the day; they left his final decision up in the air.

They were never to talk again. That evening the editor was waiting for a train to take him home to a New Jersey suburb when he inadvertently slipped off the side of a walkway, fell into the well of the tracks, and suffered a head injury. He suffered from amnesia for many months after that and had no memory of any conversation with Skloot, or any of the promises he might have made that day or decisions he had left up in the air. The editor recovered and was able to continue working after a long period of convalescence.

Skloot persuaded the editor who replaced him to release her from their contract. It took a while after that—more than a couple of years—for her to revise and strengthen her book proposal and begin to work with an agent who recognized the essential importance of the story she wanted to tell—the way she wanted to tell it. There's more to Skloot's creative nonfiction story, but in the end, twenty-five years after she first learned of Henrietta in her high school classroom, her book was finally published. It was a creative nonfiction book and a science book combined—exactly what she had intended and fought for, perhaps the most successful since the genre became an official, legitimate genre. Skloot's struggle and journey was a creative nonfiction story in itself.[5]

CHAPTER 23

THE BUSINESS OF ART? OR
THE ART OF DOING THE ART BUSINESS

I first started *Creative Nonfiction* with a surplus of a few thousand dollars left over from a fund for a conference I had directed at Pitt. That, plus the pro bono services of those grad students I mentioned, got us through the first few issues, along with my own personal contributions. But how, after that, to pay the bills?

I had not considered keeping the journal in the English department's creative writing program; the university, I knew, would not provide funding for it, unlike so many other universities for their literary publications. Like those old-line literary journals — the *Georgia Review,* the *Gettysburg Review,* the *Iowa Review* — supported by the universities whose name appeared on the masthead. Not that those folks didn't struggle for resources, fighting with administrators and paper pushers to justify their existence each year, but the basics that kept them operating were usually taken care of. Salaries, health-care and retirement benefits for employees. *Gettysburg* and *Georgia* even had their own private headquarters — cozy bungalows nestled somewhere on campus.

This would not be possible for *Creative Nonfiction;* we had no constituency, no alumni to contribute, no Creative Nonfiction University name tag to attach ourselves to. And that wouldn't work for us anyway; yes, we were a journal, but we were also a genre, a way of writing and seeing the world that went far beyond an institution, a state, or even a country. Besides, that's not what I wanted. I did not know exactly what I wanted, except that after those first few issues and the positive response the journal and the genre had received, I did not want it to fade away and die. While my initial idea was mostly to prove a point, that creative nonfiction was as much an art as fiction and poetry and that it belonged in the academy, I began to realize there was something bigger going on here. This little journal could make a difference for writers and teachers of writing, even if for no one else.

But also – the other thing important to me – to be independent, different from most literary organizations, which was in the spirit of the genre, beating our own drum. I would not rely on any one person or institution. I had good reason to feel this way. I initially tried to keep the journal at Pitt even if the university was not willing to support it, and received a seed grant from a small foundation, but when the money passed into the university system, it became very difficult for me to use the funds the way I had promised. I could see how vulnerable we would be if we remained under the Pitt – or any other university's – umbrella. What would happen if the powers that be at Georgia or Iowa decided they wanted those cozy bungalows for a student coffee shop or to excavate them for a new law school or just because money was tight and enrollment down? I thought. They'd be cooked.

As I write this, the *Alaska Quarterly Review,* published by the University of Alaska, Anchorage, since 1980, may soon disappear, along with the entire creative writing program, due to funding issues. *Tin House,* an absolutely terrific journal, ceased publication because its traditional funding source dried up in 2018. And in 2022, *The Believer* would bite the dust, mostly because of incompetence, despite very generous funding.

The original *Believer,* the one in which that controversial D'Agata essay appeared, had been sold by *McSweeney's,* a magazine and a book publisher supported by Dave Eggers, in 2017 to the Black Mountain Institute at the University of Las Vegas. The price tag, $650,000, had been donated by a philanthropist, Beverly Rogers, who had provided considerably more money in support for an increased staff, a literary festival, and many other activities. But it never was self-sustaining. Without ongoing and generous contributions by Rogers it would have folded early on. It is possible that Rogers would have continued her funding, but when its editor, Joshua Wolf Shenk, conducting a Zoom meeting while taking a bath, inadvertently exposed himself by standing up, all bets were off. Rogers withdrew funding and the magazine was sold by the university, quite irresponsibly, to Paradise Media, which operated the website the Sex Toy Collective. Subscribers to *The Believer* were inundated with advertisements and reviews for nontoxic sex toys. *The Believer* was eventually sold back to *McSweeney's*. All this happened during and soon after the pandemic.[1]

Not that I think any of this could have happened to me or *Creative Nonfiction* (I shower) and no one was Zooming in 1994, but I really thought it was important to maintain a certain independence. My father did not expand his shoe operations without knowing he could pay for it. At the agency we had a budget. You better believe we had to follow it—or else.

So how to keep on publishing *Creative Nonfiction* without interference or censorship, and not be at the mercy of other institutions or individuals who, on a whim, could wipe you out, was the problem, and the challenge. How, in essence, to pay the bills.

First, I disengaged the journal from the university and established an official Creative Nonfiction nonprofit foundation, with a board of directors and bylaws, the whole deal. This was with the help and advice of Cris Hoel, who had, you will recall, been supportive of the journal from the very beginning. If we became a nonprofit, Cris advised, we could go to foundations and other arts organizations, apply for funding that might keep us going, and be able to spend without outside interference. This wasn't too easy at the beginning. Creative nonfiction, although designated as a literary NEA category, was pretty much unproven for regular arts organizations to support, and as far as foundations and organizations supporting journalism? Well . . . creative?

We did have help early on. I staged a launch party for the second issue, "Poets Writing Prose," with readings and pitches for support of the journal. It was quite well attended, and we got a few subscribers, but two audience members who came up to talk with me when the program ended would be hard to forget—for two different reasons. The first, a tall, slim middle-aged fellow in a cardigan who encouraged more issues featuring genre-crossing. I don't remember what else we talked about because I was pretty star-struck. I knew who this guy was the moment I heard his voice. My son would have also recognized him immediately. This was a long-time Pittsburgher, then and now very famous — Fred (Mister) Rogers.

The second person I chatted with, whose first name was pronounced the same as mine, although spelled differently, Lea Simonds, was both complimentary and direct. She said she had a small foundation that supported startup arts organizations, and that she'd be happy to help. And she did — and continues to support us. But she also wanted to be a part of what we were doing by reading the work we received in our slush pile and learning how and why we decided to publish or reject submissions. I received offers like this frequently as time went on, and took advantage of them when I could, but most volunteer readers became less enthusiastic when they learned how difficult it is to put the contents of an issue together, especially as the number of submissions increased, and they soon disappeared. But Lea was serious and stuck with it. And we became, in a way, partners.

She had a big house on top of a hill on a private drive on the edge of Squirrel Hill, not far from where Mr. Rogers lived, and every week or so I would come by with a pile of essays stuffed into manila envelopes. I had already gone over the batch to eliminate the "no way" submissions — poetry, news articles, short stories. But I kept anything that had promise and possibilities. Her dining room was walled in with glass, overlooking her garden, and we sat there together, sometimes for hours, carefully reading each piece. We discussed each essay as we went along and then put them into four smaller stacks by category: "Unfortunately, no," "Maybe, has potential," "Probably," and "Yes." The "yes" stack was usually the smallest.

I hear so many complaints — all legitimate — about how long it takes for literary journals to respond to submissions, many, many months, and there are reasons for that, beginning with a lack of staff to do the busy work, recording the manuscripts submitted, digging out the self-addressed return envelopes and dropping them in the mailbox, handling correspondence and author queries. But more than anything, at least for us, it was the attention each essay received before any sort of decision about publication was made. So often, an afternoon at Lea's dining room table ended up with a smaller pile than the one I walked in with—but with no real decisions made. This would go on for weeks until there were enough essays in the "yes" pile to move ahead.

Lea and I worked and edited together, periodically joined by a third reader, Laurie Graham, a former editor for Scribner's, for the first twelve issues, and of all the *Creative Nonfiction* issues, nearly eighty of them over nearly three decades, the first dozen or so were the most satisfying to me.

I was doing exactly what I had hoped for, reading as much creative nonfiction as I could, connecting with the text, and in many cases responding to writers, especially the newbies, who ended up in our "Maybe" or "Probably" piles. What could I do—how could I help and advise them to improve their work and then, hopefully, come back to us with revisions or new pieces? This was in many ways different from my work as a teacher. While I was responding to my students in similar ways, making suggestions, being encouraging, it was not as if my students were ready to publish in *Creative Nonfiction* (although many of them after they left the university did). But publication in my journal or in any other journal—or just plain getting noticed and encouraged—was a big thing for the writers submitting to us. It really mattered, and I took their work seriously, like a concerned mentor, writing notes (often "so sorry," with rejection) and even calling them on the telephone when it seemed appropriate.

But the situation changed gradually after those first dozen issues. Lea had become much more involved with other arts organizations and with a slew of grandchildren and was increasingly pressed for time. And I was pressed for time in another direction, in addition to my teaching and my daily morning writing regimen. I am not sure now that I can say for certain that that was for the good or the bad. The good part was that *Creative Nonfiction* was growing, with more subscribers and many more writers sending their work to us. The bad part was that I was losing part of my intimate connection with the work we were receiving and subsequently publishing. There was no way that revenue from the subscriptions and the few ad dollars that could be generated could accommodate production and mailing expenses, to enable us to stay in business and continue publishing. Not to mention what would soon be a paid staff, albeit not paid very well, and a tiny office. No more dining room tables at my house or Lea's. Not that I would ever lose contact or be totally uninvolved in evaluating and selecting what we published, but there was no longer time to tear open the envelopes, hold my breath, enjoy the suspense and hope that surprises awaited me.

So I became, not just editor, but the *Creative Nonfiction* breadwinner, conjuring up ideas for funding and figuring out — often scheming — how to make our "product," to put it into business terminology, "self-sustaining," based mostly on the lessons I learned during my time with the agency. I was not complaining; I was more than a little satisfied, and even a bit surprised, with our success. Taking what many people thought was a crazy and impractical idea and making it work was a damn good thing. I eventually became consumed by figuring out ways to keep it all going — although some might say that I made a few compromises in order to do so.

The theme of each issue was mostly determined by the submissions we received — providing a focus to what we published and perhaps a thought point, a message, as with "Poets Writing Prose" and "Emerging Women Writers." The message — the thought point — was a distinguishing feature of the genre. Not that poetry and fiction lack messages or ideas, but they are often subtle and elusive. It seemed to me that the best creative nonfiction was or should be more definitive. We were not writing to throw coconuts from trees, to go back to William Gass; one way or the other through the story we wanted to get into the mud of the issue or idea and, in the process, entice our readers to dive into the muck with us. And to teach them, or inform them, at the same time.

But the theme issues pointed a way forward — with a creative nonfiction spin. In fact, this was one time when creative nonfiction had a distinct advantage over poetry and fiction — simply because it was the true story genre. Creative nonfiction offers fact — information and ideas — presented in a cinematic and compelling way, often from a personal point of view that appeals to a general readership, people who would not necessarily be interested in the information without a story to go with it. So that was the marketing spin — the selling point — the edge in our pockets. You could take the same approach for fiction and poetry, but the factual connection, or lack thereof, would be difficult to navigate.

So what if we made up our themes or potential themes and approached organizations and pitched them about a special issue of our journal that in one way or the other touched on subjects or ideas near and dear to them? Would they bite? There was certainly a lot of money around — corporations, special interest groups — if you could just figure out a way to get it — other than stealing it. So that was my pitch to anyone who would listen:

"Let us make the things that matter to you more vivid, more personal, with true, informative stories, and we will publish those pieces in our journal and introduce your ideas and passions to a literary audience. We'll get the best writers, objective voices and not those PR people on your staff who will toe the party line. And since we're a nonprofit foundation, it's all deductible. And you will be a supporter of the arts and help us do our work." Or something like that. I was doing my Johnny Carson thing many years later. Sometimes I felt like a carnival barker.

I had to do a lot of door-knocking and cold calls and letters and in-person visits to get to the right person in order to make my pitch. But once I got in the door, the unusual idea of reaching a general readership through a literary publication worked — maybe not always, but if I went after it long enough, somebody got hooked. We got money beginning with our thirteenth issue — seed grants — for a special theme issue on the brain, supported by an arts museum about to launch a major exhibit about the anatomy of the brain. From a health-care foundation driven by the scandal of medical mistakes, we received funding for a special issue on the inadequacies of the health-care system. This particular connection was to last ten years and lead to a series of books, with essays all by new writers delving into mental illness, the challenges of nursing, and the end of life.

A major corporation — a bank, J.P. Morgan Chase — wanted to score points related to diversity, which turned out to be quite lucrative for us, enough to commission work by Richard Rodriguez, Terry Tempest Williams, John Edgar Wideman, among others. Enough also to pay writers who submitted essays relating to diversity. We also offered a very attractive $10,000 award for the best essay sent to us over the transom. Most of the time we did not commission essays from famous writers at all; we just presented the theme call for submissions on our website or placed small ads in writer-oriented publications. When the funds were available, we nearly always offered a cash prize, and $10,000 was not unusual. J.P. Morgan Chase purchased an additional thirty-five hundred copies of the journal to distribute to employees.

For that diversity issue — we called it "Diversity Dialogues" — we had more submissions than we had ever received or imagined: more than two thousand yellow manila envelopes stacked on desks, floors, and even in the bathroom. (Today we often receive more than two thousand in response to calls for submission.) Submission guidelines were always very broad and general for these special issues so that writers could go in virtually any direction – be as creative as they allowed themselves. For "Diversity Dialogues," Terry Tempest Williams wrote an essay about prairie dogs who had their own diversity issues. Judyth Har-Even confronted the challenge faced by Orthodox Jewish women attempting to divorce a resisting husband, to obtain a *get,* the Jewish writ of divorce.

These weren't puff pieces. That's not what our funders were looking for or what I promised; they had their own public relations flacks to do that. And they weren't censored; we could publish what we wanted, as long as it was in good taste, which was pretty much what we were doing at the journal anyway.

Once we began getting funding for themed issues we didn't always raise enough money to make up the expenses for an entire issue, but we often had a good chunk left over to fund general issues or themes that we felt were important. The more issues we published, themed or not, the more established and recognizable we became; arts funding agencies such as the National Endowment for the Arts were more likely to consider supporting us. And they did. We also produced issues with publishing partners – the University of Pittsburgh Press, Southern Methodist University Press, and mainline publishers like Tarcher and W.W. Norton. A few of these issues were books sent to our subscribers in place of the magazine. We later worked with Norton on a book series, the *Best of Creative Nonfiction.*

It was always, in those early years, a "whatever it takes" approach to get an issue – or a book – out that we could be proud of and that would keep us going. We were open to anything that made sense, and sometimes maybe not a lot of sense, to continually promote and strengthen the genre. We eventually established our own book imprint, In Fact Books. And as our subscribers increased and the interest in the genre grew, we added an education program – an online school. Which kept us afloat much later when we were threatened, and almost made bankrupt, by the pandemic, as were so many other literary organizations. As time went by, unlike so many other literary and arts organizations, we became mostly self-sustaining.

———

I know that all of this scheming, all of these machinations, seem pretty crass and certainly not literary. I got a lot of heat from colleagues and other writers for being an unabashed promoter and even a self-promoter. Okay, maybe that was true – or partly true.

But so what? It might work. And it might save a perfectly wonderful organization, and its staff, from going under. I know that most editors of little magazines do not have a business background, and without what I learned at the agency, I might not have been as effective doing this. It is difficult to wear two hats and to reorient yourself, learn something new, practice it and make it work. And find the time to do it properly. Quite a challenge.

Many literary organizations these days are becoming much more proactive and creative in their fund-raising approaches, and some of the larger ones now have marketing professionals on staff, and those will invariably be the organizations that survive the longest in today's unpredictable economy. So maybe this isn't as literary and honorable and noble as one might have wanted it to be, but taking care of business in the "art business" can often be a question of survival. Or that other alternative.

CHAPTER 24

THE LAST CREATIVE NONFICTION "FIST-FIGHT"

Moving into the twenty-first century, creative nonfiction had become pretty well established, in and out of the academy, as was the journal, with twenty issues behind us. But not entirely. Even long after the NEA had vetted the genre and creative writing programs and English departments were adding courses and hiring faculty, reluctantly giving up part of their turf, a creative nonfictionist could not just sit back and relax and write and teach and feel secure. "If it isn't one thing, it's another," as Gilda Radner had frequently said. And as Brenda Miller was to discover.

Miller had earned a Ph.D. in creative nonfiction in the middle 1990s at the University of Utah working under Terry Tempest Williams. (She had to design her own Ph.D. program; few then existed.) With a doctorate in hand, she remembers going into the job market in 1999 as a creative nonfictionist and being aggressively recruited. She had her choice of positions and eventually chose Western Washington University, where, as the first creative nonfictionist on the faculty, she was charged with establishing and building a program.

Over the next half dozen years, Miller published three essay collections. Her work appeared in many prestigious magazines. With a co-editor, Suzanne Paola, she published what would become one of the most successful books about practicing the genre, *Tell It Slant: Writing and Shaping Creative Nonfiction.* By 2005, *Tell It Slant* had gone into a second edition (there is now a third).

Tell It Slant was a very cool title and it neatly sums up what so many writers have observed in trying to distinguish or nail how writers and readers might understand the genre. The phrase was not Miller and Paola's brainstorm, however; it comes from the first line of a poem written in 1890 by Emily Dickinson: "Tell all the truth but tell it Slant / Success in Circuit lies." By that, Dickinson meant, Miller and Paola assumed, that "truth takes on many guises; the truth of art can be very different from the truth of day-to-day life." They go on to describe the task of the creative nonfiction writer: "To tell the truth, yes, but to become more than a mere transcriber of life's factual experience."[1]

Miller's work had made a difference — or so she thought — until, in 2005, she applied for a listing in the Poets & Writers Directory of Writers — and was immediately rejected. Because she was a creative nonfictionist.

Poets & Writers was established in 1970 in New York and quickly became the representative organization for all serious writers, "the primary source of information, support, and guidance for creative writers," according to its website in 2005. E. L. Doctorow described Poets & Writers as "a saintly little service organization for writers across the country. It tells them where the jobs are, the reading gigs, the grants, the awards competitions, and it brings them news of each other. Not its least valuable service is the one that comes of all the others — the suggestion of community implicit in this lowliest and most dire of professions." But Brenda Miller and other creative nonfictionists were evidently not worthy to be part of that community.[2]

On the surface, this may not seem like a big deal, but being included in the Poets & Writers Directory, vetted by one of the most influential literary organizations in the country, and considering the very small literary world in which writers' function, was a mark of credibility and achievement. More practically, the listing provided opportunities to give readings, conduct workshops, become a "visitor" on other campuses, a source of extra income and prestige.

I had a run-in with Poets & Writers in 2003, when Carolyn T. Hughes, a contributing editor of *Poets & Writers Magazine,* called to interview me for an article she was writing about the genre. What she wanted, Hughes told me, was a distinct definition of the genre. But I resisted. I could never understand why creative nonfiction had to be defined. Could poetry and fiction be defined or limited by boundaries? I asked Hughes.

I was always so annoyed by this incessant demand to specifically define something that was in the end indefinable. Maybe I was being stubborn; surely, I could put together a few words that would satisfy Hughes, but I didn't want to be nailed down. I wanted creative nonfiction to be regarded as an art—to be open to interpretation—not definition. Instead, I described the elements of the genre, action, scene setting, characterization, etc., but that wasn't what she was looking for, and in the end, I might have seemed to her readers kind of foolish or shallow.

In the lead to her feature in *Poets & Writers Magazine,* she asked, provocatively: "What is it? When a writer says he is working on a piece of creative nonfiction, what should a reader expect? A form of writing in which structure is as malleable as the subject matter? Journalism lite? A developing genre that has yet to define its boundaries? Is the branding of creative nonfiction a failed attempt to group such discrete forms as memoir, essay and reportage? And finally, is the category necessary at all? Doesn't everything in publishing come down to good writing and bad?"

"Alas, therein lies the rub," Hughes wrote. "If one of the leading lights of a genre will not define it, the door is open for people to conclude, to echo Gertrude Stein's assessment of her home, California, 'there is no there there.'" This was obviously unfair, but I had maybe bungled the interview. Although I would not have said anything different if given a second chance.[3]

When her Poets & Writers listing was rejected, Brenda Miller first reached out to an executive at Poets & Writers, who replied: "It would be too hard for us, when screening nonfiction credits, to determine what is creative and what isn't. It's very subjective, and all nonfiction writers would want their credits listed. Consequently, the organization has decided as a matter of policy not to list writers who write creative nonfiction exclusively. (If you are also a poet or a fiction writer, then it's possible to apply for a listing.)" Miller was not mostly a poet or a fiction writer, so she was plain old "out."

What to do next? She wrote me an e-mail at *Creative Nonfiction* and explained what was going on.

This really pissed me off. There it was, happening again, I thought. Every time it seemed as if creative nonfiction had made it — that we were now a legitimate genre — there was some other roadblock, some other fist-fight that reared up. And this from such a large and prestigious organization that from its very title, its name, distinguishes between poets and writers, as if they weren't one and the same.

So, the theme for our issue twenty-six became the "Poets and Writers" issue. It featured nonfiction by poets, just as our second issue had, essays by Hilda Raz, Toi Derricotte, Terry Tempest Williams, Ted Kooser, including a piece by Kathleen Tarr, "We Are All Poets Here," which was an essay about Russian poets generally and Boris Pasternak specifically, but was more than apt in this instance. As I wrote in my "What's the Story" column, "Disregarding genre, aren't we all writers here?" In my column, I did not propose a boycott of Poets & Writers, which would have been destructive, but rather suggested a letter-writing campaign to administrators and its influential board. I said we had to take a stand with Poets & Writers and other organizations that rejected or questioned our legitimacy.

We sent copies of the issue to the board members of Poets & Writers and to those we could pinpoint that had something to do with putting the directory together.

I can't say for sure that the letter-writing campaign or the issue, and the copies we sent to the powers that be at the directory, made a difference. But the following year creative nonfiction writers were quietly included. There was no fanfare or official announcement. But if you were Brenda Miller or any other creative nonfictionist who applied, you could then be listed. If you look at the Poets & Writers website today, you will see that its mission has been amended: "Poets & Writers, Inc. is one of the largest nonprofit literary organizations in the United States serving poets, fiction writers, and creative nonfiction writers."

As I look back, I think that was pretty much the last major bastion of resistance. There were certainly issues and ideas that would be objected to about the genre and endlessly debated, but with Poets & Writers in the fold, maybe grudgingly, the battle was pretty much over with. Although *Creative Nonfiction* would continue to defend or clarify the genre whenever it seemed to be necessary.

We made a special effort, in 2005, soon after the James Frey–Oprah Winfrey scandal. Our issue, "A Million Little Choices: The ABCs of CNF," helped to explain the anchoring elements of the genre and, as we put it then, "everything you need to know to avoid the James Frey jinx." Frey's career, from that point, was pretty much in tatters. We wanted to make it clear that Frey was not writing creative nonfiction; that he was, quite simply, a fraud. *A Million Little Choices: The ABCs of CNF* was soon published as a book by W.W. Norton.

We published seven more issues over the next two years with various themes, including "Anatomy of Baseball" and "Mexican Voices," and an especially intriguing issue that has always been one of my favorites, "Imagining the Future — From the outlandish to the pragmatic — what's to come?" In it, we asked various writers and publishers to look forward and predict how literature and the business of writing would change by 2025, fifteen years in the future.

As I look back over all of the issues we published, this one is the most fun to reread. So many ideas that have not and will probably never come true — at least not yet — and wild and crazy nonetheless.

Heidi Julavits, a novelist and former editor of *The Believer,* foresaw a single, worldwide literary empire, owned by Exxon Mobil, offering a list of seven books twice per year — with blurbs supplied by eBay sellers with the highest approval ratings. "This," she wrote with assurance, "we all know, is the inevitable future."[4]

Phillip Lopate predicted a period of rapid, if somewhat primitive, experimentation. "The floating book developed in response to the rising water-levels at our coasts. The impulse book, which could be tossed in the river at completion without environmental damage, and the book-lozenge, which dissolved novella-sized works on the tongue, and the book-shot, devised for cultivated diabetics who requested a literary dose with their daily injections."[5]

Robin Hemley, the director of Iowa's nonfiction program, offered a list of terrific predictions, including the idea that books would be "printed on a tasty compound known as book jerky that can be eaten after reading. Teriyaki will be the most widely read flavor." But he saved the best for last, a rather frightening idea, which in a way hits home today. At the very least, it will make you smile and, at the same time, shudder at the possibility:

"Donald Trump, at the age of seventy-nine, will become the Greatest Love Poet Who Ever Lived after publishing a book of Petrarchan sonnets titled 'Trump!'"[6]

In 2009, the journal went on hiatus, emerging the following year as a literary magazine. No more traditional journal. This to expand the content with craft pieces and commentary, reflecting — or keeping up with — the growth and maturation of the genre. The magazine has had a couple of facelifts since then, and two major built-from-the-ground-up websites. And we're publishing quarterly, usually more or less on time. There's now a second magazine, *True Story*, pocket-sized, featuring one long-form essay, seven thousand words or more, delivered monthly by mail.

Unlike the journal, I did not go on hiatus, but I recognized that the time had come for me to imagine or reimagine my own future.

What I realized was that there was no more buzz, no more talk about how this creative nonfiction thing was evolving and might someday lead to something substantial — or might flame out. No more debates — about its existence or legitimacy. No more resistance, even to the name. Writers might prefer not to be called creative nonfictionists, editors and publishers might label what they were publishing essay or literary nonfiction or narrative nonfiction or just plain nonfiction, whatever word choice might suit their purposes and taste, but it was pretty clear that the label didn't matter anymore. It was all, in one way or another, creative nonfiction.

There were certainly debates about how one might write creative nonfiction. The line between fact and fiction, the limits of imagination, the mix of poetry and prose, and much more, but as I had told Carolyn Hughes, the boundaries of the genre would be determined by those who write it. Whatever the caveats, creative nonfiction was no longer something that might be coming. That optimistic and hopeful buzz had disappeared. We were there. We had made it. We were part of the literary ecosystem, a major and continually evolving and influential force, whether one liked it or not.

I am not sure I was aware this was happening while it was happening because it all played out kind of gradually. First there were mentions and references to creative nonfiction in publications that appealed to writers. *Poets & Writers*, no longer doubting and criticizing, was featuring informative essays about the genre and interviews of creative nonfiction writers, as was *The Writer's Chronicle*, the quarterly publication of AWP. *Writer's Digest* and *The Writer,* two magazines that appealed to a writer audience outside the academy, were giving subscribers marketing tips about submitting creative nonfiction to interested and open-to-the-genre publications. There were many of those now, especially literary journals that not long before had no interest. More jobs were available at universities and even some high schools were buying in, introducing the genre to students. More sessions at the annual AWP. And other countries were beginning to acknowledge it. Australia and New Zealand were giving it a big push. Australia became one of our theme issues, and there would be a creative nonfiction day as part of the Melbourne Festival of Books, in which the magazine was featured.

At some point, I had set up a Google alert for creative nonfiction and every day I received links about what was happening, events, awards, courses related to creative nonfiction, publications seeking submissions – mostly stuff I knew nothing about. It kept coming.

Ten years before, I was so damn delighted and excited at the mere mention of creative nonfiction – and now it was nearly commonplace. Nothing new or controversial about it anymore. Or not a lot.

In a way, I felt kind of weird about this. I had not foreseen this acceptance and growth. I think I was so involved with defending the ongoing attacks on the genre, and then my barnstorming here and there talking up the genre, and then the launch of *Creative Nonfiction,* and keeping it going, issue after issue, that it never really occurred to me, or rather I had not given much thought to when or what might happen when the goal was finally achieved. I had never thought much about goals or end points. My life was always, to me, very immediate. The next issue. The next book. The next motorcycle.

But I began wondering what my own personal next would be – or if there was to be a next. Creative nonfiction was so ubiquitous now, especially in the academy, that a "fist-fighter" wasn't needed anymore. There was no one left to fight with.

EPILOGUE

Creative nonfiction had legs way beyond English departments and creative writing programs. That's what I thought when I left Pitt in 2008 and became a writer in residence and professor at Arizona State University. Not in another English department or creative writing program, but in a science policy think tank with a mouthful of a name: the Consortium for Science, Policy and Outcomes (CSPO, referred to on campus as "Seespo").

What was I, an outsider writer with scant education, supposed to do in a think tank? What was a think tank, anyway? I had obviously heard the term before, as we all have, and I imagined a bunch of old bald-headed men sitting at a conference table, staring at one another or alone in their offices looking out into space and . . . what else? Thinking. Or sleeping sitting up.

Which was, as unlikely as it seemed for someone like me, exactly what I was supposed to do at CSPO — think. Think about how I could introduce creative nonfiction to people in other disciplines in or out of the academy — especially those engaged in science policy. And convince these wonky people that the techniques of creative nonfiction were important to learn.

What is science policy? I still don't know exactly, even after being part of CSPO for fifteen years. It is kind of an amorphous term, can be stretched in many different directions, making it difficult to pin down and define. Not unlike

---

253

creative nonfiction. Basically it means that policy wonks, in one way or the other, investigate what is happening in various fields of science and technology, assess value, potential, and drawbacks, and sometimes provide recommendations for change or compose predictions of the future in scenario form.

Complicated, vague, foggy? Yes. But challenging. This, I thought, was my next.

After all, the genre had been accepted. The journal was now a magazine, and the CNF Foundation was growing and healthy, and I needed and wanted something else, another immersion, to keep me going. I was at the time sixty-four years old. My motorcycle days were long past, but that didn't mean that I couldn't go varooming off on a new and different road. In many ways, a more important road than the one I had left behind.

The country — the world — had gone through amazing and unpredictable changes since Tom Wolfe's new journalism proclamation in 1972. Few could have imagined, certainly not I, the internet, e-mail, Twitter, Google, the iPhone, the revolutionary advances in science and medicine. Nothing is quite the same as before — whatever before means to you. We are living today — as we were in 2008 — in a world that is growing day by day less personal, less interactive, and more demanding. Instead of sitting on the porch talking to our neighbors or sharing lunch with colleagues, we are instead alone in our offices and bedrooms, hunched over computers or thumbing frantically and incessantly on our smartphones. This was especially apparent and troubling during our pandemic hibernation. With each passing year, there is so much more information, so much world-changing, eye-opening, super-complicated stuff for people to understand and make sense of and try to accept.

By "people," I mean in this context general readers, like you and me, literate, interested — those very people impacted by scientific and technological advances of all sorts, but pretty much in the dark about how they work or what they might mean. The challenge, and in many ways the mission of the nonfiction writer today, as it was in 2008 when I joined CSPO, is to bridge the gap between those in the know — experts, scientists, engineers, etc. — and, let's call us, "consumers," who want to know or should know how innovation, whatever the direction and iteration, will affect them.

We nonfictionists are well prepared to be the bridges that can make a dif-

---

ference. We can write humorous stories, poetic stories, or stories and approaches straight out of the Tom Wolfe new journalism playbook. The methods, the way we touch and connect with our readers, are up to us and are in fact—with this flexibility—the challenges and rewards that make our genre so exciting and satisfying. I am not excluding memoir here. To the contrary. Why would we write a memoir without a message? Without it being meant to be life-changing and eye-opening? What would be the point?

I don't mean that all creative nonfiction writers are required to have a big idea mission while writing their books and essays. But all creative nonfictionists in our own way understand the power and the importance of writing real life stories, even if sometimes those stories are exaggerated, or embellished or manipulated, hopefully for good reason. And we could, if we wanted to, employ what we know to inform, clarify, evaluate, or dispute the flood of ideas and information and the personal life challenges that we are all confronted with and confounded by every day.

This feeling of a mission for creative nonfictionists wasn't something I had just thought up overnight. My books, all narrative, after the ones about baseball umpires and profiles of backwoods folks like Caulkey and McCool, had been about, generally speaking, health care and technology, which was one reason the CSPO folks found me interesting. I had tackled big subjects, like the world of organ transplantation, for which I had lived side by side for four years with heart, liver, and heart-lung candidates and recipients and their families, scrubbed with surgeons, jetted through the night on organ donor harvests, and watched and reported, sometimes with joy and too often with dismay, as those who I had come to know lived or died—or, worse, often existed somewhere in between.

In other books I dug deep into the inner workings of a pediatric hospital. And in another, I captured the frustration and total helplessness of parents of children suffering from mental illness, the dysfunction of the system that had supposedly been designed to help them. I wrote about veterinarians from various perspectives, treating lions and elephants in a zoo, cattle and sheep on a farm, remarkable feats of surgery in a specialized hospital for valuable thoroughbred horses, all the while marveling at the veterinarians' passion and tenderness for the animals they treated and wishing that such sensitivity could be equaled by physicians treating their patients—people like us. I devoted, off and on, six

———

years inside a robotics institute trying to understand and communicate to my readers how these folks, programmers and engineers, worked, and how through writing code they made the creatures they built, out of scraps of metal, plastic, and duct tape, think and act — sometimes more appropriately than humans.

These books were time-consuming and brain-wracking as I labored to turn complicated issues and ideas into stories that the general public would find compelling enough to read, even if the subject wasn't at first of interest to them, and in the process of reading, learn and understand. All my time and patience had been more than worthwhile. I am not talking about reviews or royalties; I am referring to the feedback — the responses — from those affected by the issues I had confronted in these books. Parents in the case of pediatrics and child mental illness, and the families of those undergoing organ transplantation, especially. I hear from my readers often, even though most of these books were published decades ago, with appreciation for what they learned from what I wrote and for the care I took in telling their stories and explaining and dramatizing their journeys. The surgeons whose lives I documented in and out of the operating arena, an atmosphere that often resembled bloody combat, have also been appreciative. Even now, I am asked to give talks at medical gatherings, not about writing, but to share my reflections about the worlds of which I wrote.

My deep dives into these arenas were helpful, not only because I was writing clearly and concisely — okay, that was part of it — but more because I had made the information accessible to them through stories to which they could relate. In my small way — these books were not *New York Times* best sellers — I was doing what all writers, all artists, hope in their hearts their work will do: make a difference in one way or the other, have an impact, cause a change of heart or mind for those who might read them. I was certainly not making a difference like Rachel Carson or Upton Sinclair, but if I helped or impacted the lives of only a few people, that was good enough for me.

I am writing about this with the perspective of someone who has taught in a creative writing program for nearly thirty-five years. The struggle over the acceptance of creative nonfiction and new journalism was more than worthwhile. I feel now, well, maybe not triumphant, but satisfied and fulfilled. But I often thought, as the need for active verbal combat diminished and the genre I

—

championed became an equal and self-sustaining part of the literary ecosystem, that we were not thinking enough about the potential — the world-changing work we creative nonfictionists were doing. Or, more to the point, could be doing.

The courses we offered — more and more each year as the programs grew — focused primarily on style. How to write. Rather than why to write. In some ways, this is very selfish and self-centered. But I guess that's just the way writers are and need to be, focusing day and night, obsessively writing and rewriting sentences, paragraphs, or deleting half-written essays or chapters just because they didn't sound right or read right or were criticized by others in workshops or by our teachers and friends. This was the way I taught for many years, preaching style and structure and the Wolfe and Talese dogma — dialogue, description, scenes. A narrative arc; a beginning and an ending that connect. All well and good. But what about meaning and message? It took me a while to get it, to recognize, mostly because of the feedback from those books I have mentioned, the great potential of our genre and the possibility of precipitating change with our work — if we cared to, if it was part of our creative DNA.

The CSPO folks — the thinkers in the think tank — were in the process of trying to do just that, to enhance understanding and precipitate change. They were writing academic papers and convening meetings (what they often called "congresses," a meaty, more official-sounding word) focusing on, as a few examples, "Social and Ethical Implications of Research," or "The Rightful Place of Science — how we can best deal with the perpetually unfolding implications of our own ingenuity." They called this responsible innovation. One project that I became involved with in 2013 was called "The Future of Truth," very relevant then, but it would have been crucial in today's era of the Big Lie. If anyone would have paid attention.

I had thought that I knew more than a little about raising money for the work of *Creative Nonfiction* through our theme issues and my belief that there were people or institutions eager to share or donate if a project seemed worthwhile. I learned at CSPO how to think big, even if it was not completely about science or technology, but about the way science and literature could be part of the same bigger-world picture. How one could not exist in the world without the other. In my fifteen years at CSPO I was able to raise, with the help of my colleagues, nearly $1.5 million for projects related to creative nonfiction, demonstrating how using the techniques of creative nonfiction could be the essential bridge between innovation in all forms and the general public.

I also thought then—or hoped—that I could help make a path for the host of graduate students emerging from creative nonfiction writing programs—MFAs, after receiving their precious piece of paper and overloaded with debt, were suddenly, in many ways, on their own—in science and technology or whatever other discipline that was relevant. That science and health care, with dramatic real-life stories that mattered, could provide a tempting and viable option to them. I couldn't forget Diane Ackerman's plea to poets and fiction writers to consider writing nonfiction, not necessarily as a commitment and career move, but just as a way of learning new ways of writing and continuing to be productive. Maybe they'd find comfort and satisfaction venturing into creative nonfiction, she said, as many adventurous poets and fiction writers have done since. Or maybe nonfiction would sustain them until they found themselves and their voices as poets or novelists.

Or maybe even because of all they had read and studied and experimented with, they would create other ways to write, or define nonfiction—or enhance nonfiction. As I write this now, a catalogue of creative nonfiction offshoots, hybrid forms, have become a growing part of the genre. If creative nonfiction was difficult to explain or delineate a few decades ago, then what about "speculative nonfiction," or "auto(biographical) fiction" or "imaginary nonfiction"? The lyric essay, which I had thought in 1997 was quite a far reach, seems old hat today compared with these spinoffs that have emerged under the creative nonfiction umbrella. There are also new essay forms—not really new, but newly labeled and explained—like the "braided essay" (when an essay has various threads of narrative and substance, often seemingly unrelated, but eventually connected or braided together), the "hermit crab essay" (essays that merge the materials of life, like vacuum cleaner manuals or recipes, into a narrative), and the short and sweet "flash essay." We've gone way beyond the imaginative essay circa 1985 at AWP. Even wearing my editor's hat at *Creative Nonfiction,* as the submissions came pouring in, I couldn't keep up with what was happening and changing in the genre. I thought and marveled, to put it in a Tom Wolfe way: "WHATTTTTT @#$ IN THE HELLLL— —LLLLL—*&^% IS GOING ON!!!!?"

EPILOGUE

———

While at CSPO, I wrote a proposal along with colleagues to the National Science Foundation and received support for the launch of an international program bringing creative nonfiction writers and science policy wonks together to collaborate and teach one another what they knew. The program was called "Think Write Publish." The wonks taught the writers how they researched, investigated, and analyzed data and designed and fashioned predictions and policy for the future, while the writers showed the "thinkers" how to transform their ideas and research processes into story. Most of the writers participating were either working toward an MFA at various universities or had recently earned their MFA degrees. Think Write Publish had larger and more expanded iterations over the years, most recently bringing together writers and scholars to write creative nonfiction about the intersection between science and religion. The fellows selected for these programs—we had seven hundred applications for twelve fellowships in science and religion—who came from as far away as Afghanistan, were to eventually publish books and articles, which led to TV and radio interviews and appearances and featured speaking engagements at prestigious conferences and teaching positions, exactly the way in which universities establish and gauge influence and prominence.

Teaching these folks the creative nonfiction way of writing was an entirely different experience and challenge. Scientists, engineers, policy makers, took in information and ideas differently; in a creative writing class you might give your students something to read—and then in the following class you would sit around and discuss the way the writer wrote whatever had been assigned. This would go on for an entire fourteen-week semester, as structure and technique were covered, and gradually, if you were lucky, students would see the light you were attempting to shine for them.

I realized early on that this slow but steady process would not work for scientists, engineers, and policy people; they wanted information and they wanted it quickly; they were, rightly so, obsessed by the substance and the missions of their work. So I modified my teaching approach, first to the way in which scientists were accustomed to learning by using slides—PowerPoint—and meticulously deconstructing essays and articles so they could see exactly what writers

———

were doing and, in a sense, duplicate or use these techniques as guideposts for their own work. I know, you don't have to tell me, this was not the "literary way." But I found myself in a new and different world and I needed to adjust and rethink my approach to be effective and successful. If you think about it, creative nonfiction, as it evolved, also required a certain adjustment of attitude and approach, a rethinking of many basic ideas and practices, without which it might not have gained traction.

As time passed, I came to realize that *Creative Nonfiction*, and the foundation, were also more than ready for an adjustment of approach – and a successor for me. After twenty-eight years, it was time for change, I thought, and time for me to move on. A local arts foundation generously funded a nonprofit arts consultant to take a deep and intense dive into the entire organization, assessing the ways in which CNF functioned – staff, technology, marketing, leadership – all aspects. This was a challenging task – an assignment that would require many months of study and evaluation. The consultant was to eventually provide a series of recommendations to the board and for my successor – whoever that might be – to use as a road map, as he or she might choose, to expand the organization or, another possible direction, significantly limit its scope. This assessment is still in progress and has already precipitated a number of changes, many wholly unexpected. I intend to hang in and continue serving as editor and founder until the process, however long it takes, is completed.

I was also hanging in – or hanging on – to my hometown, despite my many complaints about the city and its limitations. It wasn't that I didn't like Arizona – or, later, when CSPO established an office in Washington, D.C., that I didn't enjoy my time in the capital – it was, rather, that I couldn't quite escape my Pittsburgh roots. I couldn't forget the towering and distinctive Cathedral of Learning, the CL, and what my years there had meant to me. Being part of CSPO's open and freewheeling atmosphere, I was able to consolidate my classes and – as impractical as it might seem, given the two thousand miles between Tempe and Pittsburgh – to commute.

Each time I returned to the city, I would make a point, first thing, often on the way home from the airport after touching down, to drive by the CL, even though it was somewhat out of the way from where I lived. It was also the first marker on my daily route, during my running days, before my back gave out.

The CL was where my creative nonfiction journey had started, and I never imagined or considered, despite all of the unpleasant confrontations that had taken place, that I would ever leave it. I always assumed, especially after tenure, that I would end my career there, where it all had started. But that hadn't worked out.

The funny thing is, as important as it was to me — literally and symbolically — I have only twice entered the CL in all those years since I joined ASU, both times for interviews for this book. I had, I admit, never been invited back to give a talk or reading; maybe there were still people around who were pissed off at me. I did notice, on those two occasions, though, that I was there — remembered — at least symbolically. The walls of the office wing on the fifth and sixth floors where the English department was still located, and where I had conducted those two interviews, were lined with framed posters of the writers' conferences I had put together in the 1980s.

Some remodeling had taken place over the years in the CL, but not a lot had changed. The nationality rooms were still used for classes; the Tuck Shop where I met in the evenings with my outsider nontraditional student friends was now a Chick-fil-A. I even remembered where the men's rooms were located.

It was this familiarity, this feeling of being home again along with the realization that this could never again be my home, that was quite unsettling. When I got back to my house after that second visit, I looked up the writing program faculty. I recognized some of the names, but there were only three people I knew out of dozens listed, one of whom I had interviewed. I don't want to sound maudlin here. I don't mean it that way. But it was like, weirdly, being dead and looking down at a world in which I had belonged but could no longer be a part of.

I had a similar feeling not long ago when I attended, via Zoom, the 2021 NonfictioNOW conference, which took place in New Zealand. NonfictioNOW was founded by Robin Hemley, that guy who had predicted Donald Trump's Petrarchan love sonnet collection for our "Imaging the Future" issue. The first NonfictioNOW took place at the University of Iowa in 2005, where he was then director of the nonfiction program. Hemley had since done his own barnstorming for the genre, internationally, as I had done decades before, encouraging many universities to discover nonfiction and offer courses to their students, as in Singapore, Australia, and Reykjavik, Iceland. Scanning through the program, I couldn't help thinking back to that first creative nonfiction conference I had put together at Goucher College in 1996.

You will recall that we only had a hundred people there in Towson, Maryland—compared with six hundred in New Zealand. Who would have imagined then—New Zealand? And those who came to Towson and participated were mostly beginners and not part of the academy. Just folks who had heard about creative nonfiction and wanted to learn more about it. They oohed and aahed at the sight of our special guests, as if they were celebrities and dignitaries, and I guess, to us, they were. I still remember how the discovery that Joyce Carol Oates wore sneakers had been such a surprise—she was like us! And Plimpton with an ascot? At a three-star Holiday Inn? There were workshops at Goucher, mostly for beginners, and at least two panels and a reading every day.

There were no workshops at NonfictioNOW, I noticed—no opportunity for those just starting out and exploring the genre. But there were dozens of panels with three or four speakers that focused on many issues and ideas that would have been impossible to imagine in 1996. Topics like "Synergy and Conversation Between Essaying and Performance," "Breakthrough Forms Forge New Social Structures," "How Do the Dead Speak?" and one that I really appreciated, "Yoga and Creative Nonfiction." I had, in fact, a few years before this, conducted a yoga and creative nonfiction weeklong workshop in Costa Rica.

But once again, as I scanned the program, most of the participants, obviously and evidently changemakers in the genre today, were unknown to me. I recognized a few names, two of whom had been participants in the programs I had put together at CSPO. The other? My old *Poets & Writers* friend, Brenda Miller. Some of the panels had been recorded and saved in video and I clicked on Brenda's, titled "Writing the Book on Creative Nonfiction," and I was surprised and amused at how she introduced herself in relation to creative nonfiction, as a "relic" from the past. If Brenda was a "relic," I thought, then what the hell was I?

Not that my space or distance from the genre made me sad or depressed. To the contrary; it was quite uplifting, although, I admit, a bit baffling. As I have said, I had no idea what would happen to the genre as the resistance and infighting were going on. I didn't give a lot of thought to how it would all play out.

———

EPILOGUE

I could have never predicted, as I labored to establish the first creative nonfiction MFA at Pitt, that there would, as of today, to my best count, be 226 MFA creative nonfiction programs and thirty-five Ph.D. programs across the world. But the numbers don't lie.

It had been fifty years since Tom Wolfe published his proclamation. And that was just about the same time I had started out at the CL, looking for direction and inspiration, creative nonfiction not even a glimmer in my mind. Not bad, I thought, looking back, for a barely educated motorcycle rebel who had wanted to be a writer and had no idea what in the hell to do about it or how to do it — except to read a lot of books and to close my eyes, jump in, put up my fists — and fight.

ACKNOWLEDGMENTS

Sarah Geren, my graduate research assistant at CSPO and Arizona State University's School for the Future of Innovation in Society, was a master researcher, thorough and persistent. Because of Sarah, I still have, remaining and unused, enough ideas and information to write at least one more book about the evolution of the creative nonfiction genre. Maybe even two.

Deborah S. Falik, working with Sarah's research, combined with her own efforts and resources at the New York Public Library, was a diligent and inexhaustible fact-checker. Jodi Tamewitz came to my rescue and formatted this book, a daunting task for which I was totally unprepared.

I have written many drafts of this book over the past four years — too many. Anne Horowitz responded to many of the drafts with gentle criticism and invaluable ideas and suggestions.

At some point in the writing process, feeling lost and insecure about my work, Dan Sarewitz, my former colleague at Arizona State, and Dinty W. Moore, my former student, were reassuring and calming readers.

At home, Michele Pasula, Patricia Park, and my son Sam Gutkind patiently endured my many moods as I fought through all of the ups and downs of my manuscript.

I very much appreciate how Jennifer Banks, my editor at Yale University

ACKNOWLEDGMENTS

Press, guided me through the many revisions of the book. Jennifer was always responsive to my seemingly unending questions. Phillip King, my manuscript editor, never missed a comma, a "faulty" fact, or an observation or phrase that didn't read right. Yale University Press was patient with me, allowing numerous contract extensions.

A number of great writers and editors, many of whom are featured in this book, gave their time and provided invaluable insight. This is a single-author book, but without their support and wisdom I could not have told the amazing story of the genre's chaotic evolution.

NOTES

INTRODUCTION

1. Bentley Rumble, "The Write Advice 078: Larry McMurtry," Bentley Rumble/Cumquat Productions, March 11, 2016, https://bentleyrumble.blogspot.com/2016/03/writers-on -writing-78-larry-mcmurtry.html.

2. James Wolcott, "Me, Myself, and I," *Vanity Fair,* October 1997, https://archive.vanity fair.com/article/1997/10/me-myself-and-i.

CHAPTER 1. WHO MADE THIS NAME UP?

1. Wolcott, "Me, Myself, and I."

2. Carolyn T. Hughes, "Term Limits: The Creative Nonfiction Debate," *Poets & Writers,* May–June 2003, https://www.pw.org/content/mayjune_2003.

3. John W. Miller, "What Would Barbara Tuchman Say?" *Moundsville: PBS Film & Magazine,* March 7, 2019, https://moundsville.org/2019/03/07/what-would-barbara-tuchman -say.

4. William Bradley, "Putting the 'Creative' in Non-Fiction," *Creative Nonfiction,* Creative Nonfiction Foundation, Issue 50 (2015), https://creativenonfiction.org/writing/putting -the-creative-in-nonfiction.

5. Bradley, "Putting the 'Creative' in Non-Fiction."

6. Terry Teachout, *Duke: A Life of Duke Ellington* (New York: Avery, 2013), 244.

7. John Rockwell, "Charles Mingus Dies at 56," *New York Times,* January 1, 1979, https://

www.nytimes.com/1979/01/09/archives/charles-mingus-56-bass-player-bandleader-and
-composer-dead-an.html.

CHAPTER 2. THE CHANGEMAKERS

1. Tom Wolfe, "The Birth of 'The New Journalism'; Eyewitness Report by Tom Wolfe," *New York,* May 27, 2008, https://nymag.com/news/media/47353.

2. Wolfe, "The Birth of 'The New Journalism.'"

3. Gay Talese, "Joe Louis: The King as a Middle-Aged Man," *Esquire,* June 1, 1962, https://classic.esquire.com/article/1962/6/1/joe-louis-the-king-as-a-middle-aged-man.

4. Wolfe, "The Birth of 'The New Journalism.'"

5. Gay Talese, *Fame and Obscurity* (Cleveland: World, 1970), Author's Note, ix.

6. Barbara Lounsberry, "Gay Talese and the Fine Art of Hanging Out" (2000), *Creative Nonfiction,* Creative Nonfiction Foundation, Issue 16, https://creativenonfiction.org/writing /gay-talese-and-the-fine-art-of-hanging-out.

7. Carol Polsgrove, *It Wasn't Pretty, Folks, But Didn't We Have Fun? Esquire in the Sixties* (New York: W.W. Norton, 1995).

8. Talese, *Fame and Obscurity,* ix.

9. Gay Talese, "Frank Sinatra Has a Cold," *Esquire,* April 1966 (reprinted, May 14, 2016), 1–26, https://www.esquire.com/news-politics/a638/frank-sinatra-has-a-cold-gay -talese.

10. Lily Rothman, "Why Tom Wolfe First Started Wearing His Signature White Suit," *Time,* May 15, 2018, https://time.com/5278215/tom-wolfe-white-suits.

11. Ray Gustini, "Gay Talese's Back Seat Is Too Small for Necking," *The Atlantic,* August 11, 2011, https://www.theatlantic.com/culture/archive/2011/08/gay-taleses-back-seat -too-small-necking/354035.

12. Rothman, "Why Tom Wolfe First Started Wearing His Signature White Suit."

13. Tom Wolfe, *The Kandy-Kolored Tangerine-Flake Streamline Baby* (New York: Picador, 2009; originally published by Farrar, Straus and Giroux, 1965), 76.

14. Wolfe, *The Kandy-Kolored Tangerine-Flake Streamline Baby,* 78.

15. Kurt Vonnegut, Jr., "Infarcted Tabescent!" *New York Times,* June 27, 1965, https:// archive.nytimes.com/www.nytimes.com/books/97/09/28/lifetimes/vonnegut-wolfe.html.

16. Timothy Foote, "Books: Fish in the Brandy Snifter," *Time,* December 21, 1970, https://content.time.com/time/subscriber/article/0,33009,904627,00.html.

CHAPTER 3. THE FIRST CREATIVE NONFICTIONISTS

1. Dwight Macdonald, "Parajournalism II: Tom Wolfe and The New Yorker," *New York Review of Books,* February 3, 1966, https://www.nybooks.com/articles/1966/02/03 /parajournalism-ii-wolfe-and-the-new-yorker.

2. Nicholson Baker, "The Greatest Liar," *Columbia Journalism Review,* July–August 2009, https://archives.cjr.org/second_read/the_greatest_liar_1.php?mod=djembooks.

3. Baker, "The Greatest Liar."

4. Orhan Pamuk, "What the Great Pandemic Novels Teach Us," *New York Times,* April 23, 2020, https://www.nytimes.com/2020/04/23/opinion/sunday/coronavirus-orhan -pamuk.html.

5. Michael Dirda, "'We Revel in a Crowd of Any Kind': Dickens the Journalist," *BN Review,* Barnes & Noble, February 7, 2012, https://www.barnesandnoble.com/blog/we -revel-in-a-crowd-of-any-kind-dickens-the-journalist.

6. Richard Russo, introduction to *Collected Nonfiction,* volume 2, by Mark Twain (New York: Alfred A. Knopf, 2016), ix.

7. Joseph Redgwell, "Jack London's Journey into the Abyss," *The Guardian,* October 5, 2007, https://www.theguardian.com/books/booksblog/2007/oct/05/jacklondons journeyintothe.

8. Christopher Phelps, "*The Jungle* at 100," *Solidarity,* Marxist.org, ATC 115, March–April 2005, https://www.marxists.org/history/etol/newspape/atc/294.html.

9. Phelps, "*The Jungle* at 100."

10. Karen Olsson, "Welcome to The Jungle," *Slate,* July 7, 2006, https://slate.com /culture/2006/07/upton-sinclair-s-the-jungle.html.

11. Vanessa Thorpe, "Orwell's Take on Destination, Live from Paris and London," *The Guardian,* April 28, 2018, https://www.theguardian.com/books/2018/apr/28/george -orwell-down-out-london-paris-live-performance.

12. Danny Heitman, "The Talented Mr. Huxley," *Humanities,* National Endowment for the Humanities, vol. 36, no. 6 (November–December 2015), https://www.neh.gov /humanities/2015/novemberdecember/feature/the-talented-mr-huxley.

13. Clive James, "Aldous Huxley, Short of Sight," *New Yorker,* March 9, 2003, https:// www.newyorker.com/magazine/2003/03/17/aldous-huxley-short-of-sight.

14. Heitman, "The Talented Mr. Huxley."

15. Henry Raymont, "11 Hemingway Stories 'Cub' to 'Giant,'" *New York Times,* April 7, 1970, 47, https://www.nytimes.com/1970/04/07/archives/11-hemingway-stories-cub -to-giant.html.

16. William White, ed. *By-Line: Ernest Hemingway; Selected Articles and Dispatches of Four Decades* (New York: Charles Scribner & Sons, 1967), xi.

17. White, ed., *By-Line,* xi–xiii.

18. Lillian Ross, "Profiles: How Do You Like It Now, Gentlemen? The Moods of Ernest Hemingway," *New Yorker,* May 5, 1950, 36–62, https://www.newyorker.com/magazine /1950/05/13/how-do-you-like-it-now-gentlemen.

19. Steve Newman Writer, "Portrait of Hemingway – Lillian Ross," *stevenewmanwriter*

.medium.com, May 25, 2021, https://stevenewmanwriter.medium.com/portrait-of-hemingway
-lillian-ross-f2ceaa29b68d.

20. Paul Alexander, "The Talk of the Town," *New York* magazine, April 27, 1998, https://
nymag.com/nymetro/arts/features/2553.

21. Ross, "Profiles: How Do You Like It Now, Gentlemen?"

22. Newman Writer, "Portrait of Hemingway — Lillian Ross."

23. Michael Rosenwald, "Ringing Up Lillian Ross," *Columbia Journalism Review,* November 4, 2015, https://www.cjr.org/first_person/ringing_up_lillian_ross.php.

24. Nicholas Lemann, "John Hersey and the Art of Fact," *New Yorker,* April 22, 2019,
https://www.newyorker.com/magazine/2019/04/29/john-hersey-and-the-art-of-fact.

25. Maria Popova, "Undersea: Rachel Carson's Lyrical and Revolutionary 1937 Masterpiece Inviting Humans to Explore Earth from the Perspective of Other Creatures," *The Marginalian,* February 28, 2017, https://www.themarginalian.org/2017/02/28/undersea
-rachel-carson.

26. Rachel Carson, "A Fable for Tomorrow," *Silent Spring* (Boston: Houghton Mifflin,
1962; Connecticut: Fawcett Publications, 1964), 1–4.

27. Carson, "A Fable for Tomorrow."

28. Carson, "A Fable for Tomorrow."

29. Debra Michals, ed., "Rachel Carson," *Women's History,* National Women's History
Museum, 2015, https://www.womenshistory.org/education-resources/biographies/rachel
-carson.

30. Jill Lepore, "The Right Way to Remember Rachel Carson," *New Yorker,* March 19,
2018, https://www.newyorker.com/magazine/2018/03/26/the-right-way-to-remember
-rachel-carson.

CHAPTER 4. A STATUE OF A WOMAN IN THE
PITTSBURGH AIRPORT AND ALL SHE REPRESENTS

1. Gail Sheehy, "What Tom Wolfe Taught Me About Reporting," *New York* magazine,
May 18, 2018, https://www.thecut.com/2018/05/gail-sheehy-on-what-tom-wolfe-taught
-her-about-reporting.html.

2. Harriet Baskas, "Statue of Famed Journalist and Traveler, Nellie Bly, Lands at PIT,"
Runway Girl Network, May 2022, https://runwaygirlnetwork.com/2022/05/statue-nellie
-bly-pit-airport.

3. Editors of Encyclopedia Britannica, "Nellie Bly, American Journalist," *Encyclopedia
Britannica,* accessed November 2020, https://www.britannica.com/biography/Nellie-Bly.

4. Maris Fessenden, "Nellie Bly's Record-Breaking Trip Around the World Was, to Her
Surprise, a Race," *Smithsonian Magazine,* January 25, 2016, https://www.smithsonianmag
.com/smart-news/nellie-blys-record-breaking-trip-around-world-was-to-her-surprise
-race-180957910.

5. Ellen Mahoney, "Nellie Bly: A Race Against Time," *Western Pennsylvania History Magazine,* Heinz History Center, January 24, 2018, https://www.heinzhistorycenter.org/blog /western-pennsylvania-history-nellie-bly-a-race-against-time.

6. Barbara Maranzani, "Inside Nellie Bly's 10 Days in a Madhouse," *Biography,* November 12, 2020, https://www.biography.com/news/inside-nelly-bly-10-days-madhouse.

7. Nellie Bly, "Ten Days in a Mad-House: Published with Miscellaneous Sketches. . . ." (New York: Ian L. Munro, 1877), 48, https://digital.library.upenn.edu/women/bly/mad house/madhouse.html.

8. Bly, "Ten Days in a Mad-House."

9. Annie Laurie, "A City's Disgrace," *San Francisco Examiner,* January 19, 1890, https:// undercover.hosting.nyu.edu/s/undercover-reporting/item/13090.

10. Barbara Morgan, "Black, Winifred Sweet, American Reporter Whose Versatile Reporting Helped Build William Randolph Hearst," *Encyclopedia.com,* accessed November 2020, https://www.encyclopedia.com/women/encyclopedias-almanacs-transcripts-and -maps/black-winifred-sweet-1863-1936.

11. Kim Todd, "These Women Reporters Went Undercover to Get the Most Important Scoops of Their Day," *Smithsonian Magazine,* November 2016, https://www.smithsonian mag.com/history/women-reporters-undercover-most-important-scoops-day-180960775.

12. Erin Blakemore, "The 'Sob Sisters' Who Dared to Cover the Trial of the Century," JSTOR Daily, November 10, 2017, https://daily.jstor.org/the-sob-sisters-who-dared -to-cover-the-trial-of-the-century.

13. Gilbert King, "The Woman Who Took on the Tycoon," July 5, 2012, https://www .smithsonianmag.com/history/the-woman-who-took-on-the-tycoon-651396.

14. Liza Mundy, "The Woman Who Made Modern Journalism," *The Atlantic,* January–February 2020, https://www.theatlantic.com/magazine/archive/2020/01/review-stephanie -gorton-citizen-reporters/603055.

15. The New York Public Library, "Only the Shells Whine," New York Public Library Digital Collections, accessed January 5, 2023, https://digitalcollections.nypl.org/items /c2724c7c-9e09-596e-e040-e00a180661ef.

16. Nicholas Gilmore, "The Female War Correspondent Who Sneaked into D-Day," *Saturday Evening Post,* November 8, 2018, https://www.saturdayeveningpost.com/2018/11 /the-female-war-correspondent-who-sneaked-into-d-day.

CHAPTER 5. WHAT WHITE PUBLISHERS WON'T PRINT

1. Marvel Cooke, "The Bronx Slave Market (1950)," *Viewpoint Magazine,* October 31, 2015, https://viewpointmag.com/2015/10/31/the-bronx-slave-market-1950.

2. Cooke, "The Bronx Slave Market."

3. Marilyn Bechtel, "The Marvelous Life of Marvel Cooke, Pioneer Black Woman Journalist," *People's World,* March 8, 2021, https://www.peoplesworld.org/article/the-marvelous -life-of-marvel-cooke-pioneer-black-woman-journalist.

4. "The Truth About the Revolutionary Activist Marvel Cooke," *Ross Community Center,* Ross Community Center, Muncie, Ind., accessed March 2020, https://www.rosscenter muncie.org/the-truth-about-the-revolutionary-activist-marvel-cooke.

5. LaShawn Harris, "Marvel Cooke: Investigative Journalist, Communist, and Black Radical Subject," *Journal for the Study of Radicalism,* vol. 6, no. 2 (Fall 2012), 91–126, https://drive.google.com/file/d/1uEQAIMUYf4cOs_YDeOq7uJ3b-OKd86FK/view.

6. David Smith, "Ida B. Wells: The Unsung Heroine of the Civil Rights Movement," *The Guardian,* April 27, 2018, https://www.theguardian.com/world/2018/apr/27/ida-b-wells -civil-rights-movement-reporter.

7. Ida B. Wells-Barnett, "The Red Record: Tabulated Statistics and Alleged Causes of Lynching in the United States," *Project Gutenberg,* Ebook #14977, February 8, 2005, https:// www.gutenberg.org/files/14977/14977-h/14977-h.htm#chap3.

8. Smith, "Ida B. Wells."

9. Smith, "Ida B. Wells."

10. Hurston had transferred to Barnard in 1925 from Howard University.

11. Zora Neale Hurston, "What White Publishers Won't Print," *Negro Digest,* April 1950, vol. 8, 85–89.

12. Valerie Boyd, "About Zora Neale Hurston," *Zora Neale Hurston, the Official Website,* accessed January 2021, https://www.zoranealehurston.com/about.

13. Roberta S. Maguire, "From Fiction to Fact: Zora Neale Hurston and the Ruby Mc-Collum Trial," *Literary Journalism Studies,* vol. 7, no. 1 (Spring 2015), https://s35767.pcdn .co/wp-content/uploads/2015/05/018-036-LJS_v7n1.pdf.

14. Lauren Michele Jackson, "The Zora Neale Hurston We Don't Talk About," *New Yorker,* February 14, 2022, https://www.newyorker.com/books/page-turner/the-zora-neale -hurston-we-dont-talk-about.

15. Jackson, "The Zora Neale Hurston We Don't Talk About."

16. Boyd, "About Zora Neale Hurston."

17. Jill Lepore, "Just the Facts, Ma'am," *New Yorker,* March 17, 2008, www.newyorker .com/magazine/2008/03/24/just-the-facts-maam.

18. Lorraine Glennon, "Phillip Lopate Celebrates the Personal Essay," *Columbia Magazine* (Spring 2016), https://magazine.columbia.edu/article/phillip-lopate-celebrates-personal -essay.

19. Milton J. Rosenberg et al., "Roundtable: The History of the Essay," *Fourth Genre: Explorations in Non-Fiction,* vol. 2, no. 2 (Fall 2000), 219–241, https://www.jstor.org /stable/41938574.

20. Sugar, "Dear Sugar, The Rumpus Advice Column #48: Write Like a Motherfucker," *The Rumpus,* August 19, 2010, https://therumpus.net/2010/08/19/dear-sugar-the-rumpus -advice-column-48-write-like-a-motherfucker.

21. Claire Kirch, "Strayed Comes Out as Rumpus 'Sugar' Columnist," *Publishers Weekly,*

February 15, 2012, https://www.publishersweekly.com/pw/by-topic/industry-news/people/article/50635-strayed-comes-out-as-rumpus-sugar-columnist.html.

22. Ben Brantley, "Review: Dear Audiences of 'Tiny Beautiful Things,' Prepare to Cry," *New York Times,* December 7, 2016, https://www.nytimes.com/2016/12/07/theater/tiny-beautiful-things-review.html.

23. Elissa Bassist, "Cheryl Strayed on Fame, Success, and Writing Like a Mother #^@%*&," *Creative Nonfiction,* Creative Nonfiction Foundation, Issue 47 (1997), https://creativenonfiction.org/writing/cheryl-strayed-on-fame-success-and-writing-like-a-mother.

CHAPTER 6. F*** THE ESTABLISHMENT

1. Denny Heitman, "Tru Life: How Truman Capote Became a Cautionary Tale of Celebrity Culture," *Humanities,* National Endowment for the Humanities, vol. 38, no. 3 (Summer 2017), https://www.neh.gov/humanities/2017/summer/feature/tru-lifeI.

2. Truman Capote, "The Duke in His Domain," *New Yorker,* November 9, 1957, https://www.newyorker.com/magazine/1957/11/09/the-duke-in-his-domain.

3. John Brady, *The Craft of Interviewing* (New York: Vintage, 1977), 54.

4. Norman Mailer, *The Armies of the Night: History as a Novel, the Novel as History* (New York: New American Library, 1968; Odyssey Editions, October 2013), 91–92.

5. Mailer, *The Armies of the Night,* 4.

6. Suzanne Snider, "An Interview with Lawrence Schiller," *Culture.org,* May 1, 2010, https://culture.org/an-interview-with-lawrence-schiller.

7. Joan Didion, *The White Album* (New York: Farrar, Straus and Giroux, 2009), 11–48.

8. Joan Didion, *Slouching Towards Bethlehem* (New York: Farrar, Straus and Giroux, 1968), 142.

9. Sara Davidson, "Hanging Out with Joan Didion: What I Learned About Writing from an American Master," *Lit Hub,* October 5, 2021, https://lithub.com/hanging-out-with-joan-didion-what-i-learned-about-writing-from-an-american-master.

10. Didion, *Slouching Towards Bethlehem,* 84.

CHAPTER 7. THE IMPERFECT PRIMER

1. Tom Wolfe and E. W. Johnson, eds., *The New Journalism, with an Anthology* (New York: Harper & Row, 1973), 34–35.

2. Wolfe and Johnson, eds., *The New Journalism,* 197.

3. Charles Bladen, "The Gonzo Lecture: Counterculture in the Classroom," *Compass: Journal of Learning and Teaching* (2009), vol. 1, no. 1, https://journals.gre.ac.uk/index.php/compass/article/view/14/32.

4. Bladen, "The Gonzo Lecture."

5. "Hunter Thompson Once Spread a Rumor of a Presidential Candidate's Drug Addiction and It Was Taken Seriously," *Plaid Zebra*, May 10, 2016, https://theplaidzebra.com/hunter-s-thompson-spread-rumor-presidential-candidates-drug-addiction-taken-seriously.

6. Michael Patrick Hearn, "Alex Haley Taught America About Race—and a Young Man How to Write," *New York Times*, December 12, 2021, https://www.nytimes.com/2021/12/17/books/review/alex-haley-hamilton-college-autobiography-of-malcolm-x-roots.html.

7. Alex Haley, *The Autobiography of Malcolm X: As Told to Alex Haley* (New York: Random House, 1992), 446.

8. Haley, *The Autobiography of Malcolm X*, 448–449.

9. Alex Haley, "Roots: The Saga of Alex Haley," *Slate Podcast*, August 18, 2021, https://www.stitcher.com/show/slate-presents-standoff-what-happened-at-ruby-ridge/episode/1977-roots-the-saga-of-alex-haley-86054549.

10. James Baldwin, "Notes of a Native Son," first published as "Me and My House . . . ," *Harper's Magazine*, November 1955, 54–61.

11. Baldwin, "Notes of a Native Son."

CHAPTER 8. THE SHOE DOG GOES TO COLLEGE

1. John Fedele, "The Cathedral of Learning: A History," *Pitt Chronicle*, University of Pittsburgh, March 12, 2007, https://www.chronicle.pitt.edu/story/cathedral-learning-history.

2. Association of Writers and Writing Programs, "*About, Overview*," AWP, 2020, https://www.awpwriter.org/about/our_history_overview.

3. Helane Levine-Keating, "Secret History of Writing Programs," *American Book Review*, vol. 37, no. 2 (January–February 2016), 26–27, https://muse.jhu.edu/article/613135.

4. Kimberly K. Barlow, "Obituary: Montgomery Culver," *University Times*, March 5, 2009, https://www.utimes.pitt.edu/archives/?p=8585.

CHAPTER 10. INNOCENT VICTIMS

1. Russ Walsh, "Art Williams," *Society for American Baseball Research*, accessed March 2020, https://sabr.org/bioproj/person/art-williams.

CHAPTER 11. MANIPULATING MATERIAL—AND
THE PEOPLE YOU ARE WRITING ABOUT

1. "Crime: The Fabulous Hoax of Clifford Irving," *Time*, February 21, 1972, https://content.time.com/time/subscriber/article/0,33009,905773,00.html.

2. Nicholson Baker, "The Greatest Liar," *Columbia Journalism Review*, July–August 2009, https://archives.cjr.org/second_read/the_greatest_liar_1.php?mod=djembooks.

3. U.S. Supreme Court, "Jeffrey M. Masson, Petitioner, v. *New Yorker* Magazine, Inc.,

Alfred A. Knopf, Inc., and Janet Malcolm," U.S. Supreme Court, no. 89-1799, June 20, 1991, https://www.law.cornell.edu/supremecourt/text/501/496.

4. David Margolick, "Psychoanalyst Loses Libel Suit Against a New Yorker Reporter," *New York Times,* November 3, 1994, https://www.nytimes.com/1994/11/03/us/psycho analyst-loses-libel-suit-against-a-new-yorker-reporter.html.

5. Charles Krauthammer, "Sex, Lies, and Misquotation," *Washington Post,* April 12, 1991, https://www.washingtonpost.com/archive/opinions/1991/04/12/sex-lies-and -misquotation/38f88c22-7069-45c0-bfe4-3095c3eb3912.

6. Maura Dolan, "New Yorker Writer Cleared of Libeling Psychoanalyst: Courts: Jury Rules Janet Malcolm Did Not Intentionally Err in Using Two False Quotes. Decision Ends 10-Year Case," *Los Angeles Times,* November 3, 1994, www.latimes.com/archives/la-xpm -1994-11-03-mn-58294-story.html.

7. Judith Haydel, "Masson v. New Yorker Magazine (1991)," *The First Amendment Encyclopedia,* 2009, https://www.mtsu.edu/first-amendment/article/562/masson-v-new -yorker-magazine.

8. U.S. Supreme Court, "Jeffrey M. Masson, Petitioner, v. *New Yorker* Magazine."

9. Janet Malcolm, "The Journalist and the Murderer," *New Yorker,* March 5, 1989, https://www.newyorker.com/magazine/1989/03/13/the-journalist-and-the-murderer-i.

10. Scott Manley Hadley, "Triumph of the Now," *scottmanleyhadley.com,* April 2, 2019, https://triumphofthenow.com/2019/04/02/the-journalist-and-the-murderer-by-janet -malcolm.

11. Victor Navasky, "When Journalist Bites Journalist," *Washington Post,* March 11, 1990, https://www.washingtonpost.com/archive/entertainment/books/1990/03/11 /when-journalist-bites-journalist/5c7e490f-7bc3-4b1b-979e-fe797176e200.

12. Albert Scardino, "Ethics, Reporters, and The New Yorker," *New York Times,* March 21, 1989, https://www.nytimes.com/1989/03/21/arts/ethics-reporters-and-the-new -yorker.html.

13. Tom Junod, "Rupert Murdoch, Meet Janet Malcolm—Pro Scandalist," *Esquire,* July 11, 2011, https://www.esquire.com/news-politics/news/a10507/rupert-murdoch-janet -malcolm-6075803.

CHAPTER 12. A LARGER REALITY? OR THE UNTRUE TRUTH?

1. Maureen Dowd, "A Writer for the New Yorker Says He Created Composites in Reports," *New York Times,* June 19, 1984, https://www.nytimes.com/1984/06/19/nyregion /a-writer-for-the-new-yorker-says-he-created-composites-in-reports.html.

2. Dowd, "A Writer for the New Yorker Says He Created Composites."

3. Thomas Kunkel, "What Exactly Was Joseph Mitchell Doing All Those Years at the 'New Yorker'?" *Publishers Weekly,* April 3, 2015, https://www.publishersweekly.com/pw /by-topic/industry-news/tip-sheet/article/66086-what-exactly-was-joseph-mitchell-doing -all-those-years-at-the-new-yorker.html.

4. Tim O'Brien, "'Story Truth' and 'Happening Truth' in The Things They Carried," *StudyMoose,* 1998, https://studymoose.com/story-truth-and-happening-truth-in-the-things -they-carried-essay.

5. Tom Bissell, "Truth in Oxiana," *World Hum,* February 15, 2006, www.worldhum .com/features/speakers-corner/truth_in_oxiana_20060212.

6. Bissell, "Truth in Oxiana."

7. Bissell, "Truth in Oxiana."

8. Terry Greene Sterling, "Confessions of a Memoirist," *Salon,* August 1, 2003, https:// www.salon.com/2003/08/01/gornick.

9. Sterling, "Confessions of a Memoirist."

10. Vivian Gornick, "A Memoirist Defends Her Words," *Salon,* August 12, 2003, https:// www.salon.com/2003/08/12/memoir_writing.

11. Laura Miller, "Mary Karr, Master of Memoir," *Slate,* September 23, 2015, https:// slate.com/culture/2015/09/mary-karrs-the-art-of-memoir-reviewed.html.

12. Stephanie S. Farber and Vivian Gornick, "Interview with Vivian Gornick," *Fourth Genre: Explorations in Nonfiction,* vol. 8, no. 2 (Fall 2006), 133–139, https://www.jstor .org/stable/41939390.

13. Roy Peter Clark, "Uncivil War Over the Memoir," Poynter Resources, December 14, 2006, https://www.poynter.org/archive/2006/uncivil-war-over-the-memoir.

14. Bissell, "Truth in Oxiana."

15. William Deresiewicz, "In Defense of Facts," *The Atlantic,* January–February 2017, https://www.theatlantic.com/magazine/archive/2017/01/in-defense-of-facts/508748.

16. John D'Agata, "What Happens There," *Believer,* January 1, 2010, https://www.the believer.net/what-happens-there.

17. Jennifer B. McDonald, "In the Details," *New York Times,* February 21, 2012, https:// www.nytimes.com/2012/02/26/books/review/the-lifespan-of-a-fact-by-john-dagata-and -jim-fingal.html.

18. Hannah Goldfield, "The Art of Fact-Checking," *New Yorker,* February 9, 2012, https://www.newyorker.com/books/page-turner/the-art-of-fact-checking.

19. Weston Cutter, "Missing the Point," *Kenyon Review Blog,* February 16, 2012, https:// kenyonreview.org/2012/02/missing-the-point.

20. Deresiewicz, "In Defense of Facts."

CHAPTER 13. DISSING THE MEMOIR

1. James Wolcott, "The 20-Year-Old Who Dated Her Dad—And Then Wrote a Book About It," *New Republic,* March 31, 1997, https://newrepublic.com/article/119008/james -wolcott-reviews-kiss.

2. Wolcott, "The 20-Year-Old Who Dated Her Dad."

3. Jonathan Yardley, "Daddy's Girl Cashes In," *Washington Post,* March 5, 1997, https://www.washingtonpost.com/archive/lifestyle/1997/03/05/daddys-girl-cashes-in/50dd8efc-2a36-4395-9246-fec57565e677.

4. Jonathan Yardley, "Review: 'Epilogue: A Memoir,' by Will Boast," *Washington Post,* September 12, 2014, https://www.washingtonpost.com/opinions/review-epilogue-a-memoir-by-will-boast/2014/09/12/0e21f5a2-2d3e-11e4-994d-202962a9150c_story.html.

5. Ellen Goodman, "Stranger Than Fiction," *Washington Post,* April 5, 1997, https://www.washingtonpost.com/archive/opinions/1997/04/05/stranger-than-fiction/8a436633-8ee5-4e1e-b06c-417d203d5db0.

6. Laura Barton, "The Man Who Rewrote His Life," *The Guardian,* September 15, 2006, https://www.theguardian.com/books/2006/sep/15/usa.world.

7. Barton, "The Man Who Rewrote His Life."

8. "A Million Little Lies," *the smoking gun,* January 4, 2006, http://www.thesmokinggun.com/documents/celebrity/million-little-lies?page=0,0.

9. James Frey and Nan Talese, "Oprah Duped Us!" *HuffPost.com,* May 25, 2011, https://www.huffpost.com/entry/james-frey-and-nan-talese_n_99374.

10. Larry King, "Transcripts: Interview with James Frey," *CNN-News,* January 11, 2006, https://transcripts.cnn.com/show/lkl/date/2006-01-11/segment/01.

11. Motoko Rich, "Acclaimed Memoir Proves a Fake," *New York Times,* March 4, 2008, https://www.nytimes.com/2008/03/04/world/americas/04iht-memoir.1.10684652.html.

12. Matthew L. M. Fletcher, "Margaret B. Jones, Indian Frauds: Alternet on 'Love and Consequences,'" *Turtle Talk,* April 22, 2008, https://turtletalk.blog/tag/margaret-b-jones.

13. Dan P. McAdams, "Beyond the Redemptive Self: Narratives of Acceptance in Later Life (and in Other Contexts)," *Journal of Research in Personality* 100 (October 2022), https://www.sciencedirect.com/science/article/abs/pii/S009265662200099X.

14. Marion Maneker, "The King James Version," *New York* magazine, June 11, 2001, https://nymag.com/nymetro/arts/features/4794.

15. Maneker, "The King James Version."

16. Maneker, "The King James Version."

CHAPTER 16. WRITERS INVADING THE ACADEMY

1. Philip Raisor, "The AWP/ODU Years: Occasional Grace," *Association of Writers & Writing Programs,* April 19, 2012, https://www.awpwriter.org/magazine_media/writers_news_view/2870/the_awpodu_years_occasional_grace.

2. Mary Carter, "Program Directors 'Council Report': Nuts & Bolts and DNA," *Writer's Chronicle,* February–March 1986, https://www.awpwriter.org/magazine_media/writers_chronicle_view/2099.

3. Linda Roberts, "At Play with Diane Ackerman," *January Magazine*, August 1999, https://www.januarymagazine.com/profiles/ackerman.html.

CHAPTER 18. MUD AND COCONUTS

1. David L. Ulin, "The Lie That Tells the Truth," *Los Angeles Times*, February 5, 2006, https://www.latimes.com/archives/la-xpm-2006-feb-05-bk-ulin5-story.html.

2. Peter Schneeman, "Reports from the Annual Meeting Down in the Mud or Truth or Up in the Tree of Texts," *AWP*, accessed May 2019, https://www.awpwriter.org/magazine _media/writers_chronicle_issues/september_1983.

3. Philip Connors, "Where Have You Gone, Edward Abbey?" *Salon*, October 22, 2006, https://www.salon.com/2006/10/22/abbey.

4. Rodger Kamenetz, "Reports from the Annual Meeting: Notes on Literary Culture," *The Writer's Chronicle*, September 1985, https://www.awpwriter.org/magazine_media /writers_chronicle_view/2351/reports_from_the_annual_meeting_notes_on_literary _culture.

5. Cristina Nehring, "What's Wrong with the American Essay," *Truth Dig*, November 30, 2007, https://www.truthdig.com/articles/cristina-nehring-on-whats-wrong-with-the -american-essay.

6. Heather Thomson, "On Writing About (Not So) Little Things," October 3, 2018, https://commonplacebookblog.com/2018/10/03/on-writing-about-not-so-little-things.

7. Assay Editors, "Interview with Robert Atwan," *Assay: A Journal of Nonfiction Studies* (Fall 2022), https://www.assayjournal.com/interview-with-robert-atwan-31.html.

8. Robert Atwan, "The Best American Essays: Some Notes on the Series, Its Background and Origins," *Essay Daily*, December 7, 2015, http://www.essaydaily.org/2015/12/robert -atwan-best-american-essays-some.html.

9. Atwan, "The Best American Essays."

CHAPTER 19. HOW CREATIVE NONFICTION
BECAME *CREATIVE NONFICTION*

1. George Wickes, "Little Magazines and Other Publishing Ventures," *Paris Review*, Issue 47 (Summer 1969), https://www.theparisreview.org/letters-essays/4179/little-magazines -and-other-publishing-ventures-george-wickes.

2. G. D. Dess, "The Perils and Pitfalls of the Lyrical Essay," *Los Angeles Review of Books*, May 22, 2019, https://lareviewofbooks.org/article/the-perils-and-pitfalls-of-the-lyric -essay.

3. Adam Goodheart, "Reviews: Riding the Demon," *New York Times*, June 6, 1999, https:// archive.nytimes.com/www.nytimes.com/books/99/06/06/reviews/990606.06travelt .html.

4. Carolyn Kremers, "How Tununak Came to Me," *Creative Nonfiction,* Creative Nonfiction Foundation, Issue 1 (1993), 37–51, https://creativenonfiction.org/writing/how -tununak-came-to-me.

5. Jill Carpenter, "Consanguinity," *Creative Nonfiction,* Creative Nonfiction Foundation, vol. 1, no. 1 (1993), 30–36, https://www.jstor.org/stable/i40182306.

6. Natalia Rachel Singer, "Nonfiction in First Person, Without Apology," *Creative Nonfiction,* Creative Nonfiction Foundation, No. 6, The Essayist at Work (1996), 93–102, www .jstor.org/stable/44363486.

7. Lee Gutkind, "On the Fine Art of Fist Fighting," *CNF Quarterly,* Creative Nonfiction Foundation, Issue 50 (2015), https://creativenonfiction.org/writing/on-the-fine-art-of -literary-fist-fighting.

CHAPTER 22. THE FIRST CREATIVE NONFICTION CONFERENCE

1. Michael Rosenwald, "How Many Times Did You Almost Go Out of Business with This Thing?" *CNF Quarterly,* Creative Nonfiction Foundation, Issue 50 (2015), https:// creativenonfiction.org/writing/how-many-times-did-you-almost-go-out-of-business-with -this-thing.

2. Linda Clark Rohrer, "Dear Mr. Essay Writer Guy," *Pitt Magazine* (Winter 2017), https://www.pittmag.pitt.edu/news/dear-mister-essay-writer.

3. Denise Watson Batts, "Cancer Cells Killed Henrietta Lacks — Then Made Her Immortal," *The Virginian-Pilot,* May 10, 2010, https://web.archive.org/web/20100513065957/ http://hamptonroads.com/2010/05/cancer-cells-killed-her-then-they-made-her -immortal.

4. Cristina Rouvalis, "The Writing Life of Rebecca Skloot," *Pitt Magazine* (Winter 2018), https://www.pittmag.pitt.edu/news/writing-life-rebecca.

5. Rouvalis, "The Writing Life of Rebecca Skloot."

CHAPTER 23. THE BUSINESS OF ART? OR
THE ART OF DOING THE ART BUSINESS

1. Elizabeth A. Harris and Alexandra Alter, "The Believer, a Beloved Literary Magazine, Goes Home After a Risqué Detour," *New York Times,* June 9, 2022, https://www.nytimes .com/2022/05/16/books/the-believer-mcsweeneys.html.

CHAPTER 24. THE LAST CREATIVE NONFICTION "FIST-FIGHT"

1. Brenda Miller and Suzanne Paola, *Tell It Slant,* second ed. (New York: McGraw Hill, 2012), xiv.

2. From Poets & Writers, Inc., "Fifty & Forward," *Publishers Weekly* 46, accessed November 2019, https://www.pw.org/content/from_poets_writers_inc_46.

3. Lee Gutkind, "From the Editor: The Poets & Writers Issue," *Creative Nonfiction,* Creative Nonfiction Foundation, Issue 26 (2005), https://creativenonfiction.org/writing/from-the-editor-the-poets-writers-issue.

4. Heidi Julavits, "The Writers in the Silos," *Creative Nonfiction,* Creative Nonfiction Foundation, Issue 31 (2007), https://creativenonfiction.org/writing/the-writers-in-the-silos-2.

5. Phillip Lopate, "Best of Times, Worst of Times," *Creative Nonfiction,* Creative Nonfiction Foundation, Issue 31 (2007), https://creativenonfiction.org/writing/best-of-times-worst-of-times.

6. Robin Hemley, "Introducing . . . Trump Jerky Books!" *Creative Nonfiction,* Creative Nonfiction Foundation, Issue 31 (2007), https://creativenonfiction.org/writing/introducing-trump-jerky-books.